MEMORIES AND MIGRATIONS

Memories and Migrations

MAPPING BORICUA AND CHICANA HISTORIES

Edited by

VICKI L. RUIZ AND

JOHN R. CHÁVEZ

Published in Cooperation with the
William P. Clements Center for Southwest Studies,
Southern Methodist University, Dallas, Texas

UNIVERSITY OF ILLINOIS PRESS

URBANA AND CHICAGO

Library of Congress Cataloging-in-Publication Data
Memories and migrations : mapping Boricua and Chicana
histories / edited by Vicki L. Ruiz and John R. Chávez.
p. cm.
"Published in cooperation with the William P. Clements
Center for Southwest Studies, Southern Methodist University,
Dallas, Texas"—T.p. verso.
Papers from a symposium held on Feb. 28, 2004 at the
Latino Cultural Center, Dallas, Tex.
Includes bibliographical references and index.
ISBN-13: 978-0-252-03238-7 (cloth : alk. paper)
ISBN-10: 0-252-03238-1 (cloth : alk. paper)
ISBN-13: 978-0-252-07478-3 (paper : alk. paper)
ISBN-10: 0-252-07478-5 (paper : alk. paper)
1. Mexican American women—Social conditions—20th century—
Congresses. 2. Puerto Rican women—Social conditions—20th
century—Congresses. 3. Women immigrants—United States—
Social conditions—20th century—Congresses. 4. Mexicans—
Migrations—History—20th century—Congresses. 5. Puerto
Ricans—Migrations—History—20th century—Congresses.
6. Community life—United States—History—20th century—
Congresses. 7. Sex role—United States—History—20th century—
Congresses. 8. Ethnicity—United States—History—20th century—
Congresses. 9. United States—Ethnic relations—History—20th
century—Congresses. 10. United States—Social conditions—20th
century—Congresses.
I. Ruiz, Vicki. II. Chávez, John R., 1949– III. William P. Clements
Center for Southwest Studies.
E184.M5M462   2007
305.868'72073—dc22   2007023285

Dedicado a
Gabriela Arredondo
Una Mujer Valiente

Contents

Preface

Some years ago, Vicki Ruiz, coeditor with me of *Memories and Migrations,* reviewed a book I had previously written. She had the following choice words on my *Lost Land:* "For John Chávez . . . Chicano history is precisely that—*Chicano* history. Chávez briefly mentions four notable Mexican-American women, providing no sense of women's everyday lives or even household relationships."[1] Of course, she was right. I had not consciously looked for female perspectives and had simply missed most, to put it mildly. In my own defense I can only say that I was not alone among historians of my generation. With this present book, however, I'm making up for my mistake—to Vicki and all other women, including my wife, daughter, sisters, friends, colleagues, students, and most of all to my mother and grandmothers. In this volume, Latinas take center stage with just a few comments by this repentant male.

In fall 2001, Vicki, who is professor of history and Chicano/Latino studies at the University of California–Irvine, visited us at Southern Methodist University to participate in a workshop put on by the William P. Clements Center for Southwest Studies. At the dinner afterward, hosted at the home of my colleague, the center's director, David Weber, we discussed the possibilities of a conference on Mexican-American women, realizing that such an event had not occurred in about twenty years. Because much had been written since publication of Vicki's seminal *Cannery Women, Cannery Lives,*[2] we decided to organize a symposium to celebrate and assess this maturing historical field. As a member of the Clements Department of History, as well as the center's executive board,

I lobbied for their sponsorship and received a positive and enthusiastic response. Such a project seemed thoroughly consistent with their activities and their interest in the Southwest.

The papers selected for presentation at the symposium, and ultimately for publication in *Memories and Migrations,* reflect our desire to highlight Latinas in place, as well as time. My original idea had been to focus on Chicanas in the southwestern borderlands, because historically Mexican-American women resided in the region; moreover, it made sense for the Clements Center to sponsor such a topic. Vicki, however, hoped to include other Latinas, which meant that the geography had to expand, since the traditional location of mainland Puerto Ricans (Boricuas) was in the Northeast and that of Cuban Americans in the Southeast. In addition, since at least 1980, women from other Caribbean and Central American nations had immigrated to and established themselves in earlier Hispanic regions, but also in such outliers as Washington, D.C. We had thus expected to attract scholars interested in the histories of Latinas, especially as the field related to geography—physical, cultural, conceptual, and otherwise.

The goal of our symposium and anthology was to push geographical analogies further—to reconsider regions, subregions, and localities across interstate, international, and conceptual boundaries. How had Chicanas "engendered" regions? To what extent had Chicanas placed their mark on regions, diversely defined? Conversely, how had La Reina de Los Angeles, Santa Monica, Tijuana, Española, and many other locales affected the histories of Chicanas? And how would these effects compare with similar processes between other Latinas and Little Havana, Chicago, or New York—not to mention regions of Puerto Rico, Cuba, or Mexico? Such were the nominally geographical questions to be addressed by our project.

As Vicki and I surveyed the proposals submitted, we found that most centered on the twentieth century, and despite our hopes to include other Latinas, only Puerto Rican women had submitted proposals. Papers on the twentieth-century experience of mainland Puerto Ricans and the evolution of a mainland Boricua identity fortunately reinforced our theme of the interaction between physical and mental geography. So, too, did papers that reflected the long-term migration of Mexican-origin women into the regions of the Pacific Northwest and the Great Lakes, as well as their return pilgrimages to Mexico.

In preparation for the symposium, we followed a model used at several previous symposia at the Clements Center. The participants exchanged and discussed their papers twice, once at a meeting in September 2003, in the forested mountains of northern New Mexico, where Southern Methodist has a summer campus at reconstructed Fort Burgwin near Taos. We then met in a private, all-day session on the suburban Georgian campus of Southern Methodist on the day before our public meeting in downtown Dallas, where on February 28, 2004, we held the symposium at the brand-new Latino Cultural Center, dubbed "Latina" for the occasion. Students and faculty mingled with regular people from the community, all eager to connect the stories told at the symposium with their own memories of migration and settlement in Dallas and elsewhere. We were especially honored by the presence of early civil rights leader Anita Martínez. In Vicki's gracious words, "The conference was absolutely magical."[3]

After the symposium, we revised the work further for publication as the present volume. In the course of these revisions, the original title of the proposed book changed from "Engendering Regions? Chicana/Latina Comparative Histories" to "Memories and Migrations: Mapping Boricua and Chicana Histories." Besides a narrower ethnic perspective, the new title reflected a move away from the earlier focus on region and long historical settlement, which was more evident in the nineteenth-century proposals, to one of movement from place to place, a twentieth-century experience still remembered by women alive today. Yolanda Chávez Leyva recounted the stories of children crossing the border into El Paso, while María Montoya depicted *hispanas* creating homes in Colorado; Gabriela Arredondo described *mexicanas* settling in Chicago, and Carmen Whalen *puertorriqueñas* in New York. In contrast, Marisela Chávez presented the surprising experience of Chicanas "going home" to Mexico City. On another level, Virginia Sánchez Korrol narrated her personal journey in search of space for Boricuas and other minorities in academia. Despite these changes in focus, several papers alluded to long ties to region, such as Lydia Otero's comments on Mexican Tucson and Elizabeth Salas's reference to Spanish exploration of the later U.S.–Canadian borderlands. In essence, the contributors examined ways in which Boricuas and Chicanas, whether U.S.-born or immigrant, imprinted themselves on communities and places large and small, and in turn how these places and communities imprinted themselves on these women.

Notes

1. John R. Chávez, *The Lost Land: The Chicano Image of the Southwest* (Albuquerque: University of New Mexico Press, 1984); and Vicki L. Ruiz, "Texture,

Text, and Context: New Approaches to Chicano History," *Mexican Studies/Estudios Mexicanos* 2 (winter 1986): 149.

2. Ruiz, *Cannery Women, Cannery Lives: Mexican Women, Unionization, and the California Food Processing Industry* (Albuquerque: University of New Mexico Press, 1987).

3. Personal communication, Ruiz to Chávez, March 4, 2004.

Acknowledgments

This volume would not be possible without the generous institutional support of the William P. Clements Center for Southwest Studies at Southern Methodist University. Director David Weber and associate director Sherry Smith encouraged and nurtured our collective vision. Executive director Andrea Boardman and administrative coordinator Ruth Ann Elmore handled the innumerable details of organizing the February 2004 symposium "Mapping Memories and Migrations: Re-Thinking U.S. Latina Histories" and of preparing the manuscript for submission to the University of Illinois Press. We are indebted to Ken Hamilton, director of the Ethnic Studies Program at Southern Methodist University, for underwriting the rental of the Latino Cultural Center in downtown Dallas where the symposium was held. We appreciate the hospitality of the staff at Fort Burgwin, home of Southern Methodist's summer-in-Taos program where the authors and editors met for a weekend retreat before the conference.

During the process of exchanging drafts, presenting work, and revising for publication, we made our own "memories." We acknowledge Gabriela F. Arredondo, Marisela R. Chávez, Yolanda Chávez Leyva, María E. Montoya, Lydia R. Otero, Elizabeth Salas, Virginia Sánchez Korrol, and Carmen Teresa Whalen for their astute insights, incisive scholarship, and boundless *corazón*. (And no, none of the Chávezes are related). Vicki L. Ruiz offers much gratitude to Gabriela F. Arredondo and Virginia Sánchez Korrol for their intellectual prodding. Though as a collective we had made comments on each other's written work on several occasions, the outside readers Sarah Deutsch and Monica Perales made a tremendous difference. All authors and editors should have the benefit of such conscientious, close readings of their scholarship. Their thorough command of the field and lucid, laser-point remarks proved invaluable. We thank associate director and editor-in-chief Joan Catapano and the staff at the University of Illinois Press, especially Marla Osterbur, Christina Walters, and Jennifer Clark for their encouragement, enthusiasm, and professionalism at every stage in the production of this volume. It is our hope that *Memories and Migrations* will serve as a springboard for future research and reflection.

Introduction

The year is 1930. Feeling the weight of the Great Depression, Albino Ruiz, an unemployed Mexican coal miner in Colorado's San Luis Valley, decided to move with his wife and three daughters to Denver. Without transportation, he arranged a ride with another family headed north. His daughter Erminia remembered packing a few belongings and climbing into the jalopy and onto her father's lap. Only nine years old, she cried herself to sleep with thoughts of her dog Sport standing sentinel in front of their abandoned adobe. Across the country twenty-one-year-old Elisa Santiago was also in tears. She had arrived in New York City ostensibly to care for her cousin's children. She was also there to mend a broken heart. Her beloved Eduardo, abiding by his parents' wishes, had forsaken Elisa, the Boricua from the barrio, in order to marry another, who shared his color and station on the island.[1] These narratives encapsulate the importance of mapping memories and migrations for Latina history, locating identity in the everyday as shaped by gender, generation, class, and region. The chapters that follow demonstrate to various degrees the transnational and translational nature of Latina history, a shared history marked by movement, location, and always destination.[2]

In Latina historiography, immigration, sexuality, generation, wage work, and cultural coalescence have frequently overshadowed region as a distinct category of analysis.[3] And yet region is intricately tied to Latina identity. "¿De dónde eres?" ("Where are you from?"), a familiar greeting among Latinos, emphasizes the importance of place. Many works commingling insights from political economy and cultural studies or drawing from psychoanalytic and postmodern paradigms have focused on material conditions, community activism, or the body, ignoring the impact of region. Articulations between region and gender should also be placed within the context of colonialism, past and present. Are there consonant experiences between, for example, Hispanas in Santa Fe and Boricuas in San Juan? Under what historical moments or contemporary circumstances do concepts of diaspora (figurative and physical) seem particularly insightful about the lives of Latinas?

The eight essays in this volume illuminate the ways in which women's memories and migrations shape Mexican American and Puerto Rican history over the course of the twentieth century. Moving beyond a single group or locale, this collection engages in a comparative conversation mapping political and cultural conventions through a gendered epistemology across region. Constituting three-quarters of all Latinos in the United States, Mexicans and Puerto Ricans bear the legacies of an American "culture of empire," to quote historian Gilbert González.[4] From Manifest Destiny in the mid-nineteenth century to its progeny economic imperialism in 1898, an unequal symbiotic relationship emerged between the United States and Mexico and between the mainland and Puerto Rico, especially because of Puerto Rico's ambiguous commonwealth status since 1950 and its economic dependency.[5] The transnational movements of people in the service of corporate capital is not a recent phenomenon of globalization but is evident in persistent patterns of Mexican and Puerto Rican migration to the United States. Moreover, within the continental United States, congruent patterns of economic segmentation and discrimination resonate in the lives of Puerto Ricans and Mexicans in that colonial legacies persist across families, generations, and transnational communities. The chapters that follow underscore the disjunctive diasporas in which migration, keyed to U.S. economic imperatives, mediate the formation of community spaces and cultural identities.

Intricately linked to region, history, and identity is nomenclature. For Latinos, there has never existed a single, mutually agreed-upon label of self-identification. I use Latino/a as an umbrella term signifying to all people of Latin American birth or heritage. Mexicano/a refers to those born in Mexico, with Mexican American indicating U.S. birth. Chicano/a reflects a political consciousness emerging out of the student movement of the 1960s and 1970s. Puertorriqueño/a includes everyone of Puerto Rican descent, on and off the island, while Nuyorican refers to those born on the mainland, not just New York. Boricua signifies endearment, empowerment, and unity for all Puerto Ricans. Others prefer a distinctly regional identification—Tejanos/as in Texas and Hispanos/as in New Mexico and Colorado.[6]

While geographic locale speaks volumes about perceptions of self and others, ethnoregional identity has generally been assumed, rather than theorized. A handful of scholars, such as Arnoldo De León, Sarah Deutsch, and Daniel Arreola, explore cultural agency, identity, and region. In 1984 John Chávez in *The Lost Land: The Chicano Image in the Southwest* charted a framework for remapping region within the milieu of conquests, disenfranchisement, empowerment, and homeland. Unfortunately, most Chicano and Latino historians at the time were immersed in community studies in which region became reduced in some respects to a neighborhood or factory floor.[7]

In Latina history, four books begin to situate region as central to identity formation. In *Songs My Mother Sang to Me,* Patricia Preciado Martin brings out the intimate affinities between individuals and landscape. In poignant, richly detailed oral interviews, ten Arizona natives reinscribe their memories and locate their identities in childhood soil, whether covered in saguaros or in mine tailings. Their narratives blend folk traditions, environment, and lived experiences as they point to an expansive Mexican cultural horizon in southern Arizona where one's subjectivity is not rooted in some essentialist biological mooring, but rather within Mexican cultural codes and gendered ethnoregional identification. A sense of place also resonates in the works of Sarah Deutsch, María Montoya, and Carmen Teresa Whalen. Focusing on New Mexico and Colorado, Deutsch *(No Separate Refuge)* and Montoya *(Translating Property)* bring out Hispana worldviews on imaginaries of topography, home, and history. Village loyalty and land-grant rights have resonated in the hearts and minds of area Hispanos for well over a century as they joined together in both public commemorations of the past and in legal action for future redress. Collective memory, however, does not necessarily require a layering of generations within a specific site, as is evident in Whalen's *From Puerto Rico to Philadelphia.* Whalen touches on transnational ties among Latina migrants, examining their journeys within a matrix of occupation, memory, and island and mainland cultural production and in so doing expands our notions of gendered ethnoregional identities outside the Southwest.[8]

Through poetry, short stories, and novels, Latina writers engender region in ways that are instructive for historians. As examples, Tejana poets, like Pat Mora and the late Gloria Anzaldúa, reveal the bordered body as physical landscape and mestiza soul. An excerpt from Pat Mora's "Desert Women" speaks volumes about ethnoregional identity:

Desert women know
about survival
Fierce heat and cold
have bruised and thickened
our skin. Like cactus
we've learned to hoard,
. . . .
Don't be deceived.
When we bloom, we stun.[9]

Counterintuitive to geographic space is the transnational imaginary, the homeland within the self. In "To Live in the Margins," Aura Luz Sánchez exposes a dialectic of dissonance and reclamation in which the poet "seeks solace" in a Puerto Rico filtered through family stories. A portion follows:

Her fanciful gaze wafts away
to a place where her mother was born,
a place, she has never seen.
She imagines a grove of mangoes,
flamboyant in the hair.
. . . .
She seeks solace once more
in the place where her mother was from.
There, she does not exist in the margins
of two peoples, two colors, two tongues.
. . . .
The warming womb
of imagination
transports her once more
to her mystical place in the sun.[10]

Engendering region in place and memory provides the foundation for this collection. The eight essays represent new research, fresh insight, and evidence that address transnational and translocal ties across time, enriching our understandings of gendered ethnoracial identities.[11] To frame these fascinating inquiries, three constructs seem particularly relevant—diasporic subjectivity, homemaking, and claiming region. Historian and feminist theorist Emma Pérez describes diasporic subjectivity as "always in movement, disrupting, re-creating and mobile in its representations, converging the past with the present for a new future."[12] At its most basic, home is a physical place of actual or ancestral residence. Homemaking, as conceptualized by sociologist Yen Le Espiritu, embodies "the processes by which diverse subjects imagine and make themselves at home in various geographic locations."[13] In the maw of colonialism and globalization, claiming region involves the fusion of landscape, historical memory, and lived experience. Furthermore, ethnoregional identities become manifest in part by cultural traditions, kin and community bonds, and gender in the everyday.

In teasing out the interconnections among diasporic subjectivity, homemaking, and claiming region, memory looms large in historical consciousness, individual and collective. Or as distinguished historian María Montoya astutely observed in a discussion during the first session of Mapping Memories and Migrations: Re-Thinking U.S. Latina Histories, "We use memory to situate ourselves in the world." Consequently, historical agency itself encompasses far more than personal choice or behavior but represents "the creative orchestration of cultural elements."[14] In complicating notions of gendered ethnoregional identities, these chapters remap region as physical place, process, and cultural home—as demarcated topographies or intellectual imaginaries.

Claiming space looms large in the maintenance of ethnoregional bonds that evolve and extend across generations. Latina history, however, is not tied exclusively to narratives of migration. María Montoya fuses landscape, occupation, and homemaking in her study of Hispanas in Colorado coal towns as she explores how company representations of an "American" home influenced their lives. Notions of modernity and progress did not fade from view after the heyday of Americanization programs prevalent in the Southwest during the 1910s and 1920s as evident in the scholarship of Lydia Otero. Indeed, the contested nature of public memory and public history stands out in her chapter on the grassroots efforts to save La Placita in Tucson, Arizona, from downtown redevelopment and gentrification. Focusing on local activist Alva Torres, Otero illuminates the importance of historical preservation for Latino communities, for, in Torres's words, "the buildings are not the people but they are part of the story that you try to save."

Focusing on working-class Mexican women in Chicago, Gabriela Arredondo introduces the concept of "lived regionalities" in which women's past experiences and knowledge "shape the lens through which they live and understand their lives." Gently chiding Chicano scholars who relegate women to the realm of cultural scenery in existing studies of Mexicans in the Midwest, Arredondo brings to light how diverse histories emerge when engendering narratives of migration and privileging women's experiences. Yolanda Chávez Leyva turns her attention to another lacuna in Latino historiography, the absence of children. Covering the period between 1900 and 1940, she reveals the challenges Mexican youngsters faced in negotiating border crossing and crafting border identities. The significance of their struggles cannot be dismissed, since perhaps as many as 50 percent of all Mexican immigrants who journeyed north during this era arrived as children or teenagers. Shifting from generation to occupation, Carmen Teresa Whalen interrogates the migration of Puertorriqueñas to New York City after World War II through the lens of wage work and labor activism. Tracing the connections between the Big Apple and Puerto Rico, she posits, "Puerto Rican women's sewing was central to the redefinition and engendering of their local and transnational communities."

Transnational belonging as a very public endeavor resonates in the scholarship of Carmen Whalen, Elizabeth Salas, and Marisela Chávez. Through *mutualistas,* church groups, voluntary associations, labor unions, and civil-rights organizations, Mexican and Puerto Rican women have exercised political leadership. As club women, neighborhood advocates, educators, social reformers, politicians, and feminists (to mention a few roles), Latinas have sought to improve the material conditions of their communities.[15] Elizabeth Salas examines the rise of Mexican American women as elected officials in the state of Washington, women who pursue divergent political agendas though most grew up in farmworker families. While Salas points to a maturation of political power among these contemporary public servants, Marisela Chávez complicates our understanding of Latina feminist history through a provocative intellectual coming-of-age narrative. Chronicling Chicana participation at the 1975 International Women's Year Conference in Mexico City, Chávez elaborates on the development of an international consciousness among these young feminists, but a consciousness tempered for them at the time by the disconcerting realization that they were Americans. Indeed, "Americans" and "Americanization" are more than cultural tropes to be placed under an intellectual microscope (or postcolonial thesaurus), but rather elements interwoven within Latina ethnoregional identities. As one of the first Latinas to earn a Ph.D. in history and an early leader in Puerto Rican studies, Virginia Sánchez Korrol shares a haunting autoethnography of traversing cultural and physical spaces in her coming-of-age narrative, growing up Nuyorican during the 1940s and 1950s. She was a voracious young reader who in traveling to other worlds through her local library card never found her own.

The following essays illuminate the ways in which gendered memories and migrations shape Chicana/Boricua histories. The insights of literary scholar Genaro Padilla seem particularly incisive in shifting through the messiness and contradictions within lived experiences and cultural iconographies. In his pathbreaking work, *My History, Not Yours*, Padilla refers to "the historical locus of contradiction . . . where accommodation and anger fill the same phrase and where, in the social world, an unrelenting movement between borders, countries, cultures, and languages established subjectivity as difference."[16]

Memories and Migrations embodies more than first-stage recovery research, but rather pushes the field of U.S. women's history toward innovative, interdisciplinary considerations of the intersections and intertextuality of mobility in physical place and personal memory. Congruent with incisive studies that interrogate gender and American empire (the works of Laura Briggs and Laura Wexler come immediately to mind, among others),[17] this volume helps unhitch U.S. women's history from its exceptionalist, nationalist moorings. Moreover, in moving past a contributionist or "we are here, too" approach, Latina histories reveal how transnationalism does not require travel across vast oceans but occurs within and across the Americas.

Several essays in this collection, including those by Gabriela Arredondo, Carmen Teresa Whalen, and Marisela R. Chávez, begin to situate Boricua and Chicana histories as part of larger hemispheric conversations. Taking inspiration from nineteenth-century Cuban patriot and philosopher José Martí, anthropologist Sandhya Shukla and historian Heidi Tinsman call for an innovative conceptual map of the "Americas," unfettered by the nation-state. In their words: "Following Martí, we envision such a paradigm as focusing on shared histories of connections and interactions between peoples across, beyond, and underneath national boundaries and regions."[18] Latina/o studies scholars, in general, are well poised to collaborate within this visionary discourse, *sin fronteras* (without borders).

Locating Boricua and Chicana histories within a transnational turn recognizes these narratives as born of conquest and shaped by globalization, past, present, and foreseeable future. Though rooted in specific sites, whether Seattle or Tucson, Chicago or New York, the chapters in *Memories and Migrations* express such disjunctive diasporas as crossing the border at El Paso as a child during the 1920s, growing up "Irish" in a New York parochial school during the 1940s, and discovering one's embedded "American-ness" while attending a 1970s women's conference in Mexico City. As authors and editors, we seek a fuller recounting of Latina history through locating gendered ethnoracial identities within matrices of place as landscape and metaphor, of migration and settlement, and of political space.

Notes

1. Interview with Erminia Ruiz, February 18, 1993, conducted by the author; Aura Luz Sánchez, "A Love Story," in *Laughing in the Kitchen: Short Stories, Poems, Essays, and Memories*, edited by the Streetfeet Women [Blanca E. Bonilla, Elena Harap, Mary M. McCulloch, Lin Min Mo, and Aura Luz Sánchez] (Boston: Talking Stone Press, 1998), 40–44.

2. Translational refers to the ways in which cultural meanings, memories, and practices adapt, change, and coalesce as the result of migration, including in no small measure the impact of Americanization.

3. In my previous work, I have conceptualized cultural coalescence as follows: "Immigrants and their children pick, borrow, retain, and create distinctive cultural forms. There is not a single hermetic Mexican or Mexican American culture, but rather permeable cultures rooted in generation, gender, region, class, and personal experience. People navigate across cultural boundaries and make conscious decisions with regard to the production of culture. However, bear in mind, people of color have not had unlimited choice. Prejudice and discrimination with the accompanying social, political, and economic segmentation have constrained aspirations, expectations, and decision-making."—Vicki L. Ruiz, *From Out of the Shadows: Mexican Women in Twentieth-Century America* (New York: Oxford University Press, 1998), xvi.

4. Gilbert González, *Culture of Empire: American Writers, Mexico, and Mexican Immigrants, 1880–1930* (Austin: University of Texas Press, 2004); "Nativity and Citizenship, 1990–2000," Census 2000 data analyzed by the Social Science Data Analysis Network, U.S. Bureau of the Census, *The Hispanic Population in the United States: March 2002* (Washington, D.C.: Government Printing Office, June 2003), 1, 3.

5. In 1848, under the Treaty of Guadalupe Hidalgo, Mexico ceded its northern territories (over one-half of its total land base) to the United States. Puerto Rico came under American political and economic dominion with the armistice that ended the Spanish-American-Cuban-Filipino War of 1898.

6. For more information on nomenclature, see Suzanne Oboler, *Ethnic Labels, Latino Lives: Identity and Politics of (Re)presentation in the United States* (Minneapolis: University of Minnesota Press, 1995); and Clara E. Rodríguez, *Changing Race: Latinos, the Census, and the History of Ethnicity in the United States* (New York: New York University Press, 2000).

7. Arnoldo De León, "Region and Ethnicity: Topographical Identities in Texas," in *Many Wests: Place, Culture, and Regional Identity*, edited by David M. Wrobel and Michael C. Steiner (Lawrence: University of Kansas Press, 1997), 259–74; Sarah Deutsch, "Landscape of Enclaves: Race Relations in the West, 1865–1990," in *Under an Open Sky: Rethinking America's Western Past*, edited by William Cronon, George Miles, and Joy Gitlin (New York: W.W. Norton, 1992), 110–31; Daniel D. Arreola, *Tejano South Texas: A Mexican American Cultural Province* (Austin: University of Texas Press, 2002); John R. Chávez, *The Lost Land: The Chicano Image of the Southwest* (Albuquerque: University of New Mexico Press, 1984).

8. Patricia Preciado Martin, *Songs My Mother Sang to Me: An Oral History of Mexican American Women* (Tucson: University of Arizona Press, 1992); Sarah

Deutsch, *No Separate Refuge: Culture, Class and Gender on the Anglo Hispanic Frontier in the American Southwest, 1880–1940* (New York: Oxford University Press, 1987); María Montoya, *Translating Property: The Maxwell Land Grant and the Conflict Over Land in the American West, 1840–1900* (Berkeley: University of California Press, 2002); Carmen Teresa Whalen, *From Puerto Rico to Philadelphia: Puerto Rican Workers and Postwar Economies* (Philadelphia: Temple University Press, 2001).

9. Pat Mora, "Desert Women" in *Borders* (Houston: Arte Público Press, 1986), 80.

10. Aura Luz Sánchez, "To Live in the Margins," in *Laughing in the Kitchen*, 63.

11. Transnational refers to "connecting life in two countries" and translocal refers to "connecting life in a village or region of one country and a particular city or town in another." Donna R. Gabaccia and Vicki L. Ruiz, eds., *American Dreaming, Global Realities: Rethinking U.S. Immigration History* (Urbana: University of Illinois Press, 2006), 4.

12. Emma Pérez, *The Decolonial Imaginary: Writing Chicanas into History* (Bloomington: Indiana University Press, 1999), 79.

13. Yen Le Espiritu, *Home Bound: Filipino American Lives across Cultures, Communities, and Countries* (Berkeley: University of California Press, 2003), 85.

14. Rebecca J. Lester, *Jesus in Our Wombs: Embodying Modernity in a Mexican Convent* (Berkeley: University of California Press, 2005), 305.

15. For more information, see Ruiz, *From Out of the Shadows;* Virginia Sánchez Korrol, *From Colonia to Community: The History of Puerto Ricans in New York City,* 2d ed. (Berkeley: University of California Press, 1994); Cynthia E. Orozco, "Beyond Machismo, La Familia, and Ladies Auxiliaries: A Historiography of Mexican-Origin Women's Participation in Voluntary Associations and Politics in the United States, 1870–1990," *Renato Rosaldo Lecture Series,* Monograph 10 (Tucson: Mexican American Studies and Research Center, University of Arizona, 1992–93), 37–77; Vicki L. Ruiz and Virginia Sánchez Korrol, eds., *Latina Legacies* (New York: Oxford University Press, 2005).

16. Genaro M. Padilla, *My History, Not Yours: The Formation of Mexican American Autobiography* (Madison: University of Wisconsin Press, 1993), 45.

17. See for example, Laura Briggs, *Reproducing Empire: Race, Sex, Science, and U.S. Imperialism in Puerto Rico* (Berkeley: University of California Press, 2002); and Laura Wexler, *Tender Violence: Domestic Visions in an Age of U.S. Imperialism* (Chapel Hill: University of North Carolina Press, 2000).

18. Sandhya Shukla and Heidi Tinsman, "Editors' Introduction to Our America's Political and Cultural Imaginings," *Radical History Review* 89 (Spring: 2004): 2.

PART I

A Woman's Place

MARÍA E. MONTOYA

*1. Creating an American Home:
Contest and Accommodation in
Rockefeller's Company Towns*

In 1930 Abelia López and her family were among the handful of
working families who were still living in Primero, Colorado, and making
a living at mining in the coalfields owned by the Colorado Fuel and Iron
Corporation (CF&I). While the town of Primero had seen its glory days
in the early 1920s when more than 400 families lived and worked in the
company-owned town, now fewer than 50 families lived there and some
of those households you could not even call families, for they included
boarders and other workers lucky enough to still have jobs taking the
coal out of the mines. Abelia's husband, Genario, still worked as a miner,
and her two older sons, Hermino and Filberto, rode the coal train every
morning down the line into Trinidad to attend Trinidad High School.
At home, she still had her new baby boy, José, to care for. But, as the
Depression worsened, these were comforts that she probably could not
count on since her husband could be thrown out of work at any moment
if the mine closed, and they would lose access to their company-owned
housing, which they rented for $14 a month.[1]
 Both Abelia and her husband had come from families that could
trace their roots back to neighboring New Mexico. Both had memories
of lives as farmers before they had married and migrated to Colorado, to
find work in the new coal mines that were opening as a result of World
War I and the subsequent industrial development that it spurred across

13

the American West. Now, as the Depression deepened and more and more workers were leaving on their own or being laid off, Abelia probably could not help but wonder and worry about what was to become of her and her family as they struggled to maintain her husband's job and what it provided: the security of wages, a (rented) home, and access to education for her sons.

Abelia López's concerns were not unique. Women who had formed part of Rockefeller's Colorado Fuel & Iron's company towns had been worrying and trying to build lives for themselves and their families under the constant influence and supervision of the corporation. How did working families experience life in Rockefeller's coal company towns? While historians have tended to think of work and labor as the domain solely of men in the early twentieth century, within company towns families and women in particular also had to negotiate the policies of the company and adapt to or resist them. The present essay is part of a larger project that asks how American families and American corporations have negotiated the tensions between work and home. It looks at the lives of a few Mexican American women and puts them within the larger context of how these towns were organized and places them within the context of other women, working men, a polyglot workforce, and their families. The coalfields of southern Colorado were one of the most multiethnic work and living spaces in the early twentieth-century American West. In these spaces women, Mexican Americans and others, had to learn how to negotiate and accommodate, and resist when necessary.

For these women and their families, their lives and their stories cannot be understood or discussed without understanding the violent historical context from which their lives emerged and developed. The Ludlow Massacre of 1914 is one of the most notorious episodes in American labor history. In that confrontation between government militia and the agents of the Rockefeller-owned Colorado Fuel & Iron Company on one side and the striking workers on the other, twenty people died, including two women and eleven children, when a fire erupted within the tent colony that the workers had established outside CF&I's property. The women and children had taken shelter in hastily dug cellars under the tents and had retreated there when heavy gunfire sprayed across their temporary homes from the Colorado National Guard, Pinkerton Agents, and other company proxies. Six months earlier, the workers and their families had been evicted from their company-owned homes and boarding rooms, and as a result the workers and their families had been living in the tent community as the workers' strike against the company dragged on. Company officials asserted that since the men were no longer employees of the company, they had no right to maintain residence within the company towns. The harsh and arid environment of southeastern Colorado combined with the onslaught of winter left workers and their families with no home and no protection from the elements or from the hostile government and company forces that were gathering on the boundaries of the tent colony.

How was it that these women and children came to be living in this tent colony under such difficult circumstances? What were the economic and gendered forces that drove them into this temporary housing? The segregation in the coal camps and the kind of work that miners did has rendered women and their families almost invisible on this landscape and in most labor histories. Yet the company and the miners themselves depended on the unpaid labor of these women to maintain comfortable homes and a stable workforce. Our task is to make visible the lives of these women as they moved their families into these alien, arid, and treacherous landscapes to create homes within that circumscribed social environment.

The Ludlow Massacre was viewed by CF&I company officials, and later by historians, as the watershed event that transformed labor-management relationships in Colorado's coalfields. The Rockefellers pleaded ignorance about the hideous living and working situation and vowed to improve conditions. Rockefeller corporate management proposed the Industrial Representation Plan, which was the blueprint for the corporate union that would control labor relations in Rockefeller's Colorado enterprises until the early 1930s. But despite the intentions of CF&I and the rhetoric surrounding the implementation of the Industrial Representation Plan, very little changed for workers and their families. Although the most notorious problems of living in a company town were eliminated—no payments in scrip, no company store monopoly, an open shop—there was still much social control and surveillance that continued to dominate employees' lives. Although the Industrial Representation Plan was meant to negotiate, if not eliminate, worker-employer tensions, in the end the plan did not allow worker autonomy and satisfaction. CF&I would suffer two more strikes under the Industrial Representation Plan before it was finally replaced by a union contract with the United Mine Workers in 1933.

The World CF&I Made: The Sociological Department
and the Industrial Representation Plan

Both before and after Ludlow, CF&I created a number of institutions intended to foster a content and productive workforce. At the beginning of the twentieth century the company, under the direction of Dr.

Richard W. Corwin, established the Sociological Department in order to help workers and their families adapt to industrial life in the camps. Outside observers often noted what they took to be the exceptionally favorable working conditions under which CF&I's laborers worked. For example, the *Trinidad Picketwire* noted of the emerging company-worker relationship, "The man who works for the C.F. & I., because of the fact that the company is honestly trying to make his life and that of his wife and children as pleasant as money and effort can make them, is looked upon as fortunate. The relations of the company and the workman do not end when the whistle blows in the evening and the dust-covered employe leaves the mine. It continues into his home, into his clubhouse, and through all the hours of his life."[2] The author also noted that this "pleasant" set of working and living conditions came at the expense of the company officials involving themselves in all aspects of workers' lives. Prior to the Ludlow Massacre the Sociological Department had attempted to improve the living conditions of workers by improving sanitation, living facilities, and educational institutions in the company towns. During its existence, the Sociological Department's officers influenced not only the industrial workplace of CF&I's miners, but also the "homeplace" of their wives and families. John D. Rockefeller Sr., Dr. Corwin, and CF&I president Jesse Welborn hoped that a paternalistic relationship could be formed so that workers would be content and diligent employees who would find it unnecessary to form a union under the direction of the United Mine Workers (UMW) or the more radical Industrial Workers of the World (IWW or Wobblies).

As the Ludlow incident as well as a later strikes in 1919 and 1927 made clear, workers were not satisfied with either Rockefeller's paternalistic model of industrial relations or with the working conditions and wages set by the corporation. The Ludlow Massacre, in particular, laid bare all the problems between workers and their families and the Colorado Fuel & Iron Corporation. In all three of these strikes two general concerns emerged. First, workers wanted a union contract and recognition of an independent and national union. Second, both workers and their families resented the paternalistic and domineering control of the company officials over both their work and their home lives.

The system that evolved after Ludlow, however, did very little to address the core issues that had emerged from the strike and its violence. In the post-Ludlow world that the company and workers created together, they were governed by John D. Rockefeller Jr.'s Industrial Representation Plan, an intricate blueprint for a company union that attempted to represent the interests of workers, company directors, company officers, and stockholders. Rockefeller used the metaphor of a four-legged table to explain how he saw the relationship, which he termed a square deal, between the four groups of any industrial enterprise. While giving the speech at a meeting of officers of the company and employees in 1915, Rockefeller demonstrated his analogy of the table by putting some coins on one table. He then went on to explain the preferred position that worker's held under the new plan: "Here come along the employees, and first of all they get their wages (*removing some of the coins*), every two weeks like clockwork, just what has been agreed on; they get the first chance at the pile. You men come ahead of the president, the officers, the stockholders and directors. You are the first to put a hand into the pile and take out what is agreed shall belong to you." Although the workers were the first to take their wages from the earnings of the company, this was clearly all they deserved, in Rockefeller's view. Their wages were a matter of contract and not the result of some utopian view that integrated them into the capitalist system by enmeshing them through profit-sharing, stock options, or other investments into the company's business. Compare Rockefeller's view of workers with his idea about the place of management and stockholders: "But for fourteen years, to my knowledge—how much longer I do not know—the common stockholders have gotten not one cent out of this company. I just want you to put that in your pipes and smoke it, and see if it tallies with what you have heard about the stockholders oppressing you and trying to get the better of you. That does not sound like oppression, like trying to get the best of the bargain!"[3] Although Rockefeller's speech and the Industrial Representation Plan were meant to draw men into the company as loyal and reliable workers, it in fact made it clear that they were wage laborers and could expect no higher stake in the company. In Rockefeller's view, the Industrial Representation Plan put workers first and they, in turn, should be cognizant of that and thankful for their preferred position in the corporation.

The Industrial Representation Plan, according to Rockefeller's ideal, established a company union that would address workers' grievances against CF&I. One of Rockefeller's goals was to prevent an independent union from gaining a foothold in his coalfields. Rockefeller warned of the pernicious effects of unions on men, their work ethic, and their moral fiber: "Now you know there are men going over this country from one end to the other who are saying to the workmen of the country: 'Your game is to get the shortest possible working day you can, to do the least possible work that you can get away with and not lose your job, and to get just as much as you can for what little you do.' Any man who preaches that doctrine, instead of being your friend, is your deadliest enemy."[4] Rockefeller warned that when labor does not hold up its end of the square deal, either by creating a union or striking, then the entire table collapses, and there is nothing left for anyone. Rockefeller sought to create an idealized workplace in which employees were satisfied and corporations could depend on a stable workforce. Ironically, however, unions and Rockefeller both envisioned similar roles for American labor: subordinated wage laborers who would inevitably be alienated from their work, the product, and the means of production. The only difference was that Rockefeller thought he could make it so that workers were content with their lot in life, while some unions, such as the IWW, wanted workers to remake the industrial world in which they toiled.

From the very beginning, when John D. Rockefeller Sr. and his conglomerate took a controlling interest in the Colorado Fuel & Iron Company, until John D. Rockefeller Jr. established the Industrial Representation Plan, the company's directors sought to bring the kind of corporate paternalism that had been a hallmark of Standard Oil's employee relations. The Rockefellers, with their strong Baptist background and their belief in diligence and morality as the path to success for working men, were part of an industrial elite that included other men like themselves, including Henry Ford.[5] These men revolutionized the relationship between corporation and worker by attempting to remake the home lives of the latter and their families. This corporate welfare, coupled with the benevolence of the newly created Rockefeller Foundation, laid the economic and social foundation upon which the Rockefellers sought to build an employee union that would maintain a content workforce and keep other unions, particularly the United Mine Workers of America and the Industrial Workers of the World, at bay. CF&I's Industrial Representation Plan governed these immigrant workers until it was displaced by Franklin D. Roosevelt's National Industrial Recovery Act in 1933.[6] During this period, however, the company and its workers forged a tenuous and uncomfortable working relationship that was periodically threatened by strikes and industrial accidents.

In addition to their fear of unionization, CF&I managers worried over two other issues when trying to maintain a stable workforce. First, the coal camps were isolated from cities and infrastructure, such as running water, schools, and housing; it was difficult to recruit as well as retain a consistent workforce in these remote locations. Second, the diversity of ethnic and racial groups in the camps created a polyglot workforce that caused anxiety among company officials. Managers worried about the high turnover and the incohesiveness of such a workforce. From the managers' perspective these workers came from nowhere and could run off to anywhere. Immigrants from Mexico, Italy, Greece, and Eastern Europe joined African American and Mexican American workers in the wild and chaotic world of the coal camps. Up until 1910, the CF&I had used labor agents in order to recruit its workforce. After that point, however, it is not clear how or why other immigrant groups made their way to Colorado and filled the enormous labor demands that CF&I generated.[7]

All these groups were drawn to the expanding CF&I enterprise emerging in southern Colorado with the opening of the coal mines at the beginning of the twentieth century and the production of steel at the Bessemer Steel Works (the first steel mill west of the Mississippi) in Pueblo, Colorado. Until World War II, CF&I was the major supplier of steel and coal to industry in the western United States. In addition to the mines and the steelworks, CF&I operated coke ovens in three locations, railroads, iron mines, and a timber-cutting operation in order to feed the demands of the ever-expanding corporation. By 1910 CF&I was the largest employer in Colorado, employing one-tenth of all workers in the state. The corporation boasted more than 15,000 workers on its payroll that same year.[8] CF&I formed the largest exception to Colorado's rural economy of cattle ranching and high-plains farming, an exception that lured natives and immigrants alike away from their agricultural livelihoods into a world of wage labor and company towns.

Of particular concern to both the company's management and the workers were the large numbers of mine explosions and the attendant loss of life. Managers worried that the extreme danger of the work would keep men away from the coal mines, or at the very least drive miners to strike for safer working conditions. Between 1904 and 1910, CF&I experienced five explosions, killing 193 workers in the Trinidad, Colorado, region.[9] Even by early twentieth-century safety standards, this was a large loss of life, and the company management constantly tried to lower the death and accident rate through policy and worker education. These dangerous working conditions combined with the paternalist policies of CF&I made management-labor relations tense and often violent. It was within this context, combined with a tenuous economic situation, that families created their homes within Rockefeller-owned company towns.

UNDERSTANDING THE GENDERED GEOGRAPHY OF THE COAL CAMPS

One way to understand how work, gender, and space played out on the landscape of the coalfields is to analyze how men and women inhabited their primary living spaces. For men these included the mine, the bathhouse, and the saloon: public spaces where they interacted with other men. These spaces, however, were heavily scrutinized by company officials, who feared that excessive drinking, lascivious behavior, or union organizing would occur in these company-owned public areas. For women, their space was confined mainly to their homes and yards: private areas where they had few interactions with other adults. Through the Sociological Department, and then later through other programs such as the YMCA, the company regulated all spaces of the company town, whether they were public or private. Despite such attempts at social control, both men and women transgressed company expectations by remaking spaces to conform to their own needs and desires.

Although the spaces within the company town were nominally owned and controlled by the Rockefeller Corporation, there were opportunities for workers and their families to discuss politics, organize strikes, or air petty grievances against their employer.[10] Despite CF&I's desperate and extreme measures to control social, cultural, and political space, workers and their wives were often able to transgress company norms and assert their own ideas of proper behavior. At the extreme, workers were able to overcome the obstacles established by CF&I and organize strikes, work slowdowns, and other daily acts against company authority.

Primero, which was located about twenty miles west of Trinidad in the heart of the CF&I coalfields, was the quintessential Rockefeller company town and provides a useful case study for examining how class, race, and gender played out in workers' lives. (See figure 1.1.) Primero functioned as a working mine from 1901 to 1928 and was home to approximately 400 workers. The mine had its share of industrial accidents, such as a 1907 blast that killed 24 miners and another explosion three years later that killed 75 workers.[11] Families here lived under the constant threat of industrial death or accident as well as economic ups and downs. The ethnic makeup of Primero was quite diverse: the town housed Austrian, Italian, Eastern European, Mexican, and white (American, as the company noted) workers.[12]

One observer of Rockefeller's coal camps noted the similarity in all these planned communities, and Primero was no exception to these observations: "On entering the main road, you notice first a bandstand, neat well-kept, freshly painted in gray, in the center of a 'village-green.' On one side of the green is a Young Men's Christian Association building, or miner's club, a two-story concrete building with a graceful, almost classical approach. On the other side is a school-house, also of gray concrete. Beyond the school is the miner's bath-house. Before long you notice a symmetrical relationship between the band-stand, the 'Y'

Figure 1.1. Panoramic view of Primero, Colorado, coal camp, circa 1915. Scamehorn Collection, Bessemer Historical Society, Pueblo, Colo.

club-house, the school, and the bath-house, and you exclaim, 'A civic center in a mining camp!'"[13] (See figure 1.2, a centrally designed layout of a company town.) Every aspect of the mining camps was centrally planned and was intended to convey a sense of order and surveillance. The center of the company town was surrounded by buildings that suggested the company's control and power over the miners: the YMCA, the school, and the bathhouse. One thing that did not appear in these camps was a town hall or some architectural symbol of democratic judicial arbitration. Local government was handled in the superintendent's office. Other buildings that might have reflected the communities' interests, such as churches or saloons, were kept away from the town center and in many cases placed outside company property. In a panoramic view of Primero, the most prominent features on the town's landscape were the company-sponsored Protestant church (the Catholic Church was outside the town), the mine, its tailings, the Colorado Supply Company Store, and the railroad depot and its tracks.[14] As the geography reveals, these camps represented integrated living and work spaces in which families

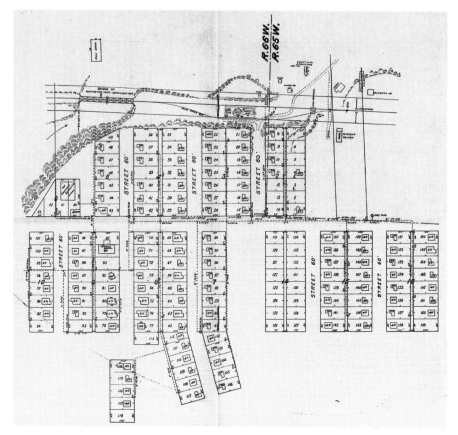

Figure 1.2. Plan of Segundo Camp, circa 1903. Annual Report of the Sociological Department of the Colorado Fuel and Iron Company.

had to negotiate daily the demands of both the workscapes and the homes they were trying to create.[15]

Gendered Male Space

One aspect of workers' lives that concerned some outside observers, particularly the Sage Foundation researchers who were surveying the successes of the Industrial Representation Plan, was the loss of manhood that might attend wage labor. The researchers commented that many of the men who worked in the mines had left or even lost their land and homes or no longer had the money to own their own piece of property because they were recent immigrants. These workers now only possessed the rights to their bodies and labor from which to gain satisfaction as men. In a report commissioned by the Sage Foundation in 1924 to survey the Rockefeller Industrial Representation Plan, the observers, Selekman and Van Kleek, made numerous references to the desire of the coal miners to see themselves as men: "A man who recently devoted some months to studying the industrial problem and who came in contact with thousands of workmen in various industries throughout the country has said that it was obvious to him from the outset that the working men were seeking for something, which at first he thought to be higher wages. As his touch with them extended, he came to the conclusion, however, that not higher wages but recognition as men was what they really sought."[16] Selekman and Van Kleek worried that the company's relationship to its workers unnecessarily fostered a paternalist relationship that left working men very little room to assert themselves as heads of households, breadwinners, or virile men. Instead, through wage labor, they were beholden to the company, not only for their livelihood, but for their very identity as men. Selekman and Van Kleek asked rhetorically: "What joy can there be in life, what interest can a man take in his work, what enthusiasm can he be expected to develop on behalf of his employer, when he is regarded as a number on a payroll, a cog in a wheel, a mere 'hand'? Who would not earnestly seek to gain recognition of his manhood and the right to be heard and treated as a human being, not as a machine?"[17] For these sociologists, manhood could only thrive under conditions that made workers independent of their employers. They saw the Industrial Representation Plan as a failure as a long-term solution to labor problems in America. In their opinion, only a democratically elected union would provide the kind of environment where workers could develop into free workers and regain their manhood.

The miners themselves appear to have had established ideas about what space constituted male versus female space, and company versus worker's space. For example, during the first elections that CF&I held for election of workers' representatives under the Industrial Representation Plan, very few men voted. As Selekman and Van Kleek noted, "At first, elections were held in buildings of the Young Men's Christian Association or in school houses. The men, however, did not come to the meetings. That is why several of the superintendents finally arranged to hold elections at the mouth of the mine or in the lamp house." Part of the problem was that men did not want to attend meetings after a long day's work. But these spaces were coded as company-controlled, and more subtly as female or domesticated space, and consequently men did not often feel comfortable conducting business there. The report continued,

"At one mine in the first year after the plan was adopted the election meeting was held in the kindergarten room of the school in the evening. From a mine employing about 225 miners, only 30 attended." While all space within the mining camps was technically owned and controlled by company managers, some spaces, such as the YMCA, schools, and the kindergarten teacher's homes, seemed to be beyond the pale of acceptable social space for men. As a result of these perceptions, once balloting and voting was held outside the mine or at the bathhouses, the participation rate rose to almost 90 percent in most camps.[18]

After the Ludlow Massacre and the implementation of the Industrial Representation Plan, the YMCA played a vital role in the development of the cultural and social life of the coal-mining camps. The Sociological Department had come to be seen as an oppressive tool of the company and was abandoned by 1915. In its place, CF&I sought to contract out the business of miners' social betterment to the YMCA. After the CF&I and the YMCA conducted a joint survey of the social terrain of the camps, the YMCA began an aggressive campaign to bring clubhouses, bathhouses, and wholesome activities to the men in the camps. Their goal was to create healthy, gender-segregated spaces where men could keep themselves physically and morally healthy and vigorous.[19]

The places in the camps that best represented the authority of the company over its workers were the CF&I company office and the superintendent's home. In Primero, as in the other company towns, both these structures differed in their quality of construction and architecture. The Primero CF&I company office is a wood-frame Victorian-era cottage with porch. (See figure 1.3.) This is a seemingly private and segregated space enclosed and secured by a white fence. Furthermore, the architectural style is not indigenous to the region and is clearly a transplant from the midwestern prairie. Indeed, most houses in the region would have been constructed of adobe with very little use of wood planking and beams because of the relatively high cost of such materials.[20] The CF&I office would have been a place occupied by mostly white men who were of the managerial class, as the five men in suits and ties in the photo suggest.[21] Rarely did working-class men venture into the offices unless they were called by company officials or had some particular piece of business with the company. Women rarely would have been seen in these offices, for they had no direct relationship with the company. The whole structure and setting give the sense of being set apart from the rest of the camp and its workers: the fence, the porch, the architecture, and its location on a hill separate the managers from the workers physically, a reflection of class and racial divisions.

Figure 1.3. CF&I Company office in Primero, circa 1915. Note the professional class of men standing in front of building. Scamehorn Collection, Bessemer Historical Society, Pueblo, Colo.

The racial hierarchy of the camps was also made explicit through the layout of the camps on the landscape. One observer from the YMCA noted, "The houses in the camp are not close together. The section given over to the colored people is in the further part of the town, along side of them are many Mexicans. This part is about a quarter of a mile from the other sections of the camp. In that section on the side of the hill near the mine, live the English speaking and the best class of foreigners. The other houses are scattered over the camp. The Japanese house is in the center of the town."[22] The company often segregated African American, Japanese, and sometimes Mexican workers from the rest of the polyglot workforce. The report makes a number of references to segregation, such as how "white" ethnics had access to the better housing, which tended to be located higher on the hills and in the choicest spots of the company town. Nonwhite workers and their families were often relegated to the lowlands and less desirable locations of the camp.

While the company offices expressed its authority over the landscape and the workers, the bathhouses were a more racially integrated space. Everyone, with the exception of African Americans, was allowed to use the bathhouses. In camps where there was a significant number of African Americans, a second bathhouse was built for their exclusive use. Figure 1.4 shows the bathhouse at Primero Camp. CF&I built similar bathhouses for each camp. The bathhouses had ample running water, showers, tubs for washing clothes, and lockers for the men to store their belongings.[23] The bathhouse was an exclusive male space, since women and children were expected to wash and bathe in the privacy of their homes, although few homes and boardinghouses had running water. The few homes that did have running water often did not have the luxury of a bathtub or shower for men to bathe after a long hot day in the mines. Also, women would have been expected to keep a fire and warm the water for her husband and sons. Consequently, the bathhouse was a labor-saving device for women, as well as a place where men could keep themselves and their clothes clean.

Figure 1.4. Men's bathhouse at Primero, circa 1915. Scamehorn Collection, Bessemer Historical Society, Pueblo, Colo.

The bathhouses worked as an extension of male workspace in close proximity to the mines and mill. The bathhouse was probably the first place that men would stop before heading home, to their boardinghouse, or to a saloon for the evening meal. The bathhouse functioned as a transitional space as the men moved from their work lives in the mines to their home lives in the camps. The bathhouses were more than just places where the men could wash themselves; they were among the few homosocial spaces where working men could speak in private with their peers out of earshot of women, families, and company managers. While company management and the YMCA viewed the bathhouse as a way to encourage both physical and moral purity, the working men saw the space as a private sphere where they could talk freely and congregate as men.

A second place where men could socialize was the saloon or clubhouse. The company, however, was uneasy about the presence of the saloon and alcohol. They worried about drunkenness and its attendant problems: loss of work hours, accidents, violence, and property damage. Although Primero was a dry camp, there were two saloons just across the railroad tracks within easy walking distance of company property.[24] Earlier, Dr. Corwin of the Sociological Department had written, "Saloons and drinking never cease to be a problem for the sociological worker. Why man created saloons no one undertakes to say. How they may be disposed of or managed, we do not feel sure. Prohibition has been tried but failed on account of blind pigs and wet bread wagons."[25] In response to his observations, the Sociological Department had advocated the opening of the "well-conducted open saloons" within the camps, which would be under the supervision of the camp superintendent. In addition to regulating the hours, there was a strict policy of "no treating," so as to minimize excessive drinking and undue influence. Corwin explained the company's logic of running a company saloon: "For such [drinking men] we are arranging to try the open reform saloon where one may obtain any sort of pure liquors, where no rules beyond good behavior are to be enforced, but where soft drinks, milk, tea, coffee, and sandwiches can be obtained and always be found conspicuously 'on tap.'" Corwin hoped that by controlling the space of the saloon, company policy would subtly persuade workers to choose socialization and refreshments over hard drink. He concluded, "Further, where, with games and music, halls, card and billiard rooms will be made more attractive than the bar room and also where it will be the duty of the barkeeper to amuse, entertain, dispense innocent drinks and food rather than sell alcoholic liquors. In other words, a real live saloon but one which shall not have for its chief

Figure 1.5. Saloon and clubhouse at Redstone Camps, circa 1921. This would have been a typical clubhouse in all of the camps. Annual Report of the Sociological Department of the Colorado Fuel and Iron Company, 1903–04, p. 28.

object monetary profit or sale of strong drinks."[26] Women rarely went into these clubhouses daily and were only sometimes invited in for special celebrations, such as holidays. The company's managers hoped that by opening these clubhouses, drinking alcohol would be the least palatable option within a wide array of other diversions. But this company policy of "damp" saloons did nothing to improve the attraction of the clubhouses, particularly because they were later run by the YMCA, which was often associated with femininity and domesticity. (See figure 1.5).

The company did not believe that it alone was responsible for creating and addressing the problem of male alcoholism. At the heart of the drinking problem, the company believed, was the fact that men did not necessarily want to leave work and return to their families and homes at the end of a long day. Corwin wrote, "The man with many clubs at his disposal is not always temperate, and the man with two rooms and five small children is not obliged to drink. . . . We have many who belong to this class; they will drink and make any excuse for drinking; small house, many children, cross wife, strikes, too long hours, too little pay, sickness, holidays and funerals; any excuse, no excuse, but drink and lose time they will."[27] The company recognized that its policies and the enforcement of the rules by the YMCA and the superintendent was not enough to stem the problems of drinking. So it began to launch a campaign to reform miners' home lives as well. In addition to the policies that the company implemented to promote sobriety, it also made a concerted effort to create welcoming homes for working men.

In addition to the bathhouses and saloons, workers could associate in the mine itself, which was the exclusive domain of men of all ages. As figure 1.6, showing the Sopris miners, suggests, these were multiethnic and intergenerational workspaces where class and racial hierarchies existed.[28] Miners worked in pairs and tended to join with relatives or men they knew well. Consequently, the pairs of men were racially and ethnically distinct. Mexican, African American, and Greek workers often complained that they were relegated to the worst parts of the mines and treated unfairly by the foremen. Although the Industrial Representation

Figure 1.6. Sopris miners, circa 1924. Scamehorn Collection, Bessemer Historical Society, Pueblo, Colo.

Plan was supposed to create a system where work was distributed eq-
uitably, and grievances aired and corrected, miners well into the 1930s
complained about the segregation and hierarchy of mine work.[29]

Female Gendered Space

The corollary to these specified male spaces was the primary social space
of married women, the company-owned homes. Relatively few unmarried women lived in the camps, and the few who did tended to live with
their families until they found marriage partners. The notable excep-
tions were the few white women who lived in the camps and worked for
the company as teachers or nurses. Private homes were where women
would entertain, visit, work, and tend to children. Men were allowed in
this space, since it was technically their space, but only after they had
passed through the bathhouse and made themselves presentable within
the "American" home created by immigrant women under the supervision of the Sociological Department, kindergarten teachers, and other
agents of social control.

The company's managers had a set of ideas about what it believed
to constitute a proper home. They also had a plan for how immigrant
women could be brought into the company's fold to aid in the Americanization project of thrift, sobriety, and hard work that the Sociological
Department, and later the YMCA, advocated. Through the kindergarten
program established by Dr. Corwin and the Sociological Department
in the early 1900s, female teachers such as those in figure 1.7 were at
the forefront of Americanizing immigrants. As Sarah Deutsch notes,
not only did the kindergarten teacher instruct young children about the
value of education and a democratic society, but "her home, too, was to
serve as a model for camp housekeepers to create a thoroughly practical
and sanitary home."[30] In addition to teaching young children, she was
expected to run classes for older girls, mothers, and wives in the home
the company provided for her, on such diverse topics as canning, keeping a house sanitary, and laundry. Dr. Corwin wrote in his annual report,
"The plan of setting apart separate houses for the use of the kindergarten
teachers has amply justified itself, for not only are the teachers comfort-
ably housed and sure of a permanent abode during the school year but
the houses have become headquarters and centers for social work. The
furnishings of the teachers' rooms are thoroughly practical and sanitary
and are intended to serve as a standard of taste from which housekeepers may realize how much may be accomplished with comparatively

Figure 1.7. Kindergarten teachers employed by CF&I, circa 1903. Annual Report of the Sociological Department of the Colorado Fuel and Iron Company, 1903–04.

small expenditure."[31] The kindergarten teacher served the company as a model of idealized American womanhood. Her house was clean, neat, and sanitary and an inviting place where immigrant women and their children could feel comfortable, but where these women could also learn by example the kind of inviting homes they should be keeping for their working husbands and fathers. (See figure 1.8).

Better Home Contests

At the pinnacle of the Industrial Representation Plan's influence, the company held a series of "Better Home Contests" in which women would compete for three monetary prizes ranging from $10 to $25. The contest was conducted yearly, and each camp had its own set of winners. According to the *Camp and Plant* editors who published the winning pictures, the winners were judged on the appearance of the woman's home and yard. Company-picked judges looked at how clean they kept their homes and how lush they could make their yards with the little water and few plants available to them. On the appointed day each woman would dress herself and her children in their finest clothes and pose for the judges and for the photographer who came to take their picture.

The result of these contests was a real competition among families in the camp to create the first-prize home. For historians the contests and the recording of the homes through photographs provide an archive that can help interpret how life within the coal camps was lived by its workers and their families. Although these photographs record the best of conditions in the camps and probably do not reflect the actuality of their lives, they do give us a sense of the vision of Rockefeller when creating these company towns.

Regardless of location or the race of the occupants, there are a few details in the pictures that are consistent across the collection of photos. (See figures 1.9–1.12.) For example, each winner had a white picket fence in front of the house. Fences were encouraged by the company, because they demarcated the "private" space of the miner and his family. They kept children within the household and away from the dangerous equipment and mine openings that were easily accessible to curious youngsters. Both the company and the YMCA saw fencing as a high priority in that it encouraged care of gardens and pride in home. "The houses in Frederick are practically all fenced in, save those whose occupants have built a crude enclosure to the little garden they cultivate. The company will possibly enclose these as it does in the other camp. It will be appreciated by the people and will stimulate greater care of yards."[32] Company managers associated the fences with an "American" ideal of property that emphasized individual ownership and occupancy while pulling miners' families away from old European or Mexican ideas about plazas and communal property.

A second aspect that is striking about the photographs is the foliage around the houses and the lush gardens. Without exception, these coal camps were located in the one of the most arid parts of Colorado. Access to water would have been limited to what the company provided its residents through their creation of irrigation ditches and aqueducts, and, in the most extreme cases, to what they trucked in and held in communal tanks. Moreover, close examination of the photographs reveals that many of the plants in the yards were not indigenous to Colorado but were transplants from other regions where water was much more readily available. The company willingly provided plants, soil, and any available water for the cultivation of the ornamental gardens. Some households also had vegetable gardens that provided supplemental food. For the most part, families were dependent on the Colorado Supply company store for their

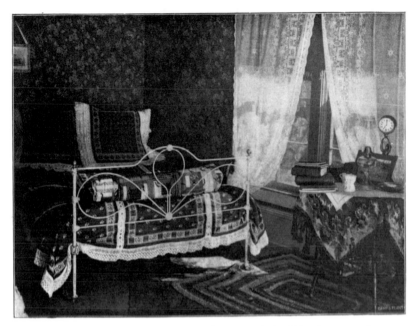

Corner of Bedroom in Miner's Cottage at Cuatro, Colorado.

Figure 1.8. Although this is captioned as a miner's cottage, it was probably a room in the model home of the kindergarten teacher. Annual Report of the Sociological Department of the Colorado Fuel and Iron Company, 1903–04.

Figure 1.9. Primero House #47. Woman and child in front of her home and exceptionally well-cultivated flower and vegetable garden. Scamehorn Collection, Bessemer Historical Society, Pueblo, Colo.

Figure 1.10. Primero House #46. Woman and child in front of home. Note the drainage ditch running in front of the yard. Scamehorn Collection, Bessemer Historical Society, Pueblo, Colo.

Figure 1.11. Woman and son in front of Primero House #42. Note the American flag. Scamehorn Collection, Bessemer Historical Society, Pueblo, Colo.

Figure 1.12. African American woman and child in front of their home at Primero House #12. Scamehorn Collection, Bessemer Historical Society, Pueblo, Colo.

food and goods, although company management did allow authorized peddlers and truck farmers into the camps to sell directly to families. In an attempt to make themselves more independent from the company store and expensive truck farmers, women grew fresh vegetables and kept chickens and milking goats. Although seemingly benign domestic activities, gardening and animal raising can be viewed as subversive daily practices on the part of women to gain control over family finances and well-being. These goods were a type of mobile property that women could take with them if they were forced to move.

All the houses are similar in layout and plan to one another. Some houses had only one bedroom and some had two, but all were built for efficiency. (See figure 1.13). The company discouraged more than one family from occupying a home; the physical layout combined with company policy fostered a sense that the nuclear family was the centerpiece of familial life. As families grew, the company preferred that they not overcrowd themselves and asked them to move into larger homes as they became available. Some families added onto their existing homes. While the company paid for the infrastructure and upkeep, these larger living quarters were reflected in the higher rents that miners paid for their homes. The only exception to the typical home layout was the superintendent's home, which stood apart literally and figuratively from

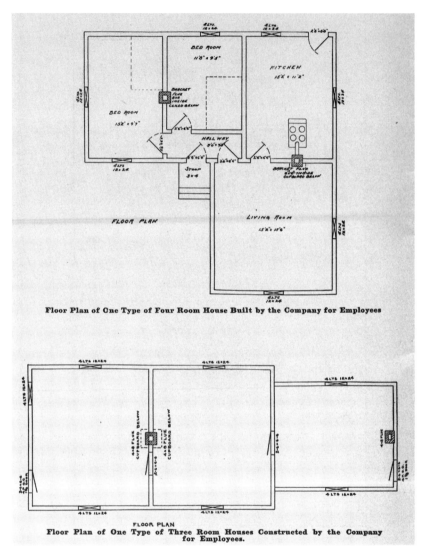

Figure 1.13. Floor plans for miners' homes. Annual Report of the Sociological Department of the Colorado Fuel and Iron Company, 1903–04.

the rest of the camp. In Primero, a two-story Victorian home stood on a hill away from the camp. Here, the superintendent and his family could look down on the camp and survey the state of its occupants.

The state of the homes and gardens, as well as the best dress of the occupants, in figures 1.8 to 1.12 suggest that these women were attempting to adhere to some outside criteria of domesticity. Both these domestic spaces—the miners' homes and the superintendent's house—reveal occupants who were performing a particular kind of domesticity based on ideas about class and "American" ideals of cleanliness and proper homes.

Daily Practices and Resistance

It is easy to read these photographs as accommodation on the part of women who seemingly embraced the company ideals of female domesticity. The well-kept yards, homes, and children seem to indicate a populace that has willingly accepted the ideal American home as established by Rockefeller's Industrial Representation Plan and embodied in the kindergarten teachers' model homes. This was clearly the image that the Rockefellers wanted to present to the outside world in the wake of the public scrutiny and criticism they sustained from the Ludlow Massacre. What better image to counteract the horrid picture of women and children murdered amidst a burned-out tent colony than happy, clean mothers and babies in front of seemingly middle-class, or at least upwardly mobile, homes on Rockefeller property?

Nevertheless, all was not as well as it appeared in the photographs. There was constant tension between the women in the camp and the superintendent, who was responsible for managing the homes and families as well as the workers and the mine. One of the downsides for the company of having a widely distributed newsletter—*Camp and Plant*—was that news of improvements in one camp circulated widely through the other camps. Women in one camp complained that they did not have sinks and running water in their kitchens when they heard or read that other camps had this luxury. Through women's complaints, superintendents were often pushed into providing a level of comfort and service that they might not necessarily have wanted to supply. Often these complaints were a result of cultural misunderstanding and particular desires expressed by women. For example, one woman had a very different idea of what she thought was an appropriate color for her kitchen. "A Mexican woman, wife of an employe at the Segundo Coke Ovens, did not fancy any of the colors offered her by the company for a coat of paint in her kitchen," wrote one observer of the camps. The woman complained that white was too boring, and she preferred to have her kitchen a brighter color to cheer it up. Despite her desires and her request, however, the company prevailed through the interference of the Industrial Representation Plan union representative, "also a Mexican and member of the committee on housing, [who] persuaded her to like one of them, chiefly by convincing her that she was fortunate to have her kitchen painted at all when it already looked better than his own."[33] While the woman felt comfortable using the Industrial Representation Plan and its grievance procedure as a way to lodge her complaint, she still did not get her wish. For the most, conformity was highly valued and pursued by company officials.

Extraordinary Practices

Women not only made their displeasure with the company's policies known through their daily interactions over issues such as home improvement and access to schools, but they also created havoc for company officials when they joined strikes. Frances Valdez was an eight-year-old girl during the 1913 Walsenburg upheaval that preceded the Ludlow Massacre.[34] Although her age prevented her from playing a key role in the union struggle, her observations of how the strike affected her family and how she subsequently came to perceive the union is particularly telling. Her perspective demonstrates how ethnic, religious, and gender divisions even among strikers and company supporters were fluid within the mining towns owned by Rockefeller.

Valdez's father was a fire boss for the company and was "naturally on the side of the companies." Her uncle was also a "company man" and a mine guard. Her cousin "Shorty" Martínez was an undersheriff, who had been elected on the Republican ticket, and he was decidedly antiunion. Her brother Moises, however, "was a strong union man," as were many of her other relatives. Frances remembered that in her family, "It was a rather strange situation. You didn't know which side to be on, because you had relatives on both sides." The strike was not the only thing that divided the family. Part of her family was Hispano, and part was Anglo. Her grandparents on one side were Presbyterian, and on the other, Catholic. In spite of these ethnic and religious differences, and opposing sympathies on the subject of unions, Frances insisted that the family came first. Jack Burke, a pro-union Irishman who boarded at their house for many years, was considered a member of the family as well. While Frances's father and uncle supported CF&I during the strike, Moises and Jack Burke hosted notable union leaders, such as Mother Jones and John Lawson, head of the United Mine Workers, at the family dinner table. In spite of passionate ideological differences, it was Moises who guarded the family home at night to protect his father and family from angry strikers.

Frances received a very personal, if informal, education on the union. She learned of the "terrible conditions in the coal mines and all the dangers of the coal mines, and the rate of their pay" from the miners themselves, for they stayed in her mother's boardinghouse. She said of her childhood attraction to the union, "Mother Jones was, well, a dynamic little person. And I remember how much I favored the union, all because of Mother Jones, not because I understood too much about working conditions." Mother Jones was instrumental in organizing the strike but, as Frances pointed out, the miners and their families "were ready for organization" because of the dangerous working conditions and oppressive living conditions. And, she insisted, "The miners clearly understood what they were fighting for."[35]

When asked about the role of women in the strike, Frances replied, "Well, women were more militant than the men were." According to her older sister Anna's eyewitness report, it was a group of women who initiated the confrontation at Walsenburg. When armed company guards came to move the wife of an antiunion man out of town, "a group of women . . . stepped into the yard and were throwing the shoes and all they could find at the wagon, at the guards. . . . They broke a large mirror that was on the wagon. . . . As to whether the guard fired the first shot or the miner, [Frances's sister] heard the shot and saw the guard fall from his horse. . . . Everything broke loose when the first shot was fired." These women were careful to police the boundaries of their home and community. When officials locked them out of company towns, women insisted that their children be allowed to cross picket lines and enter company property in order to attend school. Men on both sides stood aside as women and children crossed this economic and political boundary to create their own educational and domestic space.[36]

In the IWW strike that rocked the Colorado coalfields in 1927, women were once again central to calling the strike and to its success. The issues in the 1927 strike revolved mainly around union recognition, and there was a battle between the UMW and IWW to see who would represent the miners. Also central to the cause was a demand by workers and families to be released from the paternalistic hold that Rockefeller-owned CF&I had on them. In particular, workers wanted an end to the Industrial Representation Plan and the company-controlled housing. While workers appreciated the relatively high quality of the homes and some of the best living conditions that could be expected in industrial America, the paternalistic offerings did not grant the kind of dignity that the families desired. As they organized for the strike in both the southern and northern coalfields, union organizers realized it was essential to have women on the picket lines, because their presence kept in line company officials who did not want to have another Ludlow incident on their hands. Women would put on their finest clothes and fur coats to walk picket lines for their husbands. (See figure 1.14.) For families in Colorado's coalfields, strikes were a family event and enterprise that required the work and sacrifice of all its members.

Figure 1.14. Women standing on the picket line. Circa 1927. Bessemer Historical Society, CF&I Archives, BHS-RMSM/CF&I Audiovisual, Industrial Relations, Photo CFI-IND-006.

Conclusion

While the Ludlow Massacre is often viewed as a watershed event that
marked a clear change of attitude and policy on the part of CF&I, in reality
not much changed for workers in their day-to-day lives. Their wages and
working conditions were still set by company officials with very little
input from workers or their representatives. Wives and families lived
in homes owned and run by the company; they did not own their own
property. As the Sage Foundation report made clear, the men, the women,
and their families would not find true satisfaction until they were independent, free to contract on a more equal basis with CF&I. Whether it
was Ludlow, the 1919 strike, or the 1927 IWW strike, one issue remained
paramount: Only union recognition and the attendant freedom and responsibility that came with such recognition would satisfy the miners.
Colorado miners, their wives, and families were willing to struggle for
this goal from the beginning of the twentieth century until they were
finally granted union recognition in 1933. For through the union, men,
women, and their families expected to map their own space—to be free
to own their homes, free to send their children to schools of their choosing, free to associate where and with whom they wanted, and even free
to choose the color of their kitchen walls. While company officials and
YMCA leaders often labeled these as petty desires, for these workers
and their wives they were necessities at the core of what it meant to be
independent workers and to raise a family in America.

Notes

1. U.S. Bureau of the Census, 1930 manuscript census, Enumeration District
36–15, Supervisor's District #10, J. M. Romero enumerator, Town of Primero. We
also know from the census that Abelia had her first son Hermino two years before
she married Genario. Was Genario Hermino's biological father? Unknown, but
possible. Hermino was born in 1913, and we know that Genario fought in World
War I. It is possible that Genario left before he could marry Abelia and upon his
return he married her and had a second son, Filberto. Or was Abelia a widow?
Possibly she and Genario had only recently married and become parents of the
one-year-old, José. Unfortunately for historians, the census can give us only clues
to the stories that lie behind the names, but with extrapolation we can speculate
about the rich lives that these women and their families lived.

2. "An Honest Effort to Help the Working Man," *CF&I Industrial Bulletin*, 1,
no. 8, (July 31, 1916), as reprinted in the *Trinidad* (Colorado) *Picketwire*.

3. John D. Rockefeller Jr., "Address of John D. Rockefeller Jr. at the Joint Meeting of the Officers and the Representatives of the Employees of the Colorado Fuel
and Iron Company," Pueblo, Colo., October 2, 1915, pp. 12–13.

4. Ibid., 14.

5. The best and most recent biography of John D. Rockefeller and his family is Ron Chernow, *Titan: the Life of John D. Rockefeller, Sr.* (New York: Random House, 1998).

6. H. Lee Scamehorn, *Mill & Mine: The CF&I in the Twentieth Century* (Lincoln: University of Nebraska Press, 1982), 80.

7. I do not have specific data about how and why immigrants made their way to Colorado. I am, however, intrigued by Gunther Peck's study of the western labor markets of mining companies; he points out that there were labor agents in foreign countries who were hiring workers for CF&I; see Peck, *Reinventing Labor* (Cambridge, U.K.: Cambridge University Press, 2001). See also Howard Lamar, "From Bonded to Contract Labor: Ethnic Labor in the American West, 1700–1890," in *The Countryside in the Age of Capitalist Transformation: Essays in the Social History of Rural America*, edited by Steven Hahn and Jonathan Prude (Chapel Hill: University of North Carolina Press, 1985), and Ben M. Selekman and Mary Van Kleek, *Employees' Representation in Coal Mines: A Study of the Industrial Representation Plan of the Colorado Fuel and Iron Company* (New York: Russell Sage Foundation, 1924), 116.

8. Scamehorn, *Mill & Mine*, 3, 14, and 15.

9. Ibid., 33.

10. Tim Cresswell suggests that geography can be used to understand how people transgress social norms to create lives that have meaning for themselves and which can hopefully improve their social and economic place in society— Cresswell, *In Place/Out of Place: Geography, Ideology, and Transgression* (Minneapolis: University of Minnesota Press, 1996), 21. In discussing the transgressive behavior of workers and their families within the context of company towns, I have also been influenced by cultural theorists of space and place, especially Jürgen Habermas, *The Structural Transformation of the Public Sphere: An Inquiry into a Category of Bourgeois Society* (Cambridge, Mass.: MIT Press, 1989); Pierre Bourdieu, *Outline of a Theory of Practice* (Cambridge, U.K.: Cambridge University Press, 1977); and Bourdieu, *Distinction: A Social Critique of the Judgment of Taste* (Cambridge, Mass.: Harvard University Press, 1984). See also Antonio Gramsci, *Prison Notebooks* (London: Lawrence & Wishart, 1973); and Michael de Certeau, *Practice of Everyday Life* (Berkeley: University of California Press, 1984). For historical applications of these ideas I found the following particularly useful: Geoff Eley, "Nations, Publics, and Political Cultures: Placing Habermas in the Nineteenth Century," in *Habermas and the Public Sphere*, edited by Craig Calhoun (Cambridge, Mass.: MIT Press, 1992), 289–339; and Mona Domosh, "'Those Gorgeous Incongruities': Polite Politics and Public Space on the Streets of Nineteenth Century New York City," *Annals of the Association of American Geographers*, 88 no. 2 (1998): 209–26.

11. Scamehorn, *Mill & Mine*, 33.

12. "Report of the Possible Service by the YMCA in the Mining Communities of the Colorado Fuel and Iron Company Based upon a Survey by Dr. Peter Roberts of the Industrial Department, International Committee," pp. 2–5, Folder 30, Box 1, Scamehorn Papers, Bessemer Historical Society, Pueblo, Colo. The original is at the Rockefeller National Archives Center, Tarrytown, NY (hereinafter Roberts Survey).

13. Selekman and Van Kleek, 118–19.

14. Panoramic View of Primero, Colorado coal camp, circa 1915, Scamehorn Collection, SCM 7–45, Bessemer Historical Society, Pueblo, Colo.

15. I use the term *workscape* deliberately and in reference to Thomas Andrews's "Road to Ludlow: Work, Environment, and Industrialization in Southern Colorado, 1870–1914" (Ph.D. dissertation, University of Wisconsin, 2002), in which he describes the industrialization of Colorado's landscape as a result of the increase in coal production in the southern fields.

16. Selekman and Van Kleek, 31.

17. Ibid.

18. Ibid., 82.

19. For a full description of the mining camps in 1915, see the Roberts Survey.

20. Regarding the relative values of adobe versus wood frame construction in the region, see María Montoya, *Translating Property: The Maxwell Land Grant and the Problem of Land in the American West, 1848–1900* (Berkeley: University of California Press, 2002), 138–43.

21. Scamehorn Collection, SCM 7–27.

22. Roberts Survey, 28.

23. Photo of man in front of Primero bathhouse, circa 1915, Scamehorn Collection, SCM 7–24, Bessemer Historical Society, Pueblo, Colo.

24. Scamehorn, *Mill & Mine*, 89.

25. Ibid., 10.

26. Ibid., 11.

27. Ibid., 10.

28. Photo of Sorpis Miners, circa 1924, Scamehorn Collection, SCM 11–27, Bessemer Historical Society, Pueblo, Colo.

29. Andrews, "The Road to Ludlow" in chapter 3 discusses work within these coal camps and how it was divided by race and ethnicity.

30. Sarah Deutsch, *No Separate Refuge: Culture, Class, and Gender on an Anglo-Hispanic Frontier in the American Southwest* (New York: Oxford University Press, 1987), 97; and Annual Report of the Sociological Department of the Colorado Fuel and Iron Company, 1903–1904, 22.

31. Ibid., 22.

32. Roberts Survey, 10.

33. Selekman and Van Kleek, 97.

34. Oral interview with Frances Valdez Nelson, October 7, 1987, Herman County Oral History Collection, Pueblo Municipal Library, Pueblo, Colo.

35. Ibid.

36. Selekman and Van Kleek, 101.

2. *La Placita Committee: Claiming Place and History*

One day in April 1967, Alva Torres unexpectedly became a historical preservationist in her hometown of Tucson, Arizona. During the course of a routine schedule that revolved around her three children, she ran into an elderly Rodolfo Soto. They were related by marriage and their families had known each other for generations. Like many established families whose labor had built the desert city, both Torres and Soto referred to themselves as *tucsonenses.* Soto possessed a keen knowledge of history, and, in fact, descended from one of the city's founding families who had inhabited the Spanish presidio in the late eighteenth century.[1] Noticing his distress, Torres approached Soto with concern and in the hope of providing comfort. He lamented to Torres, *"Ay, Alvita, como estoy triste de lo que están haciendo en el centro"* ("I am saddened about what they are doing downtown"). Torres asked, *"¿Por qué, Señor?"* ("Why, Mr. Soto?"). *"Porque se les va a olvidar donde empezó el pueblo, se les va olvidar todo. Están tumbando La Placita, y el Barrio Libre y no se van a acordar de nosotros y nadie le va importar"* ("Because they are going to forget Tucson's origins, they are going to forget everything. They are tearing down La Placita and Barrio Libre and nobody's going to remember us and nobody's going to care"). Caught off guard, but feeling compassion for her lifelong friend, Torres consoled Soto and assured him that his fears were unwarranted.[2]

A coalition of local boosters and elected officials initiated the transformation of the downtown area. It came under the guise of a national policy of urban renewal. This approach radically changed the physical and social landscape in Tucson and in cities across the United States. Urban ethnic communities became targets for eradication in an era that proposed to improve poor people's quality of life by destroying their communities.[3] In 1966 Tucson voters approved Arizona's first urban renewal project, the Pueblo Center Redevelopment Project. The centerpiece would be a new civic center complex, the Tucson Community Center (TCC). Designed to be close to downtown, construction of this new expansive structure required that the city's oldest barrio be destroyed. Most Tucson residents knew this area as Barrio Libre, or simply as el barrio.[4]

Torres's conversation with Soto kept resurfacing, and soon she too began to feel Soto's panic and sense of loss. She felt that something needed to be done to prevent the destruction of Mexican American space in a city where Sonoran culture had always thrived. Torres began to question the motives that underscored urban renewal policy and "the city's attempt to show that an area was devastated, [to] get their hands on money and build a community center."[5] Unfortunately, by this time much of the barrio had already been destroyed. City officials had already relocated most of the residents and destroyed most the area's homes and businesses.[6] The only site that remained intact, and which Torres considered irreplaceable, was the area known as La Placita. It, like numerous plazas throughout the Southwest, symbolized revered historical and spiritual communal space.[7] Infused with memories and cultural meanings, it represented the intersection of place, community, and identity to much of the tucsonense community. As the focal point and public square of the barrio for close to one hundred years, it fostered deep feelings of belonging in Tucson. La Placita also continually reminded tucsonenses of their long history in the area.

Alva Torres calls her conversation with Soto and her revelations regarding urban renewal's agenda her "baptism with fire." She changed her entire life and vowed to devote all her time and efforts to saving La Placita.[8] Torres came to understand that the loss of tangible evidence that testified to and confirmed a long history of Mexicans and Mexican Americans in the area would ultimately distort historical memory. Alva Torres initiated a public battle not only to save a place, but to preserve an essential part of southern Arizona history. At the core of the debate lay the fate of an aging Tucson landmark. An examination of historical preservation efforts to save La Placita provides insight into crucial issues of conflicting visions of the past that Tucson residents wished to celebrate and the future they hoped to construct. The Society for the Preservation of Tucson's Plaza de la Mesilla, known as the La Placita Committee, a group composed mostly of women, emerged to challenge the cultural arrogance that lay at the heart of urban renewal policies. Led and organized by Torres, the committee waged a battle over space and memory. This grassroots organization, armed with their collective memory of the past, rallied for social change.[9] Mexican American women's voices appealed for the right of tucsonenses to control public space and history.

Historical preservationists such as the Daughters of the American Revolution (DAR) and the Mount Vernon Ladies' Association have long been recognized as the traditional women's historic preservationists.[10] An examination of the La Placita Committee, a Mexican American historical preservationist movement that contested the possibility of being forgotten, or further marginalized, complicates historians' understanding of layered claims to space. The historical preservationist movement demanded that Mexican and Mexican American contributions be recognized and that tucsonenses' collective connection to the past also be openly acknowledged. Like women from the DAR, the committee recognized the need for the public sites that testified to their, and the barrio's, significance in history and to the area's development. The power of place, which historian Dolores Hayden calls "shared time in the form of shared territory,"[11] formed the glue that bonded La Placita Committee members as they rallied to gain support. Their history, however, was one that urban renewal advocates hoped to minimize. It challenged the local narrative that highlighted Anglo Americans, dude ranching, military exploits that triumphed over Apaches, and cowboys. An examination of the committee's actions, recorded minutes from their meetings, and public statements indicate that they recognized the importance of historic representations to identity formation and to the construction of positive or demeaning perceptions of Mexican people. In this case, they demanded that a slice of history that highlighted their ancestors' extensive tenure in southern Arizona be preserved. Despite bureaucratic obstacles, and lack of institutional support, the La Placita Committee claimed a dignified place for Mexican Americans in the local and national imaginary.

In the politics of place, La Placita Committee's activism recognized and appreciated the importance of communal space in cultivating and maintaining the social networks that strengthened the ethnic cohesiveness of tucsonenses. In an era of burgeoning social movements, the committee recognized the importance of community space for civic identity and potential political mobilization. That they chose to stage a battle over La Placita denotes an astute political consciousness. The committee did not seek to save a site associated with a famous person, but concentrated instead on a place recognized by tucsonenses as important shared public space. These grassroots historical preservationists understood the dangers that underscored urban renewal directives, which could foster a sense of "placelessness" in future generations. Historian David Glassberg delineates the link between place and identity that underscores the importance of the past. He argues that "a sense of history locates us in society, with the knowledge that helps us gain a sense of *with whom we belong*, connecting our personal experiences and memories with those of a larger community, region, and nation."[12]

Urban planners, however, had designed a major thoroughfare to traverse and destroy the plaza area. The Pueblo Center Redevelopment Project not only called for the destruction of the old placita, but also proposed to replace it with a multimillion-dollar *new* La Placita Village. According to the approved plans, this modern concrete shopping, office, and restaurant complex would best complement the city's new vision and its celebrated civic center. Although city officials framed their project as a "community effort" designed to benefit all Tucson residents, their actions suggest that they deemed the barrio a local eyesore. Boosters and city officials hoped to infuse the former "slum" with Anglo American culture. In contrast to the barrio's distinctive ethnic ambiance, urban renewal proponents envisioned their project as creating a new place "where singers, athletes, Boy Scouts, square dance people and others can come."[13]

La Placita, initially known as La Plaza de la Mesilla, dates back to the Mexican period. In the mid-nineteenth century, early Anglo American newcomers desired the presidio area, and they began to take over this coveted space. Displaced tucsonenses began to establish homes and business southward in the direction of La Placita and toward Barrio Libre. The exact date of La Plaza de la Mesilla origins remains uncertain, but it appeared in the first map of Tucson commissioned by Major Fergusson of the Union Army in 1862, only six years after the final evacuation of Mexican troops. After the *Tratado de la Mesilla*, better known as the Gadsden Purchase, which made southern Arizona part of the United States, this plaza became the social hub of tucsonenses, who represented the majority population until the turn of the century. It also marked the final stop of a wagon trail route that connected Tucson to Mesilla, New Mexico. Typically, La Plaza de la Mesilla marked the end of the trail that drew people to the area to meet passengers, hear the latest news, gossip, and speculate why each new arrival had chosen the desert town as their destination.[14] Transportation advancements, first the railroad, and later the automobile, eventually brought hundreds of thousands of people to Tucson. These newcomers' insistence on simulating their former social and physical environments dramatically transformed southern Arizona.

Around 1863 the rapidly displaced tucsonense community desired
and felt the need for a new church in their newly established neighborhood.[15] This inspired them to construct one in La Plaza de la Mesilla,
on present-day Broadway and Church Streets. Firmly committed to the
project, wealthier tucsonenses provided the funds, but the faithful of all
classes helped build the new church. According to Ana María Comadurán Coenen, "After each morning's religious services the community
made the adobes. . . . The entire church was built by the people of the
parish." Anastasia Santa Cruz Hughes adds more detail and remembers
that "the men made the adobes and the women carried water in *ollas* on
their heads for the mixing of the adobe dirt. The finished adobes were
also carried by women, who fashioned a ring of cloth and placing it on
their heads, placed the adobes on it and carried it to the men, building
the walls."[16] This San Agustín Church, named after Tucson's patron
saint, was completed along with an adjacent school by 1868.[17] The open
courtyard or plaza that stood in front of the church became known as
La Plaza de San Agustín after the newly erected church and in time became recognized simply as La Placita.[18] Many small, Mexican-owned and
-operated businesses that catered to the Mexican American community
arranged themselves around the perimeter of the church's plaza. Most
notably, it denoted a unique place that tucsonenses created to encourage
face-to-face exchanges and a space to celebrate their Sonoran traditions,
particularly as they experienced hardship and downward mobility due
to the growing Anglo American presence.

Most of Tucson's major celebrations took place in La Placita. The
yearly celebrations of Tucson's patron saint, San Agustín, lasted for more
than two weeks. Anthropologist Thomas Sheridan describes this festival as beginning with a mass at the church, "followed by a procession
around the church plaza, the old *plaza de la Mesilla. . . .* It was Tucson's
celebration of its Catholic heritage, its rural heritage, and above all, its
Mexican heritage."[19] He also asserts that San Agustín festivals died out in
the early part of the twentieth century when "a part of Tucson's Sonoran
soul died." Sheridan overstates his observation because tucsonenses have
always remained closely affiliated with Sonora. He also overlooks the
importance of memory and the strength of the oral tradition within the
Mexican American community.[20] A festival of this magnitude, and the old
church itself, continued to be remembered by subsequent generations of
tucsonenses, and it became one the main motivating factors that inspired
and fueled the La Placita Committee's historical preservation efforts.[21]

After becoming a part of the United States, southern Arizona also fell
under the command of the Diocese of Santa Fe. Catholic Church officials

increasingly took control and decided that "the old church ceased to serve its community."[22] Father Peter Bourgade sold the old church after a new cathedral, St. Augustine's Cathedral, currently located on Stone Avenue, had been built. In 1898 the old church became the San Augustine Hotel and eventually deteriorated to a brothel. The old San Agustín Church was demolished in 1936. When Frank C. O'Rielly, the last owner of the property, was asked what was to be done with the remaining stones, he replied "Dump them into the nearest bank of the [nearby] Santa Cruz River."[23]

In the coveted downtown, La Placita that symbolized a Mexican past posed a problem for mid-twentieth-century boosters. In order to justify urban renewal, city leaders increasingly began to construe the barrio as a dangerous place that had deserved to be obliterated for decades. These boosters believed concrete and steel high-rises represented a contemporary city and considered the barrio's Sonoran architecture and its large tucsonense population in the midst of an urban environment as belonging to an earlier era. Boosters identified themselves and their visions as forward-looking ones that exemplified progress and used urban renewal as an opportunity to solidify the city's identification as an "American" place. In turn, they sought to raze a community that conflicted with the imagery and notions associated with a cowboy fantasy heritage. They encouraged entertainment, excursions, and a lifestyle based on an exaggerated and manufactured western past. This resulted in the proliferation of dude ranches, a rodeo extravaganza, and the creation of Old Tucson: The Motion Picture Locations and Sound Stage. Established by Columbia Pictures in 1939 for the filming of "Arizona," the studio intended to "build a replica of the real Tucson of the 1860s." It incorporated a *masculinist* viewpoint typical of the cowboy fantasy heritage. In the studio's imagined past, "If you weren't a dangerous hombre or a shopkeeper, you probably became a rancher."[24] This movie set and the films that it produced never presented a realistic portrayal of the area. In 1860, before Arizona received territorial status, fewer than one thousand people lived in Tucson. The 168 Anglo American residents at that time composed less than 20 percent of the population, and Mexican Americans still composed the majority population, numbering 653 residents.[25]

Increasingly, after the beginning of the twentieth century, various booster organizations actively became invested in revising negative perceptions of the city, particularly recurring claims that the area was too "Mexican," or "backward" and "uncivilized" evident in various stages of the state's development.[26] In 1931 a local newspaper article titled "Good bye America—hello Mexico" alluded to crossing the international border, but only metaphorically. Instead, the article highlighted what boosters had long tried to conceal, that steps away from downtown thrived Meyer Street, the barrio's main commercial fairway where "the same sensations . . . are felt [as] when crossing the International line at Nogales. Geographically we may be still in the United States; but in every sight and sound and every varied impression we're in the heart of old Mexico. As we proceed down this bizarre old world rialto we realize that we have left the land of the hot dog for the land of the chile con carne; the land of the go-getter for the land of mañana [sic]. . . . And to think that America is up there, a block away on Congress street."[27] Promotional literature frequently referred to Tucson as "the gateway to Old Mexico," but advertisements carefully situated the city as unconditionally American, free of any Mexican influences.[28] Boosters committed themselves to the concept of a "gateway" because it clearly outlined the geopolitical boundaries that placed Tucson on the American side of the "gate" while also heightening the distinction between a modern city and conditions in Mexico. An examination of the tourist industry literature indicates that boosters, in collaboration with city officials, manipulated ethnocentric and nationalistic ideas of Mexican "backwardness," stasis, and poverty as a construct to highlight the "Americanness," modernity, and prosperity of the city. Ideas advanced by boosters and historians reveal the cultural assumptions shared by local economic and intellectual elites. Historian Matthew Frye Jacobson argues that "public images and expressions [have] the power to articulate and to influence racial conceptions." An examination of boosters' tactics reveals that they did more than manipulate images and silences. They also used "race [as] a kind of social currency" and selectively sought to recruit a certain race and class of people, in this case moneyed European Americans, to the city.[29] The actions of the boosters and urban renewal advocates demonstrated a refusal to recognize Mexico and Mexican-origin people as vital members of society and of its history.

Their biggest problem, however, derived from the fact that Mexican Americans in Tucson refused to disappear or to appear only when summoned. Tucsonenses not only claimed the barrio and La Placita as their space, they also claimed the popular downtown area. Inevitably, tourists ventured to the city's central business district and witnessed for themselves the large tucsonense presence. Reducing these types of encounters required more than sophisticated misrepresentations in local cultural productions. It required the eradication of the barrio. Urban renewal forced a large number of tucsonenses to relocate away from the downtown area and destroyed irreplaceable historical cultural spaces in the late 1960s. In their quest to "rehabilitate" the city's image, however, local leaders wielded substantial power to transform the urban landscape but encountered unexpected resistance in their attempts to destroy a vital Mexican American landmark, La Placita.

As the focal point of the barrio, the La Placita area defied and inverted the local economic and social hierarchy. Since its inception, it emerged and remained the barrio's main commercial and ceremonial center for more than one hundred years. La Placita and its surrounding businesses provided tangible evidence of a place that survived and thrived because of the Mexican people's patronage, solidarity, and loyalty. The bandstand, or kiosk, which sat at the center of the plaza, was added in the 1950s. On the perimeter of the plaza stood the Belmont Hotel, El Charro Restaurant, Ronquillo's Bakery and El Edificio de Piedra (the stone building that housed some small shops), Rosequist Gallery, Zepeda Shoe Shop, and Half-Moon Chinese Food—all operational in 1967.[30] This space projected Mexican American success and entrepreneurship. The La Placita Committee tried not only to save the kiosk and the plaza, but also prioritized saving the surrounding businesses. They urged city officials to preserve the older structures and surviving businesses instead of destroying them. No other area in Tucson served as a focal point for Mexican and Mexican American culture, history, and economic advancement as did La Placita. (See figure 2.1.) The desire to defend Mexican American space and memory compelled Alva Torres to take action. The media had openly debated and discussed the urban renewal issue, but Torres remained unaffected. At first, she trusted the city's press campaign that affirmed that preserving historically significant sites was an integral part of the urban renewal agenda. Unfamiliar with politics, Torres claims that her family responsibilities kept her too busy to notice the changes and destruction occurring in the city's oldest sections of downtown.[31] Torres, however, had strong ties to the barrio. While Anglo Americans painted the barrio as a place to fear, Torres never felt afraid and often shopped and socialized with family and friends who lived in the barrio. Before her marriage, she had worked at Lyric Outfitters, a clothing store, on Meyer Street in the barrio. Torres attended local schools and graduated from high school in 1950. She also married Arthur Torres, an electrician, that same year. Unusual for Mexican Americans of her generation, Torres attended the University of Arizona and received a two-year liberal arts degree. She lived in the Armory Park area a few blocks from the barrio for decades before she became a political activist. She also belonged to a Mexican American women's social club that had met in the barrio since she was fifteen. When I interviewed her, she recalled the numerous fiestas at La Placita, noting that she often coordinated booths for her club there. These

Figure 2.1. La Placita, circa 1968. In the center of the plaza sits the kiosk, surrounded by various businesses. The large vacant lot behind St. Augustine's Cathedral provides evidence that much of the barrio had been razed by 1968. Courtesy of Arizona Historical Society, PC 177–1300.

fiestas meant more than fun; they strengthened personal and community bonds. Tucsonenses, and all Tucson residents, celebrated feast days of the saints, Mexican Independence, and the Fourth of July, but they mostly celebrated themselves. Torres had always considered the barrio a vital part of Tucson, and La Placita indispensable.[32]

Sociologist Mary S. Pardo defines grassroots activism as that which "happens at the juncture between larger institutional politics and people's daily experiences. Women play a central role in the often unrecorded politics at this level."[33] It is not surprising that the most visible and effective resistance to urban renewal arose from the leadership of an inexperienced activist from the Mexican American community. Torres combined the private role of mother with the more public role of social and political activist.

With no prior experience in local politics or personal knowledge of dealing with city hall, Alva Torres approached the issue in a rather naïve and improvisational fashion. She first approached Bill Mathews, the editor of the local newspaper, the *Arizona Daily Star*, because Torres felt he wielded substantial power. Torres recalls that Mathews was not particularly friendly, but he listened while she outlined her new mission. She proposed that "instead of destroying everything, why not at least save La Placita?" He informed her that a group called the St. Augustine's Placita Committee or St. Augustine Committee was already in place to deal with concerns about that area. Mathews suggested that Torres talk to Don Laidlaw, the chief urban renewal officer at city hall. Recognizing Torres's status as a political neophyte, he advised her to "tell him Bill Mathews sent you." Without Mathews's referral, Torres felt that Laidlaw would have ignored her.[34]

As 1966 came to a close, Laidlaw felt that the proposed new La Placita Village's objectives "appeared satisfactory to all concerned," but a few months later, in May 1967, he met Alva Torres. At that meeting she outlined her ideas for La Placita. He later recalled this meeting in a memorandum: "She stated her understanding that the hour was late, but she added that she was determined to make every effort to see that certain other objectives were achieved . . . to retain substantially the same street pattern and almost all the buildings. . . . She stated that this was the Tucson Mexicans knew and stated further her belief that the area should be preserved more or less as it is."[35] At that meeting Laidlaw informed Torres for a second time that a committee already existed to deal with La Placita, and he suggested that Torres meet with the St. Augustine Committee. Torres recognized that she was "getting the runaround," but the fear of impending bulldozers and the understanding that La Placita's days were numbered convinced her to set up a meeting with the St. Augustine Committee.[36]

Torres expected bureaucratic obstacles in her initial efforts to save La Placita, but she never expected to encounter blatant discrimination, and on such a personal level as she did in her experiences with the St. Augustine Committee. She received a telephone call from "a very unreceptive and patronizing" chairwoman of the St. Augustine Committee, Dorothy Haas, who questioned Torres's motives. According to Torres, Haas attempted to discourage and discredit her by saying "Who are you to get involved? Where do you get the authority?" Caught off guard by the hostile manner and tone expressed in the phone call, Torres responded by saying, "I was born here, this is my town, I have as much right as anybody else and I think I have a good idea." This dismissive conversation made Torres keenly aware of her outsider status. Ultimately, the St. Augustine Committee rejected Torres and denied her access to their meetings, although a handful of other Mexican Americans, primarily from the Tucson elite, served on the St. Augustine Committee.[37] The

St. Augustine Committee never attempted to implement any plan or to garner community support to save La Placita. Their strong affiliation with St. Augustine's Church prevented them from challenging urban renewal, since the church benefited from the removal of older structures located adjacent to the cathedral. Indeed, the Catholic Diocese worked with the city in order to acquire 77,000 square feet to expand the cathedral and parochial school as part of the Pueblo Center Redevelopment Project.[38]

Although Torres had been brought up Catholic, her grandfather, a Methodist minister, strongly influenced her. She often referred to herself as "Christian," preferring a more inclusive religious identification. Born in 1932, a fourth-generation tucsonense, her maternal and paternal ancestors arrived in Tucson in the early nineteenth century. Her father's family traced its origins not to Mexico, but to Peru. After living in Tucson for many generations, and marrying into a Mexican community with whom they shared an ethnic background, they considered themselves *mexicanos.* Although not from the elite, Alva Bustamante Torres was well connected in the Mexican American community, and these people recognized her as being from an old tucsonense family. In a time of crisis, she turned to her staunchest allies, her large network of family and friends.[39]

Feeling powerless, but not defeated, Torres formed a prayer committee. She shared her and Soto's concerns with her family and friends and convinced them to pray to persuade God to get involved in saving La Placita. It must be noted that many tucsonenses, like Torres, never forgot the relationship between La Placita and religion. In 1967 a Greyhound Bus Depot stood in place of the old San Agustín Church, but many still considered La Placita to be linked to a sacred place. This understanding eventually prompted the La Placita Committee to push to have a chapel built on the old church site. With no other tools, this prayer group of Mexican American women (most were Catholic, but several Methodists took part as well) formed what would become the core of the committee. Armed only with the inspiration derived from shared religious beliefs, these women prayed so that God would intervene and grant Torres strength and direction.[40]

Hoping to find a solution, Torres walked around La Placita in the spring of 1967. It was at this point that she understood that she needed to organize more than a prayer group. Understanding the limits of individual effort and living in a political era that promised change, Torres consciously recognized the advantages of a collaborative and collective effort. She made numerous phone calls and visits to friends and family members. The first meeting of the Society for the Preservation of Tucson's Plaza de la Mesilla took place in Torres's home. According to

Torres, this group was never elitist or exclusive in its assumptions. Anyone interested in saving La Placita was welcome to join. Torres never consciously intended for the group to be principally Mexican American, but she invited people she knew, and since she associated with mostly tucsonenses they made up the bulk of the group. Although committee membership hovered at only twenty, they became the city's most vocal and public critics of urban renewal.[41]

Many angry and resentful barrio residents forced to relocate did so grudgingly, but they remained silent. In 1997 Leticia Jacobs Fuentes remembered that "We saw it all go down. It was bad. I didn't want to see it. . . . People weren't very happy. They'd been there all their lives. It was quite a trauma for us, for everybody. . . . We were a happy family there. We lost that neighborhood."[42] Many others also felt betrayed by a city that had masterminded the destruction of their community. As they witnessed the eradication of irreplaceable historic space, still others, like Rodolfo Soto, harbored private feelings of fear, loss, anger, and disappointment. He, like many, shared these sentiments with like-minded or sympathetic ears, as he did with Torres. These nonconfrontational behaviors and sentiments characterize what James C. Scott calls "hidden transcripts." He describes them as a "critique of power," a "discourse that takes place 'offstage,' beyond direct observation by powerholders."[43] In this distressed and dislocated community, Alva Torres broke the silence and voiced a previously veiled but heartfelt discourse.

Grounded in resentment and feelings of powerlessness, Torres turned the hidden transcripts into a public issue. City officials called for a special meeting in 1967 to address "the situation . . . [because a] good deal of controversy is being generated over the questions of preserving La Placita." The "situation" they referred to was Torres's La Placita Committee. This underscores the committee's effectiveness in contesting urban renewal's designs and its efforts to raise the public's awareness of the changes taking place downtown. Torres came to understand that the erasure of Mexican American space and history amounted to blatant historical misrepresentation, and that many in Tucson as well as future generations would suffer the cultural consequences of this exclusion. Through her leadership and actions, the preservationist concerns of many tucsonenses finally found public expression.[44]

The committee employed a personal approach to reach the community. They sent invitations to influential officials and friends announcing the dates of forthcoming meetings. Invitations read, "We hope to make a coordinated community effort to preserve this historic area in Tucson and would appreciate an opportunity to discuss it with you at this meeting." The group's secretary, Ann Montaño, personally signed each letter.[45] It proved an effective strategy, for more than one hundred people attended a large community meeting at El Charro Restaurant on Friday, August 11, 1967.[46]

It was unsurprising that the local papers, which had jumped on the urban renewal bandwagon, chose not to cover the activities of the La Placita Committee. The press even ignored this persistent and visible group of women who stood on various downtown street corners, gathering signatures in 100-degree-plus temperatures. They worked at street corners, at grocery stores, and at numerous gatherings during the hot summer months, gathering support and signatures. Asserting their right to petition and appeal to the state, they convinced a large number of Tucson residents to support their cause and demand that the city implement their plan designed to save the La Placita area. Altogether, they collected more than 8,000 signatures, mostly from Mexican Americans, evidence that the committee had significant backing from the community.[47]

The committee's demands are best outlined in its "Plan for the Preservation, Restoration and Uses of the Plaza de la Mesilla Area, within the Pueblo Center Redevelopment Area." Committee members presented this plan in 1968 to the mayor and city council along with their petitions. The following summarizes the highlights of the four-page plan, which included complicated details on the subject of street boundaries. The La Placita Committee first demanded that the city declare the Plaza de la Mesilla area and its surrounding structures a "Historic Area for the City of Tucson, Arizona." Second, it demanded that the city "provide for authentic restoration." This demand specifically stated that only structures that dated back to the nineteenth century should be restored. Committee members always recognized the importance of religion to the area and called for the construction of an "inter-faith chapel" and museum in their plan. They insisted that the plaza remain an open area so that the festivals, celebrations, and public meetings would continue and that a "perpetual restriction against any buildings" be enforced. This plan mandated that only the kiosk, the new chapel, and museum be allowed in this open area. As part of the new construction, the committee requested that the city include a "750 seat theatre suitable for both movie and legitimate theatre productions in Spanish."[48]

The La Placita Committee insisted that its plan be "considered as a whole, a unified plan. . . . It must be added that it is critically important to save everything authentic in such a uniquely historic area, continuously successful for over 100 years." As boldly as the committee outlined its plan, it was clear that it did not have the funds to take on or to even assist in the rehabilitation of the old structures. The committee's intent was to make its demands known, get as many people as possible to support the plan, and force the city to adopt its proposals for La Placita. This was made clear in its "Plan for Restoration," which urged city officials "to explore fully all possibilities for the use of Federal, State and Foundational Funds available for historic restoration and development."[49] This was not an improbable request, as city officials had enthusiastically supported, with substantial funding, the restoration of the "Fremont House," named after territorial governor John C. Frémont, an icon of western expansion and Manifest Destiny.[50]

Torres's conviction that place shapes identity corresponds with the view of historian Dolores Hayden, who argues that "Identity is intimately tied to memory: both our personal memories (where we come from and where we have dwelt) and the collective or social memories interconnected with the histories of our families, neighbors, fellow workers, and ethnic communities."[51] Urban renewal not only threatened to eradicate La Placita, but by this time had already obliterated the largest repositories of Mexican American memories, including the Alianza Hispano-Americana building. It had housed a prominent mutual-aid organization designed to help Mexican Americans as they increasingly lost economic and political power at the turn of the century. The Alianza began in Tucson and grew to be a national organization. The Alianza Hispano-Americana building, along with grocery stores and clothing stores—not to mention entire streets—disappeared, as did most of the barrio.

Part of the La Placita Committee's tactics consisted of a letter-writing campaign to influential politicians. In a letter to Congressman Morris Udall, Torres cited the indifference of local officials and identified the city's hidden agenda by stating, "It is not enough that many citizens of Mexican descent who have lived in the area for many years are being relocated and being caused some financial hardships since most are pensioners, but it appears to us that the main effort is to destroy once and for all any identification with the Mexican-American community."[52]

Various tucsonenses also wrote letters of support to the committee. Local supporter Irma Villa wrote that "for years it has been proven that people were supposed to be proud of their cultural background, but if symbols of this cultural background are destroyed in the name of progress there is very little that the people of today and our future generations have to be proud of. There are many instances in our history where some of the greatest cultures became extinct because the very symbols of this great culture were destroyed in the name of progress. A very good example is what happened to the great Aztec culture."[53]

Despite community criticism, the city refused to deviate from its blueprints. Alva Torres summed up the situation by stating, "The problem at heart centers around the alignment of a street."[54] With the help of an architect, the committee devised an alternative route for Broadway that would circumvent the La Placita area. This plan required that the location of the proposed new hotel for the civic center be modified.[55] Torres continued to insist that if Broadway were moved only "ten feet to the north," most of the plaza would be saved and a new chapel could be built on the site where the old San Agustín Church once stood.[56]

Since their inception, Tucson's urban renewal plans called for a special retail complex that stressed "quality development" in contrast to the old *placita*. City-approved plans described the new La Placita Village as "retail specialty shops, personal or business service establishments, offices, art exhibits and sales including on premises creation of artifacts and handicrafts, restaurants and places serving food and drink." In response to the committee's proposal, city officials insisted that "the street pattern as presently designed is necessary to meet requirements for vehicular and pedestrian safety." These considerations took precedence over community concerns and preserving Tucson history.

Increasingly, city officials stipulated that the La Placita Committee come up with and shoulder a fiscal plan that would pay the costs of restoring and bringing the older buildings up to code. This placed an immense financial burden on Torres and the committee.[57] After endless meetings with unresponsive city officials, the committee made a major concession by agreeing that "If Broadway MUST transverse the original Plaza site, then the street should be moved further North, if at all possible and certainly no further South." This dramatic shift marks the committee's understanding that the city would not deviate from its proposed plan. Coincidentally, Torres, the main force behind the La Placita Committee, began to be plagued with health problems. Despite the support garnered by the committee, the inflexibility of urban renewal officials on the location of Broadway, and the city's refusal to shoulder any fiscal responsibility for restoration caused the committee to abandon its plan. Overwhelmed, committee members increasingly pursued a strategy to preserve as much of the plaza area as possible.[58] La Placita Committee's intervention, however, did result in the preservation of a small triangular patch of green grass where Congress and Broadway Streets intersect, which still exists. Torres calls it the "most attractive area downtown" in stark contrast to the surrounding concrete buildings. The committee's activism and intervention also forced the city to agree to leave the kiosk in the original spot where it stood in the old La Placita. The kiosk also contrasts with the new La Placita Village because it looks old and its authenticity visually marks it as different from the surrounding structures. Moreover, some of the businesses, such as Ronquillo's Bakery, that stood near La Placita received assistance from the city to move to a new location. As she looks back on her struggle for historic preservation, Torres laments, "It hurts my feelings that when things come up [about historical preservation] they do not mention us. There is no permanent record of us. It is too painful. I think we failed. We were successful in making urban renewal a public issue. But we were not able to preserve [the] environment that made La Placita special, and we should have been able to save it."[59] Torres's use of the "we" indicates that she spoke for the Mexican American community. (See figure 2.2.)

The intense energy Alva Torres put into the petition drive and into saving La Placita eventually made her physically ill. When it came time to submit the petitions to the mayor and city council, Torres could not attend because she was hospitalized. She never completely recovered from the battle to save La Placita. Even after her health forced her retreat, the demolition of each additional structure caused her great pain. As Torres recalls, "It was as if they were killing one of my kids."[60]

La Placita Village, a $10.2 million, three-acre complex that included 200,000 square feet of new office, shop, cinema, and restaurant space on five levels, "decorated in an authentic Southwest style," opened on May 3, 1974.[61] Mariachis wandered through the new complex, as did jazz musicians, barbershop quartets, and clowns. If the defeat of La Placita Committee and the destruction of most of La Placita failed to remind those tucsonenses who attended of their "place" or "historical erasure," then the staged conquest reenactments did. According to press reports the "highlight of the day was the re-enactment of the arrival in old Tucson of the Mormon battalion on December 16, 1846 [conquering forces that arrived during the U.S.–Mexican War], . . . [and] wandering throughout the sun-drenched La Placita for several hours were the authentically garbed Tucson Mountain Men showing interested groups what was worn by the stalwart explorers who first brought the sound of the English language to what is now Pima County."[62]

In the end, similar development projects designed to level large areas and displace communities could never happen again in Tucson as a result of La Placita Committee's activism. Members of the committee eventually forced the mayor to create a Tucson Historic Committee. The former "outsiders" lobbied for a place on the Tucson Historic Committee from its inception, eventually becoming "insiders" who affected local policy.[63] Alva Torres served on this committee for six years. The roots of the

Figure 2.2. The old kiosk at La Placita Village. Photograph by author, October 10, 2002.

Tucson–Pima County Historical Commission, which currently remains an active and powerful voice in historical preservation matters, can be traced back to the efforts of Torres and the La Placita Committee. In 1972 committee members pushed forward and passed the Historic Zone Ordinance that currently protects older structures from destruction and dramatic alterations.[64] Today, the kiosk that once graced La Placita, El Tiradito, and the Sosa-Carrillo-Fremont and Samaniego Houses, among others, have Arizona Historical markers that mention Mexican American contributions to local history. Alva Torres claims that she insisted that the text on all historical markers be in both English and Spanish.[65]

The La Placita Committee disbanded after most of its members became part of the Historic Committee, but they remained friends and potential allies in historical preservation issues. When El Tiradito (Tucson's old wishing shrine) stood in the path of the proposed freeway, they received telephone calls asking for help. Committee members joined the protests and helped guarantee the site's survival. Some individual committee members also worked to save the home of a longtime and influential tucsonense family, the Samaniego House. Deservingly, Torres was selected as Woman of the Year by the Tucson Advertising Club in 1976. She was the first Mexican American woman to receive the award. Torres eventually became a journalist and wrote a popular weekly column in the 1980s for the local newspaper raising community concerns and issues. She also worked as director of the Legalization Amnesty program for the Catholic Community Services of Southern Arizona and served on various charities and community boards. She remains a committed activist to this day, and in 2002 Torres received the YWCA's Lifetime Achievement Award for Women Who Make Tucson Better.[66]

Representations of the past are important for how individuals and communities construct their present and envision their future. Alva Torres and most of the members of the La Placita Committee forged a common identity that centered on a shared investment in the past and hope for a more inclusive future. The culture, environment, and history that La Placita represented had shaped generations of tucsonenses, making it an important place in Chicana/o identity formation.[67]

Although Alva Torres and other members of the committee never self-identified as *Chicana* or *Chicano*, they formed an important and unrecognized component of the early development and ideology of the unfolding Chicana/o Movement. Historian Rodolfo Acuña argues that "by the late 1960s, there was no defined Chicana ideology. Nor was there a defined Chicano ideology for the total community. Anger and reaction to an unjust system, whether macro or micro, was being acted out. There was a call for Chicanismo that took on different meanings to different people. Generally, it meant pride of identity and self-determination."[68] Using this heterogeneous standard, the La Placita Committee's historical preservation efforts embodied an unrecognized, but vital, component of Chicanismo.

Clearly, "pride of identity and self-determination" characterized the committee's organizational ideology. This Chicana/o historical preservation movement challenged an urban renewal agenda intent on marginalizing and fragmenting the Chicana/o community and struggled to integrate Chicana/o history into the historical record and into Tucson's public spaces.[69] Members of the La Placita Committee never betrayed their roots, culture, or heritage. Their plan demanded that city officials embrace and celebrate their ethnicity, and they went as far as demanding the construction of a Mexican American museum.[70]

Other than allowing the kiosk and some of the green area that surrounds it to remain, the new La Placita Village complex planners failed to include any major recommendations made by the La Placita Committee. The new complex turned out to be a commercial disaster and a virtual ghost town. According to Torres, "They cheated everybody and built something that for years did not make them money because they did not do it right. When you do something wrong it comes back to you and that's what the city did. La Placita would have been a natural asset to the city. People could have come out and seen how the city once was. Our grandchildren and tourists would have loved it. It's like we had a little diamond and we gave it away for a zirconium. I love Tucson, and the buildings are not the people, but they are part of a story that you try to save."[71] What remains of La Placita stands as testimony to Chicana/o resistance in the city's quest for progress and represents a collective effort toward controlling space and self-determination.

Even after the La Placita Committee abandoned its plan, Torres continued to walk the area and monitor ongoing construction. In 1970, when another historic building again faced demolition, she wrote city officials a letter. Her words echo her extraordinary historical imagination and reveal why the city never felt invested in preserving the area: "It is the last remaining edifice in Tucson where many of us often went to enjoy ourselves with our loved ones. Not one other building standing in Tucson is of as much value in a non-monetary way as this one. . . . Personally I place a great value on intangibles. Intangibles are after all the only indestructible forces or energies left to us. . . . Please do not begin to measure in money what it would cost to restore the 'El Charro' building, otherwise you will probably give up. . . . In order to save an important spirit in the 'Old Pueblo,' first you must love it—if you do not, I doubt that anything I can say will make you want to save it."[72]

In 2002 the National Register of Historic Places, known as the "nation's official list of cultural resources worthy of preservation," lamented, "Considering the enormous impact that Hispanic culture has had upon the United States, especially in the Southwest, West, and lower Southeast, it is surprising to learn that Hispanic cultural heritage is under represented in the National Register." Apparently, what occurred in Tucson took place throughout the Southwest because of urban renewal policy and ethnocentric historic preservation goals. As of 2002, of the 67,000 properties listed in the Registry, only 73 were nominated for representing "Hispanic ethnic heritage."[73]

Notes

1. Ethnic and racial classifications are often issues of contention. I use "Mexican" or "Sonoran" to refer to the strong cultural influences that forever will continue to transcend borders, endure, and flourish in the United States. Unless I am referring to the Mexican period in southern Arizona, I try to avoid referring to Mexican people simply as "Mexican(s)." Documents, oral interviews, and a variety of promotional literature indicate a strong Anglo American preference and persistence in classifying all Mexican people as "Mexicans," regardless of citizenship status. Additionally, I use "Mexican people" to refer to the aggregate population of Mexican origin people, Chicanas/os, Mexican nationals, and those from earlier generations who may have identified as Spanish. I often use "Mexican people" and "tucsonenses" interchangeably. Ethnic Mexican Americans, some whose families had lived in southern Arizona before it became a part of the United States, and who claim Tucson as their home, then and now, refer to themselves as tucsonenses. A multilayered and linked relationship between region and ethnicity form the main constituents of this distinctive and unifying identity, which at the core denotes a strong historical, geographical, and cultural connection to Sonora. See Cynthia Radding, *Wandering Peoples: Colonialism, Ethnic Spaces, and Ecological Frontiers in Northwestern Mexico, 1700–1850* (Durham, N.C.: Duke University Press, 1997); and Thomas E. Sheridan, *Los Tucsonenses: The Mexican Community in Tucson, 1854–1941* (Tucson: University of Arizona Press, 1986), for more on this regional identity. Tucsonans refers to all the people who live in Tucson.

2. Alva Torres, interviewed by author, tape recording, Tucson, Arizona, December 6, 2002.

3. See James Robert Saunders and Renae Nadine Shackelford, *Urban Renewal and the End of Black Culture in Charlottesville, Virginia: An Oral History of Vinegar Hill* (Jefferson, N.C.: McFarland, 1998), June Manning Thomas and Marsha Ritzdorf, *Urban Planning and the African American Community: In the Shadows* (Thousand Oaks, Calif.: Sage Publications, 1997); Michael E. Jones, *The Slaughter of Cities: Urban Renewal As Ethnic Cleansing* (South Bend, Ind.: St. Augustine's Press, 2004); John M. Goering, Maynard Robison, and Knight Hoover, *The Best Eight Blocks in Harlem: The Last Decade of Urban Reform* (Washington, D.C.: University Press of America, 1977); and Thomas J. Sugrue, *The Origins of the Urban Crisis: Race and Inequality in Postwar Detroit* (Princeton, N.J.: Princeton University Press, 1996).

4. Generally, the barrio destroyed in the late 1960s was known as Barrio Libre, although some former residents resented this label. Before urban renewal, this area, the city's principal barrio, was simply called el barrio. For simplicity, I too will refer to it as such. Parts of an adjacent barrio called El Hoyo were also leveled. A small section of the barrio, south of 14th Street, still remains today and

is known as Barrio Histórico or Barrio Viejo. Currently, nearby South Tucson is increasingly being referred to as Barrio Libre by locals.

5. Torres interview.

6. According to Bonnie Newton, *Pueblo Center Redevelopment Project, 1967–1969* (Tucson: City of Tucson, Department of Community Development, Urban Renewal Division, 1969), 7–8, urban renewal destroyed a total of 269 structures, many of them multiple-occupancy dwellings and businesses. The "official" record indicates that the city managed to relocate "118 individual householders, 142 families, and 105 businesses." This is a vast undercount, particularly since census records indicate that this was the most densely populated area in the city. Many barrio residents did not seek or refused relocation assistance for a variety of social and economic reasons.

7. Setha M. Low, *On the Plaza: The Politics of Public Space and Culture* (Austin: University of Texas Press, 2000); and William David Estrada, "Sacred and Contested Spaces: The Los Angeles Plaza (California)" (Ph. D. diss., University of California, Los Angeles, 2003), provide detailed information on the importance and history of plazas.

8. Torres interview.

9. I use Susan A. Crane's notions of collective memory and historical memory outlined in "Writing the Individual Back into Collective Memory," in *The American Historical Review*, December 1997. Crane defines collective memory as that which people remember, or their personal "lived experience." Accordingly, historical memory is the "preservation of lived experiences" that are institutionally and professionally commemorated or remembered through museums, exhibits, texts, historical place markers, and the like. La Placita Committee members rallied to save a particular memory of Tucson. Collective memory inspired their activism. Likewise, what remains of La Placita in downtown Tucson has a historical marker denoting its historical significance. Newcomers gain knowledge, despite the severe limitations, from the information provided by commemorative inscription. This is an example of historical memory. I also refer readers to Iwona Irwin-Zaecka's *Frames of Remembrance: The Dynamics of Collective Memory* for a richer analysis of these discursive issues. She claims that "a 'collective memory'—as a set of ideas, images, feelings about the past—is located not in the minds of individuals, but in the resources they share."

10. See Barbara J. Howe, "Women in Nineteenth-Century Preservation Movement," in *Restoring Women's History through Historic Preservation*, edited by Gail Lee Dubrow and Jennifer B. Goodman (Baltimore: Johns Hopkins University Press, 2003), 17–36.

11. Dolores Hayden, *The Power of Place: Urban Landscapes As Public History* (Cambridge, Mass.: MIT Press, 1995), 9.

12. David Glassberg, *Sense of History: The Place of the Past in American Life* (Amherst: University of Massachusetts Press, 2001), 20 and 7.

13. "Editor's Urban Renewal Opinions Are Disputed: Architect Nelson Defends 'Center,'" *Arizona Daily Star*, 23 February 1966.

14. Maria Isabel MacLaury, "La Placita: Vantages of Urban Change in Historic Tucson" (Master's thesis: University of Arizona, 1989), 37 and 38.

15. See Bernice Cosulich, "Chapel Was Important Part of Presidio: Established by Spaniards Here in 1776," *Arizona Daily Star*, no date available, in Ephemera:

Places—Tucson—Churches—Catholic—St. Augustine, Arizona Historical Society, Tucson.

16. Ana María Comadurán Coenen, interview with George Chambers and G. T. Urias, 1927, Arizona Historical Society; and "Sacrifice of Pioneers recalled As Walls of Old Convent Tumble," *Tucson Daily Citizen*, June 30, 1932, in Ephemera: Places—Tucson—Churches—Catholic—St. Augustine, Arizona Historical Society.

17. C. L. Sonnichsen, *Tucson: The Life and Times of an American City* (Norman: University of Oklahoma Press, 1987), 67–68. Note that there were many different churches, functional in different periods, named in honor of San Agustín in the Tucson area. The presidio's full name was Presidio de San Agustín del Tucsón. A small military chapel within the presidio was also called San Agustín. That Mexican people chose to build their new church within walking distance of their homes testifies to the marked racialized demographic shift taking place in the town. Built in 1896, the current St. Augustine's Cathedral (note the Anglicized spelling) still stands at 192 South Stone Avenue and is the only remaining church with this name that has survived. Tucsonenses usually refer to it as "La catedral."

18. Alva Torres to Mayor Lew Murphy, October 14, 1973, MS1134, Torres, Alva, box 2 of 4, f.18, Plaza de la Mesilla—Correspondence, 1968–1974, Arizona Historical Society.

19. Sheridan, *Tucsonenses*, 151 and 163.

20. Carlos Vélez-Ibañez, *Border Visions: Mexican Cultures of the Southwest United States* (Tucson: University of Arizona Press, 1996).

21. Sheridan, *Tucsonenses*, 151 and 163. For example, my grandmother shared stories of the huge San Agustín festivals with my mother who in turn related the stories to me. During her interview, Torres also shared her recollections of the festivals with me. Many of La Placita Committee's demands centered on incorporating and re-creating the area's religious and festive past.

22. George W. Chambers and C. L. Sonnichsen, *San Agustín: First Cathedral Church in Arizona* (Tucson: Arizona Historical Society, 1974), 26. The Arizona Historical Society restored the church's portal and it stands at the entrance of their building in Tucson.

23. Ronni Neufeld, "Santa Cruz River Project May Be Last Chance to Preserve Tucson's Birthplace," *Changing Tucson*, October 1974. Published by Citizen Participation Division of Department of Urban Resource Coordination, in MS1134, Torres, Alva, box 2 of 4, f.15, Historic Preservation: Tucson 1969–1980, Arizona Historical Society.

24. Jack Williams, "Tucson Was Dude Ranch Capital for Ranching Experience," *Nogales International*, 22 July 1987. For a summary of dude and guest ranches, refer to Frank Blaine Norris, "The Southern Arizona Guest Ranch As a Symbol of the West" (Master's thesis, University of Arizona, 1976); Louis De Mayo, *Old Tucson: The Classic West* (Phoenix, Ariz.: De Mayo, 1972); and a letter from Jack N. Young, February 2, 1972, in Records Relating to the Publication, Arizona's Heritage, folder 3, Special Collections, University of Arizona Library. For more information on fantasy heritages, see Carey McWilliams's discussion of the Spanish fantasy in California in *North from Mexico: The Spanish-Speaking People of the United States* (New York: Greenwood Press, 1990).

25. These statistics are garnered from Thomas E. Sheridan, *Tucsonenses*, 37

and Appendix A, 259–262. Although Sheridan is credited as the author, this book is the culmination of a larger local community effort of predominantly Mexican Americans who actively participated in recovering their history, called the Mexican Heritage Project, housed at the Arizona Historical Society.

26. I discuss these perceptions and developments in my dissertation, "Conflicting Visions: Urban Renewal, Historical Preservation, and the Politics of Saving the Mexican Past" (Ph.D. diss., University of Arizona, 2003), 63–69.

27. "Romance of Old, 'City within City' Revealed by Strolling down Meyer: Quaint Atmosphere of Old Mexico to Be Found a Few Steps from Bustling East Congress Street and Unusual American Sights," *Tucson Daily Citizen*, July 4, 1931.

28. Nancy K. Vardaman, "Everybody's Dudin' It: Winter Ranch Vacations in the Southwest," *Traveler*, Fall Issue, 1955.

29. Matthew Frye Jacobson, *Whiteness of a Different Color: European Immigrants and the Alchemy of Race* (Cambridge, Mass.: Harvard University Press, 1998), 11.

30. Torres interview.

31. Ibid.

32. Ibid.

33. Mary S. Pardo, *Chicana/o Women Activists: Identity and Resistance in Two Los Angeles Communities* (Philadelphia: Temple University Press, 1998), 5.

34. Torres interview.

35. Donald H. Laidlaw to Committee on Municipal Blight setting a meeting date of October 4, 1967, MS1134, Torres, Alva, box 2 of 4, f.17, Plaza de la Mesilla—Correspondence, 1967, Arizona Historical Society. This letter, written on City of Tucson letterhead, is not dated.

36. Torres interview.

37. Torres interview; and "La Placita Restoration Plans Told: Group Seeking Historical Link," *Tucson Daily Citizen*, September 14, 1967. Found in MS1134, Torres, Alva, box 3 of 4, f.20, Plaza de la Mesilla—Newspaper Clippings, 1967–1986, Arizona Historical Society.

38. Diocese of Tucson to Donald Laidlaw, December 21, 1967, in City of Tucson Archives, City Clerk, box 2 of 2, M/C History File, binder #5, Report on Planning Proposals, Code No. R-214. The church bought 77,000 square feet to locate a "diocesan structure on the land between Corral, Stone, McCormick and Convent Streets."

39. Torres interview.

40. Ibid.

41. The following people, at one time or another, served as members of La Placita Committee: Alva and Arturo Torres, Ana Montaño, Viola Terrazas, Grace Esperon (acting chairman when Torres was unavailable), Carlitos Vásquez, Alberto Elias, Ruben Villaseñor, Aileen and Paul Smith, (Alva's sister and brother-in-law) Julieta and Ernest Portillo, (Alva's brother) Miguel Bustamante, Arturo Soto, Rodolfo Soto, (Arturo Torres' brother) Alberto Torres, and Felizardo Valencia. The following people were listed as members on subsequent lists: David Herrera, Eddie Jacobs, Natalia Nieto Slana, Alberto Montiel, Mr. Illeano, Tito Carrilo, Sybil Ellenwood, Louis Barassi, Cheto Valencia, Lorraine Agular, John Gabusi, Clarence Garrett, Basilio Morrillo, Dr. and Mrs. Marrow, Dr. Floyd Thompson, Kieran McCarthy, and María Urquidez. Aileen Smith stands out because of the

strong relationship she forged with Alva Torres. She rallied endlessly for historical preservation and other social causes through La Placita Committee and in
other groups through the city.

42. Margaret Regan, "There Goes the Neighborhood: The Downfall of Downtown," *Tucson Weekly*, March 6–12, 1997.

43. James C. Scott, *Domination and the Arts of Resistance: Hidden Transcripts*
(New Haven, Conn.: Yale University Press, 1990), xii and 4.

44. Laidlaw to COMB (undated), MS1134, Arizona Historical Society; and Torres interview.

45. The letters read, "Members of the Society for the Preservation of Tucson's
Plaza de la Mesilla would like to extend a cordial invitation to you, and hopefully
to several members of your group to attend a meeting." Ann Montaño to Mrs.
Walter Fathauer, August 30, 1967. MS1134, Torres, Alva, box 2 of 4, f.17, Plaza
de la Mesilla—Correspondence, 1967, Arizona Historical Society.

46. Minutes, August 24, 1967, MS1134, Torres, Alva, box 2 of 4, f.16, Plaza de
la Mesilla—Minutes, 1967–1968, Arizona Historical Society.

47. Torres interview.

48. From Society for the Preservation of Tucson's Plaza de la Mesilla to the
Honorable Mayor and Council of Tucson, Arizona. No date on document, but the
petitions were presented to the mayor and council in September 1967. MS1134,
Torres, Alva, box 2 of 4, f.17, Plaza de la Mesilla—Correspondence, 1967, Arizona
Historical Society.

49. Ibid.

50. I refer to the Fremont House in quotes because the territorial governor's
connection with the house continues to be matter of debate. It was renamed the
Sosa-Carrillo-Fremont House in 1992.

51. Hayden, *Power of Place*, 9.

52. Undated letter, Alva Torres to Congressman Udall, MS1134, Torres, Alva,
box 2 of 4, f.17, Plaza de la Mesilla—Correspondence, 1967, Arizona Historical
Society.

53. Irma Villa to Society for the Preservation of Tucson's Plaza de la Mesilla,
October 18, 1967, MS1134, Torres, Alva, box 2 of 4, f.17, Plaza de la Mesilla—Correspondence, 1967, Arizona Historical Society.

54. Undated letter, Alva Torres to Congressman Udall, MS1134, Torres, Alva,
box 2 of 4, f.17, Plaza de la Mesilla—Correspondence, 1967, Arizona Historical
Society.

55. Donald L. Woods to Mrs. Torres, September 28, 1967, MS1134, Torres, Alva,
box 2 of 4, f.17, Plaza de la Mesilla—Correspondence, 1967, Arizona Historical
Society.

56. "La Placita Restoration Plans Told," *Tucson Daily Citizen*, September 14,
1967, MS1134, Torres, Alva, box 3 of 4, f.20, Plaza de la Mesilla—Newspaper
Clippings, 1967–1986, Arizona Historical Society

57. Donald H. Laidlaw, urban renewal administrator to Alva B. Torres, August
10, 1967, MS1134, Torres, Alva, box 2 of 4, f.17, Plaza de la Mesilla—Correspondence, 1967, Arizona Historical Society. In their effort to preserve the "Fremont
House," the Tucson Heritage Foundation, a group of well-connected, mostly
European Americans, offered to purchase the house. The mayor and council willingly complied and set in motion a title transfer in exchange for about ten cents
a square foot. The mayor even directed the city's lobbyist in Washington, D.C.,

to prioritize securing federal funds for the preservation effort. See "Foundation Has Funds Restoration Work Due," *Citizen*, March 20, 1971.

58. Minutes of Combined Meeting, December 13, 1967, MS1134, Torres, Alva, Box 2 of 4, f.16, Plaza de la Mesilla—Minutes, 1967–1968, Arizona Historical Society, and Torres interview.

59. Torres interview.

60. Torres interview.

61. "Festive Opening at La Placita," *Tucson Daily Citizen*, May 4, 1974, MS1134, Torres, Alva, box 3 of 4, f.20, Plaza de la Mesilla—Newspaper Clippings, 1967–1986, Arizona Historical Society.

62. "La Placita Dedicated May 3 with a Fiesta Spirit" in *Noticias de La Placita* 1, No. 1, June 1974, MS1134, Torres, Alva, box 2 of 4, f.21, Plaza de la Mesilla—Miscellaneous, 1969–1974, Arizona Historical Society.

63. Tucson City Council Minutes, September 7, 1971, Box 1 of MS1706, File Ordinances, Tucson Historic Committee, 1971–1973, Arizona Historical Society.

64. Ibid.

65. Torres interview.

66. Romano Cedillos, "YWCA Recognizes Women Who Make Tucson Better," *Tucson Citizen*, December 27, 2002.

67. In analyzing Chicana/o social movements, political scientist Benjamin Márquez argues that "Identities provide a frame of reference through which political actors can initiate, maintain and structure relationships with other groups and individuals." Márquez, "Choosing Issues, Choosing Sides: Constructing Identities in Chicana/o Social Movement Organizations," *Ethnic and Racial Studies* 24 (March 2001): 220.

68. Rodolfo Acuña, *Occupied America: A History of Chicanos* (New York: Longman, 2000), 357–58.

69. In 1967, in what would later be recognized as the Chicana/o Movement in Tucson, generally younger, more militant college students started to organize. Salomón "Sal" Baldenegro had just founded the Chicana/o student association (MASA) at the University of Arizona. Baldenegro, Guadalupe Castillo, and Raúl Grijalva became the city's most visible self-identified Chicana/os. They formed the Chicana/o Liberation Committee. This group organized walkouts at local high schools and demanded Chicano history and studies courses in the high schools and at the University of Arizona. They used more confrontational tactics to force the city to convert the El Rio Golf Course, located in the heart of a Chicana/o neighborhood, into a community center in the early 1970s. Francisco A. Rosales, *Chicano! The History of the Chicana/o Civil Rights Movement* (Houston: Arte Público Press, 1996), 211.

70. It should also be noted that La Placita Committee never furthered the idea that Mexican people should pursue a "white identity."

71. Torres interview.

72. Alva Torres to Mr. Royal, February 20, 1970. MS1134, Torres, Alva, box 2 of 4, f.18, Plaza de la Mesilla—Correspondence, 1968–1974, Arizona Historical Society.

73. Sarah Dillard Pope, "Hispanic History in the National Register of Historic Places." Retrieved April 15, 2007, from http://crm.cr.nps.gov/archive/20-11/20-11-5.pdf.

PART II

Migration and Settlement

3. *Cruzando la Linea:*
Engendering the History of
Border Mexican Children during
the Early Twentieth Century

In the summer of 1917, fourteen-year-old Beatriz Orrellana of Mexico City applied for entry into the United States through Nogales, Arizona. This case, found in the transcripts of the Records of the Immigration and Naturalization Service, reflects the anxieties that permeated U.S. border society when it came to Mexican children crossing the border. Beatriz's older sister, Trinidad, and her older brother, Alfonso, accompanied Orrellana. According to their testimony, their mother and two other sisters had moved to El Paso two to three years earlier and worked at the Star Theater as actors and singers.[1] Appearing before the immigration board, the three siblings faced intense questioning. Repeatedly, immigration officers questioned Trinidad and Alfonso about the occupations of their mother and sisters. They also interrogated the two about their younger sister: "Now, how about this 14–year old sister of yours? Has she ever done any work at all, either in the theater or around home, or for other people, for wages?" Both Trinidad and Alfonso stated that she had not. Basing their decision on what they perceived as acceptable appearance and hygiene, the board allowed them to enter, concluding, "The little 14–year old girl is clean and well dressed, and shows evidence of good care."[2]

Two weeks later, the acting supervising inspector reprimanded the inspector in charge, writing, "As you know, the Mexican dancers and singers employed in cheap variety shows on the border are, for the most part, of an irresponsible, immoral class, and it seems to the writer in this case an investigation properly should have been conducted at El Paso to determine, if possible, the character of the relatives living here and their mode of living before favorable action was taken upon the application."[3] The reprimand was imbued with thinly disguised references to prostitution. A Mexican woman or girl crossing the border at the turn of the century, particularly if from the working class, ran the risk of such suspicions. Scholars such as Eithne Luibhéid have demonstrated the "distinctions between women who get labeled as prostitutes and other women derive not from any inherent characteristics within the women themselves but from social relations of power."[4] Outside the model of a normative family (a husband, wife, and children), Beatriz Orrellana, her mother, and her sisters were questionable entrants to the nation. An increasingly codified and exclusionary immigration system, created in part to uphold women's morality, viewed girls outside the control of a nuclear family as possible threats to the nation.

Writing children into history transforms the way we look at the U.S.–Mexico border as well as Mexican American history. At the most basic level, it allows us to understand the day-to-day lives of the majority of the Mexican population on the border. But centering children's experiences and representations does more. It also enables us to realize more clearly the obstacles faced by the Mexican community and the strategies employed by adults and children to assert agency. Writing children into border history provides us a glimpse into the creation of the contemporary border. At the beginning of the twentieth century, the border as we know it now was only fifty years old. Efforts to demarcate the line geographically were followed by attempts to demarcate the line socially and culturally. The migration of children threatened these intentions, making Mexican children lightning rods of controversy.

Despite historians' views of Mexican migration as largely a movement of adult men, evidence points to the youthfulness of many migrants. Historian George J. Sánchez's sample of Mexican immigrants who came to the United States between 1900 and 1930 gives evidence of this—of 2,622 individuals in his sample, 37.7 percent of the females had crossed as children, and another 19.2 percent had crossed as adolescents (between 13 and 18 years of age). Of the males in the sample, 30.1 percent had crossed as children, and 22.6 percent had crossed as adolescents. In all, children made up 32 percent of the sample while adolescents comprised almost 22 percent.[5] Marcus S. Goldstein's 1943 study of Mexican immigrants in Texas also substantiates the youthfulness of many immigrants. According to Goldstein's survey of 325 Mexican mothers and fathers (whose childhood coincided with the period 1880–1930), almost 37 percent of the fathers and 58 percent of the mothers had immigrated to the United States as children or adolescents. In fact, almost 30 percent of the mothers had come to the United States between birth and the age of 15.[6] A 1910 report from inspector Frank R. Stone to the commissioner general of immigration in Washington revealed that children represented 28 percent of the statistical Mexican aliens admitted through El Paso between June 1, 1909, and May 31, 1910.[7] Although excluded from much of the scholarly study of Mexican migration, evidence indicates that they comprised a significant segment of the immigrant community.

At the beginning of the twentieth century, a time of accelerating Mexican immigration, Mexican children crossed many borders. "*Cruzaron la linea*" (they crossed the line) physically as they migrated across the geopolitical boundary. Developmentally, they moved through the stages of childhood and adolescence, and what is as significant, they crossed cultural and racial boundaries.[8] Was the inspector truly concerned about the future living conditions of Beatriz Orrellana? Did he hope to protect the young girl from an "immoral" life, or was he worried that she was already part of the "irresponsible [and] immoral class"? After all, by the turn of the century immorality had become a central issue in immigration policy, reflecting the greater national efforts of reformers to protect women and girls. Just as domestic legislation officially sought to protect women and girls from prostitution, immigration laws sought to protect the nation from prostitutes.[9] The same year that fourteen-year-old Beatriz Orrellana crossed the border at Nogales, Congress passed the Immigration Act of 1917 that specifically banned women and girls from entering the United States for "immoral purposes" and made it possible to deport women and girls who "acted in immoral ways after arrival," even decades after their entry.[10] Such regulations gave immigration officials tremendous power to judge young Mexican immigrant women and their suitability as potential residents of the United States.[11] Both gender and class shaped the interactions between Mexican children and the institutions they would encounter in the United States. Class standards, euphemistically referred to in terms of "cleanliness" and "dress" combined with gendered expectations to determine the futures of young Mexican immigrants.

In significant ways, the growing presence of Mexican children defined critical aspects of the modern border. Both Mexicans and Euro-

Americans responded to the growing presence of Mexican children. The Mexican community sought creative ways to negotiate on behalf of its children, understanding that the treatment of the children reflected the position of the larger Mexican population. The children's presence also acted as a mirror whose reflection propelled Euro-Americans to define "American" in an increasingly rigid and exclusionary manner. This understanding shaped public discourse and government policy, ranging from the implementation of educational policies outlawing the speaking of Spanish, to immigration policies focusing on the control of children, to the debates over Mexican children's worthiness. Although these children held no institutional power, their presence was vital to the formation of a modern border space at the beginning of the twentieth century.

By viewing the experiences of Mexican children crossing the border and the binational response to that movement, we can begin to appreciate the complex ways in which Mexican immigrant children negotiated a racialized and gendered childhood and adolescence. At the turn of the century, new institutions of control emerged along the border, often situated within the structures of local governments and churches. Institutions intended to control children, including schools, juvenile courts, and social service agencies flourished along the 2,000-mile geopolitical divide. Yet, in their interactions with such institutions, Mexican children also navigated creatively. For example, at Rose Gregory Houchen Settlement House in south El Paso, founded in 1912, missionaries focused on Americanization, including citizenship, English, and Bible classes, the essential elements of assimilationist efforts. But Southside children could also take advantage of the playground and entertaining activities such as scouting.[12] Mexican children found themselves at the often contradictory junction of these institutions of control, as described later.[13]

To write of childhood in the late nineteenth and early twentieth centuries is to grapple with multiple definitions of "child." For urban, middle-class youth in the late nineteenth century, childhood extended into the teenage years as parents extended the length of their children's education, postponing their entry into the work world.[14] For Mexican children, however, such categories operated less clearly than for their white middle-class counterparts. Poverty, immigration, and other circumstances often pushed children into carrying out the responsibilities and roles associated with adults at extremely early ages. As part of the family, for example, very young Mexican children often entered the workforce in order to provide extra income for their families. When writing about Mexican children, the category of "child" often remains clouded by the familial needs and survival. Children frequently lived, worked, and existed in an adult world in which they were in fact, if not by legal definition, adults. This does not mean, however that young people saw themselves as adults even while acting as adults. Their parents controlled their wages more often than not despite their adult-like participation in the labor force.

This essay employs several indicators to determine the status of child, minor, or nonadult. Institutions and schools, for example, often considered sixteen to be the age when adolescents became young adults. Legislation made education compulsory through age fourteen. Another indicator is whether the individuals considered themselves children. During the Mexican Revolution of 1910, for example, young boys fought alongside adult men, yet did they consider themselves men? Referring to themselves as "chamacos" or "muchachitos" in later remembrances often provides the clue. In looking at the situation for girls, other questions made themselves evident. Did marriage, sexual activity, and childbirth make girls adults? When Julia Hinojosa Chinas described her first sexual encounter at the age of fourteen with a much older man, she added that "I never had children with him because I was too young."[15] For girls, the line between childhood and adulthood could be fuzzy indeed. Trinidad Escobar, for example, recalled that she married at twelve. The happiest times at the beginning of her marriage were when her husband went out of town. It was then she could play with her dolls.[16]

In the early decades of the twentieth century, the increasingly frequent entry of Mexican immigrant children into the United States amplified their visibility. The Mexican population on both sides of the border was very young. For example, school censuses reveal the growing population of young Mexicans and Mexican Americans in El Paso. In 1914 the El Paso school census reported 7,545 Mexican children between seven and seventeen. Only one year later, the population had increased to 9,141. At the same time, the number of "American" children decreased from 4,732 to 4,022.[17] These numbers are considerable, in light of the total population of the city, which was 77,560 in 1920 according to the U.S. Census. An estimate for 1916 places the Mexican-origin population of the city at 32,724.[18]

This heightened visibility coincided with a period of intense scrutiny of children in general and of immigrant children in particular. During this time, reformers and government agencies studied them and recommended new laws and policies to protect and control children.[19] To local governments, immigrant children represented an additional burden on the schools, the welfare system, and at times, the courts. To reformers, teachers, and employers, Mexican children represented future productive (and low-paid) workers. For American nationalists, the children represented an invasion of unassimilable youngsters who would remain loyal to Mexico, a threat to the integrity of American society.

On the Mexican side of the border, children also held great power as symbols. To Mexican nationalists, the movement of children to the United States represented the loss of the nation's patrimony. During the Revolution of 1910, leaders and governmental officials hoped the younger generation would be the beneficiaries of a new society. As in the United States, Mexican capitalists saw the children as future workers. Finally, to their working-class families, they could represent both *hijos queridos* (beloved children) and workers who could bring in much-needed supplemental income to assist the household.

Economic Development along the Border

The changes occurring along the U.S.–Mexico border were the consequences of several historical processes. First, the war between the United States and Mexico in the late 1840s had initiated a process wherein the international boundary would become increasingly fixed, dividing already existing communities (the El Paso–Ciudad Juárez region, for example) and creating new ones (Laredo and Nuevo Laredo, for example). The new dividing line partitioned not only communities but families as well. Increasing migration at the turn of the century also changed the demographic landscape. Although the borderlands had a long history of migration from central Mexico, dating back to the colonial period, the new geopolitical boundary made this migration even more financially rewarding and more scrutinized and controlled.

In the late nineteenth and early twentieth centuries, socioeconomic change came to both sides of the border simultaneously, driven by capitalism and modernization through which both sides of the border grew increasingly interdependent.[20] In the Mexican North and the U.S. Southwest, agriculture, railroads, and mining drove economic development and population growth. Employers recruited Mexican men, women, and children to work in these nascent industries. Railroads, above all, enabled the population of the border to grow as the twentieth century was ushered in.[21] While railroads provided the means, higher wages in the North of Mexico and yet higher wages on the U.S. side provided the incentive for migration.

Wage differentials within Mexico brought thousands northward. Wages in the less-populated North were higher than in the more densely populated central Mexico. For example, in 1899 the average daily wage for unskilled workers in Guanajuato, with a population density of 92 people per square mile, was 18 to 37 cents. In Chihuahua, with a population density of three per square mile, the average wage was \$1–\$1.50 per day.[22]

On the U.S. side the wages could be even higher.[23] In 1902 wages in Texas ranged from \$1.00 to \$1.25 per day for unskilled labor on railroads. Other southwestern states claimed even higher wages. According to two immigration scholars, unskilled workers "on north Mexican railways deserted by the hundreds for higher wages across the border. Mexican miners did the same, and then agricultural workers."[24] Economist Paul S. Taylor noted that the completion of the St. Louis, Brownsville, and Mexico Railroad in 1904 allowed South Texas commercial agriculturalists access to Mexican workers who provided the labor, which built South Texas into "a garden of Eden, producing all manner of fruits and vegetables, as well as cotton."[25] As railroads and commercial agriculture both enabled and encouraged the migration of Mexicans to the border region, the population of the border cities skyrocketed. Not only did the border population grow, it also became noticeably younger. Children were sometimes employed by railroads, but often their experience was as residents of boxcar communities. Boxcar settlements, often home to Mexican children, "symbolize[d] the most significantly visible evidence of Mexican immigrant ties to the railroad industry in the United States and especially in the Southwest."[26]

Migration of Women and Children during the Mexican Revolution

In the 1910s, as the migration of Mexican men accelerated because of the economic development of the Southwest, the movement of women and girls also accelerated but for very different reasons. During the Mexican revolution (1910 to 1920), the migration of women and children across the border increased as they fled the violence and destruction of the war. During the Revolution, as in contemporary conflicts, women and children represent the great majority of refugees.[27] The experiences of Mexican women and girls diverged from that of men and boys in significant ways. In those years thousands of women and children crossed into the United States, both temporarily and permanently, fleeing rape, abduction, and other forms of gendered violence by entering the United States. With few other options available to them, Mexican women and children, understanding the safety afforded them, took advantage of the international boundary to seek sanctuary. Their movement across the border drew the attention of the military, the immigration service, and the media.

One such incident occurred on the Texas-Tamaulipas border in June 1915. E. P. Reynolds, inspector in charge, reported to the supervising inspector at El Paso. "One thing is certain, however," Reynolds wrote, "large numbers of Mexicans (mostly women and children) are arriving in Matamoros and Reynosa, and a very small per cent of them are applying for admission to the United States."[28] Reynolds's report described the "the intolerable conditions in the interior" and asserted that "train service between Monterrey and Matamoros [had made] it possible for them to come to the border."[29] This scenario points to the fact that for many women, crossing the border lacked the permanency feared by American politicians and xenophobes. Rather, they were simply moving across the dividing line as an expediency.

Several years later in 1919, *El Paso Times* reporter Harry Morgan described the scene as migrants crossed the border from Ciudad Juárez to El Paso in the face of intense battle.

> Genuine pathos marked the flight of the Mexicans. Half clad women, their hair loose, fear written on their faces, ambled across the bridge, holding scantily dressed, crying babies to their breasts. Shawls and blankets trailed in the dirt. To them the night of terror was just another page in Mexico's lengthy chronicle of revolution. To flee from their homes, leaving behind everything they possessed of worldly goods which, meager as it might be, was their all, was only a repetition of former experiences. To leave their humble homes in the wake of war and at the mercy of their fellow countrymen was not a novel thing, but its repetition made it no less terrible. Little children old enough to walk but incapable of understanding tagged along at their mothers' skirts, their eyes tearful, yet full of innocent wonderment. They had been born in the throes of revolution, and to them life had been little more than a recurring series of bloodshed.[30]

For these children the war created a life in which experiences that should have been "extraordinary and temporary" were instead "normal and constant."[31] During the Mexican Revolution, women crossed the border as a survival strategy, bringing their children with them.

Children and Immigration Policies

While the motivations for children to cross the border during the Mexican Revolution are evident, other motivations for migration are difficult to examine. Children's lives and decisions intertwine so profoundly with those of the adults around them, particularly their parents, that uncovering children's agency seems problematic. Furthermore, legal, social, institutional, and familial power structures allow children, particularly young children, little control or voice. An additional obstacle to understanding the migration of children lies in the lack of firsthand contemporary accounts of such crossings. Until the passage of the Immigration Act of 1917, crossing the border from Mexico into the United States was very simple. A lack of inspectors, along with lax surveillance, meant that many Mexican immigrants simply walked across the border without going through any legal procedure whatsoever; as a result, thousands of children crossed without documentation. For much of the first two decades of the twentieth century, children crossed the U.S.–Mexico border without scrutiny of immigration inspectors. As Charles Armijo, who crossed from Ciudad Juárez to El Paso as a child in 1910, remembered, "There were no restrictions then about Mexicans coming over. They were free to come in and go out without any passport, without anything else. Everybody was allowed to go back and forth whenever they wanted."[32] The testimonies of Mexicans living on the border in the early twentieth century tell the same story.[33]

This ease of entry began to change in the late 1910s as U.S. fears of unrestricted immigration led to changes in policy. The Immigration Act of 1917, for example, levied a head tax and required immigrants to take a literacy test before being admitted to the United States. The growing "medicalization" of the border also imposed new requirements for immigrants, and in 1917 a disinfection station was built in El Paso for the examination of immigrants crossing into the city.[34] By 1924 the creation of the Border Patrol hastened the construction of the U.S.–Mexico border as an impermeable line dividing the two nations.

Eithne Luibhéid argues that immigration controls created an "exclusionary sexual order derived from the fact that the model of family codified in immigration law involved a husband, a wife, and children born to the couple."[35] Women and children became central to this new system of control and exclusion, since both represented threats to the sovereignty and maintenance of the nation-state. Mexican women, as bearers of children and culture, and children, symbolic of the future, were threatening to the U.S. racial hierarchy. Furthermore, government officials feared that Mexican women and their children would become "public charges" because of their prevalent poverty and lack of education. For such reasons, it became essential to control their movement across the border.

Mexican children found themselves targets of exclusion a decade before the passage of the 1917 Immigration Act. An act of 1907 that outlined categories of "excluded classes" who could not enter the United States included children unaccompanied by their parents. The case of Beatriz Orrellana, with which we began this chapter, illustrates the implementation of this law. Other excluded people were "undesirables," such as persons with tuberculosis or physical and mental disabilities.[36] This is not to say that children did not enter the United States without their parents, but it demonstrates U.S. immigration policy's intent to ensure that Mexican children would be under the control of a conventional nuclear family unit. Because of this law, immigration inspectors interviewed children and their adult companions extensively. Transcripts indicate that class, racial, and gender expectations shaped recommendations whether to allow a child to enter the United States. The 1907 law left behind a legacy of documents that described the interactions between inspectors, children, and their companions. Despite their problematic nature, these documents allow us to examine the variety of circumstances under which children crossed the border.[37] Often the children came with relatives— older siblings, aunts, uncles, or grandparents. Occasionally legal guardians or even teachers accompanied them. Their reasons for migrating ranged from temporary visits to see relatives and friends or, even as in the case of fourteen-year-old Fernando Ceseña, to "buy clothes." Those who sought moves that were more permanent were also represented, as in the case of thirteen-year-old orphan Guadalupe Muñoz, who sought entry into the United States to live with her uncle in El Paso.[38]

The class differences among children evident in the interview transcripts are striking. For middle-class Mexican parents, the opportunity to send their young to school was often the motive behind the movement of these children across the border. For example, in July 1917 Amblard Emanuel applied for admission to the United States, accompanying two young men, Odilon Mendoza, age thirteen, and Ignacio Calderón, age twelve. The two young men were destined for a Marist college in San Antonio, Texas.[39] Similarly, fifteen-year-old Santos Zaragoza sought admission in order to attend St. Cecilia's College in Los Angeles.[40]

Documents also reveal the lives of working-class immigrants, for example, in the case of Ana María Ramírez. In June 1918, Dolores G. Viuda de García and her seven-year-old orphaned granddaughter, Ana María Ramírez, arrived in Nogales, Arizona, from Tepic, Nayarit. "I have raised [her] as my own daughter," García told inspectors. García and her granddaughter were en route to Caléxico, California, to join Luisa Sarilla. García had worked for Sarilla's family for many years, "raising her ever since she was born." García received room and board for herself and her granddaughter and $10 per month.[41] The details of working-class immigrants' lives often disclose the importance of kinship and the creative ways in which Mexican immigrants cared for family members.

Family Networks

Family reunification proved a strong motive and goal for children's immigration. At times geography divided families, with some living on the Mexican side of the border and others on the U. S. side. Such transnational family networks both facilitated and encouraged the movement of children across the border. Interview transcripts from the Records of the Immigration and Naturalization Service give us a glimpse into the complexity of such family networks. In the summer of 1917, seventeen-year-old Raymundo Valdez accompanied his fourteen-year-old sister Luisa Valdez from San Antonio to Saltillo, Coahuila, to visit their father and grandfather. Luisa lived in San Antonio with her mother, who ran a rooming house for Mexican families and worked in a clothing store. When asked why his parents lived apart, Raymundo answered, "Because my mother has 3 brothers and two sisters living here; all of her family lives in the U.S. and also for the purpose of educating my little sister."[42] Raymundo's presentation of his mother was in opposition to stereotypical representations of Mexican women as exclusively devoted to their husbands.

The importance of family and family reunification is particularly evident in the stories of the most vulnerable groups of children—the poor and the orphaned. The financial circumstances of the family networks were crucial in determining the fate of the children. As evidenced by the transcripts of special boards of inquiry at the border, older siblings and grandmothers frequently accompanied children across the border. In October 1917, thirty-three-year-old Matías Adriano passed through the Immigration Office at Laredo, Texas. Earlier that month he and his family had left their home in Ossawatomie, Kansas, in order to visit his family in Viesca, Coahuila. He brought back his seventeen-year-old sister, María, and eleven-year-old brother, Francisco. In comparison to other immigrants, Matías was relatively well off. Employed as a firefighter in the railroad shops, earning $2.50 daily, he owned his home. His two children were Kansas-born, and he had applied for citizenship. He testified that he was bringing his two young siblings to the United States because "they don't want to stay in Mexico." Further, although they had both attended school in Mexico, Francisco had "left school on account of the Revolution." Attesting to the strength of family ties, Matías stated that he intended to keep his brother and sister with him "until I die." Immigration inspectors allowed the children to enter the country with their older brother, confident that they would not become public charges.[43]

Transcripts provide important clues into the ways that kinship worked and how families organized to provide for orphaned children. Repeatedly individuals described their relationship with their orphaned relatives in similar terms. Adults spoke of raising the children "as their own" while children spoke of their relationship with their female guardians as being one of mother and daughter. Such relationships were essential to the survival of children whose parents had died, a growing occurrence during the Mexican Revolution, or who were too poor to care for them.

The following case demonstrates the complex intergenerational reliance that allowed families and children to survive. In May 1917, Isabel Mariscal, accompanied by her sisters, thirteen-year-old María and twenty-five year old Clotilde, and Clotilde's seven-year-old son, Guadalupe, entered the United States through El Paso's port of entry. Isabel testified that their mother had died about ten years before and their father four years earlier. Since that time, she had reared María. Although María had attended school for two years, she could neither read nor write. She testified that she had "not learn[ed] anything in school." María also testified that she had "always been with my sister and she has looked after me as if she were my mother."[44] Such relationships were essential to the survival of vulnerable children, but they also point to the lack of resources on the Mexican side of the border. This strategy was particularly important for families that could not depend on governmental assistance or private charities to provide support for their young relatives. Furthermore, the practice of taking in children, whether related by blood and not, had a long history among Mexican families.[45]

Life in the United States

The growing movement of children across the border in the early twentieth century coincided with growing societal concerns over child labor and education. Legislators and others had debated compulsory education laws and child labor legislation since the turn of the century. Middle-class reformers argued that the future of the nation depended on a well-educated citizenry. The duty of parents, therefore, was to ensure that their children attended school. As legislatures began to incorporate these values into local and state law, immigrants and working-class people found their children often excluded from such protection.

For example, in 1903 the Texas House of Representatives considered the passage of a child labor law that would prohibit the employment of children under fourteen in mills and factories. The *San Antonio Express News* reported that the "bill is an outgrowth of the agitation against child labor which has been going on throughout the South since the advent of factories."[46] All across the country, reformers and legislators attempted to protect children from exploitation in the workplace. Middle-class norms could not allow children to work when their place was in the classroom. Despite the good intentions, however, the legislation would have little effect on protecting Mexican children from exploitation. These children were concentrated in agriculture, and the law did not cover agricultural work.[47] In Texas and other southwestern states, the passage of such laws had specific implications for Mexican children; they reveal the ambivalence with which legislators and policy makers viewed these youth. In a period of an increasingly protective stance toward children, U.S. society excluded the Mexican young from the vision of a future in which they would be equal participants. Instead, educators and employers intended for them to provide low-paid work as their parents had.

The second issue, compulsory education laws, also demonstrates the hesitancy of American legislators when dealing with Mexican children. When El Paso government officials and educators debated the passage of such a law in 1916, there was strong resistance against enforcing it for Mexican children. First, enforcement would require building new facilities and hiring new teachers for the many hundreds of Mexican children who would be compelled to attend school. Second, according to the *El Paso Herald*, "members of the school board are not in favor of enforcing the law strictly in reference to the Mexican children whose parents are residing here temporarily and who move from place to place and who are a charge on the community in many cases."[48] Such policy decisions—to exclude child agricultural workers from protective legislation and to omit them from compulsory education laws—were based on the prevailing belief that these children were not worthy citizens nor genuine members of U.S. society. In the minds of legislators and local policy makers, Mexican children and their parents were temporary interlopers who would soon return to Mexico.

Education and work were primary concerns for the inspectors, whether the children testified that they sought only temporary entry or more permanent residency in the United States. When Josefa Altamirano and her young sister, Rosario Altamirano, aged five, applied for reentry to the United States after a brief visit to a cousin in Nogales, Sonora, inspectors questioned whether Josefa and her parents "appreciate[d] the benefits of a good education." She assured them that the child would enter school and would not have to work. "We earn enough to maintain ourselves decently," Josefa declared.[49]

When crossing the border, children with work experiences were singled out and interrogated more consistently. As a result, inspectors asked questions not only about future work plans but also about whether the child had worked in Mexico. When Michaela Quintero, aged fourteen, applied for entry through the port of Naco, Arizona, in the summer of 1917, inspectors questioned her about such experience. Although Quintero testified that she was going to Douglas, Arizona, simply to visit her aunt, Josefa Ocano Chacón, inspectors asked what kind of work she would seek if she decided to stay. She had been working in a ticket office and in the confectionery store at Cananea Consolidated Copper Company for three months. Inspection officers admitted Quintero only after the testimony of her aunt, who affirmed that she would reside in Arizona only temporarily and would be under her care.[50]

In addition to the anticipated questions on whether the child would ever become a public charge, inspection investigators also focused on the child's future work plans. To varying degrees, immigration inspectors questioned the adults who accompanied them, and often the children, about whether the child would work. The answer was rarely yes. María Mariscal, aged thirteen, was an exception. When asked what she would do if admitted to the United States, she answered, "If there is work, I expect to go to work."[51] More common were the answers that emphasized the family's plans for the child to attend school. Work would be unpaid labor at home.

Interviewees often dismissed the work of women and children within the home as less than true "work." Matías Adriano provided a typical response when he testified about his young brother and sister: "They will help my wife around the house with house work and attend school."[52] When immigration officials pressed a grandmother, María C. Viuda de Lastra, about her intentions to keep her young granddaughter in school if allowed into the United States, the grandmother testified, "I want her to learn a whole lot." The only work the eight-year-old had done in Mexico was "taking care of the little children at home, outside of school hours."[53] Lastra's response, based on an understanding of what the immigration inspectors wanted to hear, also reflected the devaluation of women's and girls' work inside the home.

Gendered Work

Immigration officials and much of the American public feared that Mexican children would work and that they would become charges of the state. Euro-Americans feared that children would not attend school, yet they did not apply compulsory education laws equally. Americans were caught between two contradictory pressures. One was grounded in the growing idea that society was responsible for protecting children, for they were the most vulnerable. Legislation requiring compulsory education and limiting child labor demonstrated the desire of lawmakers and other groups to provide this protection. The other pressure was grounded in widespread fears that immigrants entering the United States would take advantage of the system. Although the welfare system was limited in the early twentieth century, American lawmakers sought to ensure that immigrants would not benefit from relief. These fears manifested themselves in notions of proper gendered behavior on the part of immigrant children.

These conflicting impulses are evident in the questions asked by immigration inspectors. In the 1910s immigration inspectors consistently asked three kinds of questions of the children who came to the United States and to the adults who accompanied them: Who would support the child? Had the child ever worked for wages, and would the child work for wages in the United States? Had the child ever been to school, and would the child go to school as required by American law?

While working to help support their families remained a norm in the early decades of the twentieth century, boys and girls found that their work differed in significant ways, reflecting gendered expectations of girls' and boys' roles in the family. Although some families expected boys to help with some household chores, a large part of housework fell to their sisters. The chores that Mexican families expected their daughters to perform at home were both more varied and more time-consuming than those expected of their brothers. Evangeline Hymer found in 1923 that both boys and girls contributed to the family income, but in addition girls were expected "to share the burden of washing and housework which the mother with her large family finds too great." Because of their household obligations, girls attended school less frequently than boys, particularly on washday.[54] Indeed, two decades later, researcher, Ruth Lucretia Martínez, found in the 1940s that laundry continued to be time-consuming tedium. "Wash day in the Mexican home is a day of drudgery. For most families it means the lighting of a fire in the yard, the heating of water in the old-fashioned galvanized tub, the use of a rubbing board, and clouds of steam followed by back-aches from the labor expended on dirty overalls and the play clothes of the children."[55]

In her 1921 sample of thirty-five Mexican families in Los Angeles, Alice Culp found that almost two-thirds of the children worked in the home, doing housework and caring for younger children: "The treatment of the children by their parents is shown also by the work the children have to do about the house."[56] She reported that children as young as five worked in the home and that older children taking care of younger siblings "take them to school with them where there is a nursery for them."[57] Such heavy family responsibilities had serious consequences for girls. Culp worried that children forced to work at home, particularly daughters who were obligated to do housework before and after school, would miss the benefits of "wholesome recreation."[58] Not only was recreation lost, but Mexican girls also found that the additional household duties cost them educational opportunities.

Girls' work, despite its significance, was invisible work.[59] Carried out within the confines of the home and considered "free" labor, girls' work was less visible than that of their brothers. Furthermore, their work allowed their brothers to attend school more frequently. But younger girls also worked in the home in order to allow their older sisters to work outside the home. In its 1943 study of the children of agricultural workers, the Children's Bureau of the Department of Labor found that the "boys in the study were employed more frequently than the girls, owing, no doubt, to the fact that girls were often assigned to care for the home and younger children in order to release others in the family for work." While girls as a whole were employed outside the home in smaller numbers than boys, the difference was greatest among girls under fourteen; "That the younger girls were often assigned to household chores, in order to permit their older sisters with greater earning power to work in the fields, perhaps accounts for this difference."[60]

Interviews reveal that working-class girls often worked as domestics as well, mirroring the unpaid labor they already did in their own homes. The transcripts of the Immigration and Naturalization Service provide a glimpse of the working conditions encountered by child domestics on the Mexican side of the border. In August 1917, Albertina Velásquez applied for temporary admittance to the United States. Accompanying her were her fourteen-year-old brother, Luis, who was destined for school in Baja California, and her fourteen-year-old "servant," Altagracia Olvera. Olvera had been orphaned three years earlier and had worked for Velásquez for more than a year. In return, she received monthly wages of three dollars, clothing, soap "to keep clean with," and a room. Velásquez, whom immigration inspectors described as "of the better class of Mexicans," was on her way to join her husband in Ensenada, Mexico. When inspectors asked Olvera about her employment, she related that after her parents' death, she had lived with a family friend who eventually took her to a woman who placed her as a servant with Velásquez. Olvera testified that Velasquez "has taken charge of me forever, I expect to remain with her."[61] With few other options, Mexican girls like Olvera turned to domestic work in order to survive. While immigration inspectors interrogated other children to ensure that they did not have expectations of working, middle-class privilege allowed Velásquez to bring a child servant into the United States.

Similarly, in July 1917, eleven-year-old Constancia Castillo applied for admission to the United States before a Board of Special Inquiry at Laredo. She testified that she was the servant of Lucinda Saunders, who had been admitted the previous day. Constancia declared that immigration officers had turned her back at that time "because my head was not clean." Constancia was an orphan. "I only have grandparents," she told inspectors. Both the girl and Saunders stated that Constancia had worked as a servant for six years. Lucinda Saunders declared, "This child's parents died when she was about 4 years old. There were several in the family. The grandparents left this child with me and the others in different families." When asked if she paid the child wages, she replied, "No, I just take care of her—give her clothes and meals and I send her to school." Saunders told inspectors that they were entering the United States to go to San Antonio on a pleasure trip. Ironically, in describing her servant, Saunders commented, "I look upon her as an adopted child, and wherever I go this child goes with me."[62] While inspectors positioned themselves as protectors of children, girls like Constancia Castillo were vulnerable to exploitation. Class position outweighed progressive ideals about the protection of children. While middle-class markers, such as dress, facilitated the entry of children into the United States, children from the working class were less protected when they crossed the border.

Conclusions

In the early twentieth century, Mexican immigrant children crossed many lines—cultural, racial, and geographic. Responding to events beyond their control, from civil war in Mexico to the growth of border capitalism, children moved across the new border in increasing numbers. They entered a society where definitions of "Mexican," "American," "man," "woman," as well as "child," and "adult" were already in place. Their mounting presence challenged each of these categories. Often excluded from Progressive definitions of childhood, and therefore from the societal and legal protection afforded to children, Mexican youth experienced a different kind of childhood from that of middle-class Euro-Americans. In the early twentieth century, limited educational opportunities and early entry into the workshop shaped generations of Mexican Americans to come. Mexican parents actively sought equal education for their children, understanding that schooling or lack thereof would mold their futures. The sheer numbers of Mexican children along the border forced policy makers and reformers to engage them.

Mexican girls would challenge norms as well as live lives limited by those norms. If Progressives viewed children as vulnerable, girls were doubly at risk. Legislation and attitudes aimed at protecting women and girls played out differently for *mexicanas*. Like the young woman at the beginning of this chapter, they encountered American institutions unsure about the place of Mexican women in the United States. At times, reformers and other representatives of institutions treated them as a group to be protected, especially from the dangers of immorality and exploitation. But because of stereotypes and fears, they often represented immorality to those protectors of society. Through it all, Mexican children and adolescents, along with their parents and families, sought to create productive lives. Each child's story provides a glimpse into the determination of the Mexican families and children who crossed the border seeking better lives. Centering Mexican children in understanding the historical development of the border has much to teach us about the ways in which race, class, and gender worked together to create identity and region.

Notes

This article is part of a larger work in progress, *Crossing the Line: Mexican Children along the U.S.–Mexico Border, 1880–1940*. The manuscript argues that at the beginning of the twentieth century, Mexican childhood at the border provided a critical site where numerous groups struggled over the creation of gendered identities and their maintenance, as well as their challenges.

1. "In the Matter of Orrellana, Trinidad, et al.," *Records of the Immigration and Naturalization Service*, Series A, Subject Correspondence Files (microfilm), Reel 8 (Bethesda, Md.: University Publications of America, 1992), hereafter referred to as *Records of the INS*; for a different interpretative focus on this case, see Vicki L. Ruiz, *From Out of the Shadows: Mexican Women in Twentieth-Century America* (New York: Oxford University Press, 1998), 12.
2. "In the Matter of Orrellana, Trinidad, et al.," *Records of the INS*, Reel 8.
3. Ibid.

4. Eithne Luibhéid, *Entry Denied: Controlling Sexuality at the Border* (Minneapolis: University of Minnesota Press, 2002), 38.

5. Sánchez, *Becoming Mexican American*, 34.

6. Marcus S. Goldstein, *Demographic and Bodily Changes in Descendants of Mexican Immigrants* (Austin: University of Texas, Institute of Latin-American Studies, 1943).

7. Report of inspector Frank R. Stone to the commissioner general of immigration, Washington, D.C., June 30, 1910, *Records of the INS, Series A, Part 2 (Mexican Immigration, 1906–1930)*, Reel 2. These children numbered 1,138 out of a total 4,017 statistical immigrants, representing 28 percent; the children constituted a much smaller number of nonstatistical immigrants—1,089 out of 35,886 (4 percent).

8. Several historians have addressed the history of Mexican American adolescence in the early part of the twentieth century; see for example, Douglas Monroy, *Rebirth: Mexican Los Angeles from the Great Migration to the Great Depression* (Berkeley: University of California Press, 1999); George J. Sánchez, *Becoming Mexican American: Ethnicity, Culture, and Identity in Chicano Los Angeles, 1900–1945* (New York: Oxford University Press, 1993); and Ruiz, *From Out of the Shadows*. Scholars have also paid some attention to gender and childhood in contemporary Mexican immigrant communities; see Pierrette Hondagneu-Sotelo, *Gendered Transitions: Mexican Experiences of Immigration* (Berkeley: University of California Press, 1994); and Abel Valenzuela Jr. "Gender Roles and Settlement Activities among Children and Their Immigrant Families," *American Behavioral Scientist* 42 (January 1999): 720–42.

9. "In the Matter of Orrellanam Trinidad, et al." *Records of the INS*, Reel 8.

10. Luibhéid, *Entry Denied*, 31–54.

11. While similar fears were expressed about the entry of other immigrants, the vast majority crossing the U.S.–Mexico border were Mexican; see Patrick Ettinger, *Tenacious Immigrants: Crossing the Border, 1880–1930*, Pass of the North Heritage Corridor Booklet Series (El Paso, Tex.: El Paso Community Foundation, 2002); and Luibhéid, *Entry Denied*.

12. Ruiz, *From Out of the Shadows*, 33–50.

13. The Progressive era institutions of control were heir to earlier efforts by white middle-class women to do "woman's work for woman" as Peggy Pascoe describes in *Relations of Rescue: The Search for Moral Authority in the American West, 1874–1939* (New York: Oxford University Press, 1990); the racial hierarchies evident in Pascoe's study of Protestant home missions were evident in border institutions as well where both Mexican women and children were seen as in need of instruction and correction.

14. David I. Macleod, *The Age of the Child: Children in America, 1890–1920*, Twayne's History of American Childhood Series (New York: Twayne, 1998), 139.

15. Colección Divulgación, *Mi Pueblo Durante la Revolución*, vol. 1 (México, DF: Instituto Nacional de Antropología e Historia), 20–21.

16. Trinidad Escobar, interviewed by Ray Burrola, Center for Southwestern Studies, University of New Mexico, Albuquerque.

17. *El Paso Herald*, June 22, 1914, and July 1, 1915.

18. Oscar J. Martínez, *Border Boom Town* (Austin: University of Texas Press, 1978), 159–60.

19. See Linda Gordon, *Heroes of Their Own Lives: The Politics and History of Family Violence, Boston 1880–1960* (New York: Viking, 1988), for the ways in which child protection developed in the late nineteenth century from efforts of Christian, middle-class women volunteers to professional programs that were integrated into the new social work profession in the Progressive era.

20. Oscar J. Martínez, *Border People: Life and Society in the U.S.–Mexico Borderlands* (Tucson: University of Arizona Press, 1994).

21. Arthur F. Corwin and Lawrence A. Cardoso, "Vamos al Norte: Causes of Mass Mexican Migration to the United States" in *Immigrants—and Immigrants: Perspectives on Mexican Labor Migration to the United States,* edited by Arthur F. Corwin (Westport, Conn.: Greenwood Press, 1978), 45; Jeffrey Marcos Garcilazo, "Traqueros: Mexican Railroad Workers in the United States, 1870 to 1930," Ph.D. diss., University of California at Santa Barbara, 1995, for an in-depth description of the ways in which *mexicanos* formed an essential part of the railroad industry in the Southwest.

22. Corwin and Cardoso, "Vamos al Norte," 39–41.

23. Although southwestern wages were higher than Mexican wages, a dual wage system existed throughout the region, which placed wages paid Mexican and Mexican American workers below those paid Anglo American workers; there also existed a dual wage system in which women were paid lower wages than men. As these two wage systems intersected, Mexican women often found themselves at the bottom of the scale.

24. Corwin and Cardoso, "Vamos al Norte," 45.

25. Ibid., 47.

26. Garcilazo, "Traqueros," 244.

27. In fact, in the late 1980s women and children represented approximately 80 percent of all refugees who fled across borders; see Gary W. Ladd and Ed Cairns, "Children: Ethnic and Political Violence," *Child Development* 67 (January–February 1996): 15.

28. Report of E. P. Reynolds, inspector in charge, to supervising inspector, Immigration Service, El Paso, Texas, June 18, 1915. *Records of the INS, Series A, Part 2 (Mexican Immigration, 1906–1930),* Reel 5.

29. Ibid.

30. Quoted in Oscar J. Martínez, *Fragments of the Revolution: Personal Accounts from the Border* (Tucson: University of Arizona Press), 295.

31. Peter S. Jensen, "Children As Victims of War: Current Knowledge and Future Research Needs," *Journal of the American Academy of Child and Adolescent Psychiatry* 32 (July 1993): 697.

32. Sánchez, *Becoming Mexican American,* 51.

33. For another example, see Enrique Acevedo interviewed by Robert H. Novak, May 17, 1974, transcript on file at the Institute of Oral History, University of Texas at El Paso.

34. Alexandra Minna Stern, "Buildings, Boundaries, and Blood: Medicalization and Nation-Building on the U.S.–Mexico Border, 1910–1930," *Hispanic American Historical Review* 79 (February 1999): 45. See Stern's more recent *Eugenic Nation: Faults and Frontiers of Better Breeding in Modern America* (Berkeley: University of California Press, 2005).

35. Luibhéid, *Entry Denied,* 3.

36. William C. Van Vleck, *The Administrative Control of Aliens: A Study in Administrative Law and Procedure* (New York: Commonwealth Fund, 1932), 10; this law also created the Dillingham Commission, which set out to study the condition of immigrants and reported its findings in a forty-two-volume set published in 1911.

37. *The Records of the INS* represent one of the few contemporary sources that allow us a glimpse of the children's words. Most of the interviews, however, are translations of the Spanish originals. In addition, it is certainly possible that the children had been somehow coached on their answers, although it seems from many of the adults' responses that they knew how to answer the Board of Inquiry's questions.

38. "In the Matter of Fernando Ceseña," and "In the Matter of Múñoz, Guadalupe, and Múñoz, Manuel," *Records of the INS*, Reel 9. In addition, in October 1917 immigration inspectors allowed Justina Díaz, her infant, and her thirteen-year-old sister, Carmen Díaz, to enter the United States temporarily; they were on their way to "San Antonio to shop." "In the Matter of Justina Díaz et al.," *Records of the INS*, Reel 8. On the same microfilm reel are the cases of sixteen-year-old Mariano Valenzuela and six-year-old Epifanio Valenzuela from Cananea, Sonora, who were visiting a family friend in Bisbee, Arizona; fifteen-year-old Presentación Altamirano from Pilar, Mexico, who was admitted through Del Rio, Texas, to go shopping; five-year-old Carmen Muños, who accompanied her grandmother from Hermosillo, Sonora, to visit her sick uncle in Tucson, Arizona; fourteen-year-old Ramiro Martínez from Villaldama, Nuevo Leon, who crossed over to Laredo to go shopping; and on Reel 9, twelve-year-old Refugio López, who went from Cananea, Sonora, to South Bisbee, Arizona, to visit a family friend whose husband had died recently.

39. "In the Matter of Amblard, Emanuel, et al.," *Records of the INS*, Reel 8.

40. "In the matter of Zaragoza, Santos," *Records of the INS*, Reel 9; Zaragoza's uncle, Leonardo Camou, was from an influential Sonorense family. For a history of Sonora that refers to the influence of the Camou family, see Miguel Tinker Salas, *In the Shadow of the Eagles: Sonora and the Transformation of the Border during the Porfiriato* (Berkeley: University of California Press, 1997).

41. "In the Matter of García, Dolores G. Vd. de, et al.," *Records of the INS*, Reel 9.

42. "In the Matter of Valdez, Raymundo, et al.," *Records of the INS*, Series A: Subject Correspondence Files, Part 2: Mexican Immigration, 1906–1930, Reel 8.

43. "In the Matter of Adriano, Matías, et al.," *Records of the INS*, Reel 8.

44. "In the Matter of Mariscal, Isabel, et al.," *Records of INS*, Reel 8.

45. See Yolanda Chávez Leyva, "El Amparo de las Viudas: Widows and Land in Colonial New Mexico," in *Writing the Range: Race, Class, and Culture in the Women's West*, edited by Elizabeth Jameson and Sue Armitage (Norman: University of Oklahoma Press, 1997). Colonial records of the impoverished settlement of New Mexico demonstrate a similar survival strategy; poor and orphaned children depended on relatives to raise them while adults depended on grown children to support them.

46. "Child Labor Bill," *San Antonio Express News*, January 17, 1903, p. 3.

47. Child labor debates in the early twentieth century often romanticized farm-

work as an opportunity for children to work outside and learn a strong work ethic. See Bill Kaufmann, "The Child Labor Amendment Debate of the 1920s," *Essays in Political Economy* 16 (November 1992): 11.

48. *El Paso Herald*, September 14, 1916.

49. "In the Matter of Altamirano, Josefa, et al.," *Records of the INS*, Reel 8. Although the family had been living in Tempe, Arizona, for about eight years, their five-year-old daughter Rosario had been born in Nogales, Sonora, a fact that surprised the immigration inspectors. Her older sister testified that their mother had crossed to the Mexican side of the border to have the baby.

50. "In the Matter of Micaela Quintero," *Records of the INS*, Reel 8.

51. "In the Matter of Mariscal, Isabel, et al.," *Records of the INS*, Reel 8.

52. "In the Matter of Adriano, Matías, et al.," *Records of the INS*, Reel 8.

53. "In the Matter of Lastra, María C. Vd. de, et al.," *Records of the INS*, Reel 8.

54. Evangeline Hymer, "A Study of the Social Attitudes of Adult Mexican Immigrants in Los Angeles and Vicinity," master's thesis, University of Southern California, 1923, 37.

55. Ruth Lucretia Martínez, "The Unusual Mexican: A Study in Acculturation" (master's thesis, Claremont Colleges, 1942), 37.

56. Alice Bessie Culp, "A Case Study of the Living Conditions of Thirty-five Mexican Families in Los Angeles with Special Reference to Mexican Children" (master's thesis, University of Southern California, 1921), 38.

57. Ibid.

58. Ibid., 50.

59. See Jeanne Boydston, *Home and Work: Housework, Wages, and the Ideology of Labor in the Early Republic* (New York: Oxford University Press, 1994), for a history of the increasing invisibility of women's work in the home.

60. Amber Warburton, Helen Wood, and Marian M. Crane, *The Work and Welfare of Children of Agricultural Laborers in Hidalgo County, Texas* (Washington, D.C.: U. S. Department of Labor Children's Bureau Publication, 1943), 21.

61. "In the Matter of Velásquez, Albertina, et al.," *Records of the INS*, Reel 8.

62. "In the Matter of Castillo, Constancia," *Records of the INS*, Reel 8.

GABRIELA F. ARREDONDO

4. *Lived Regionalities:*
Mujeridad *in Chicago,*
1920–40

Mujeridad

In August 1926, Señora Carmen de Blasco stopped in Chicago during her travels throughout the United States. She was billed by several newspapers as "the representative of the modern Mexican woman."[1] In an interview she granted to Chicago's largest Spanish-language newspaper, she explained that the current crisis in Mexico (referring to the postrevolutionary unrest) was caused in large part by the backwardness of Mexican women. "Mexican women," Carmen insisted, "have not learned nor have they been taught anything more than what their mothers learned." She went on to clarify that they "have neither ambitions nor perspectives; neither can [they] see ahead nor can they envision the Mexico of the future." She, however, apparently could. Like several women activists throughout Latin America during this era, Carmen sought to include the rights of women in the postrevolutionary remaking of the Mexican nation-state.

Unlike progressive Anglo women in the United States, many activist women in Latin America considered "emancipation" or the equality of the sexes to be a threat to home and family. In their version of progressive "new womanhood," or what I am calling *mujeridad* they sought instead "neither 'sameness' with men nor . . . a status quo that perpetuated female legal, professional, and economic inferiority."[2] They worked to restructure civil codes, increase education, improve wages and work conditions, and only eventually to gain political enfranchisement.[3] Like Carmen de Blasco, Mexico's progressive women came largely from the affluent classes, and they remained a small but vocal group through much of the first half of the twentieth century. They maintained ties with other prominent progressive women in the Americas, yet they only gradually achieved the changes they sought.

Carmen de Blasco must have been impatient at the rate of change, so much so that she abandoned Mexico entirely and decided to settle in the United States. In making this choice she explained that she fully expected "to live with all the characteristics of a modern life and within a liberal atmosphere that supported the freedoms of women."[4] Carmen's views on women's rights, then, must have been more liberal than those of the majority of progressive women in Mexico. Her decision to live in the United States makes it very likely that her vision of the rights of women diverged from the *mujeridad* summarized above and aligned more with the visions of New Womanhood held by Anglo progressive women in the United States who sought equality of the sexes.

In coming to this country, Carmen de Blasco experienced these two competing sensibilities about women's roles and women's relation to men. Other Mexican women who came to Chicago, particularly those of the lower and middle classes, also experienced the tensions within divergent notions of womanhood and of the "proper roles" for women. They, like Carmen, discovered life in the United States provided women more freedoms than life in Mexico.[5] Indeed, these women encountered new gender norms and expectations that often clashed with those of their birthplace. This essay focuses on some of these Mexican women who embraced new opportunities and whose lives challenged traditional gender norms and behaviors. In doing so it sheds light on the experiences of otherwise invisible women whose lives made plain contemporary visions of what I will call *mujeridades*, that is, the competing visions and beliefs about what Mexican women could and should do. This concept of *mujeridades* provides a way to capture the multiple, often conflicting meanings of Mexican "womanhood" that affected various aspects of their lives from migrations to marriages, families to workplaces. *Mujeridad* is also distinct and separate from notions of womanhood developed around middle-class Anglo women.[6] The distinction is critical, for Mexican women juggled expected behaviors related to both *mujeridad* and womanhood—as embodied in the New Woman of the 1920s—once they arrived in Chicago. In addition, Christian-infused normative expectations of them as *mujeres decentes* (decent women) dictated repressive behaviors and restricted life trajectories, while modernizing moves, particularly in urban centers in Mexico and the United States, offered new modes of behaving and new life options.

Moving out of familiar contexts left behind in Mexico—often small towns in the countryside where women's behaviors were effectively policed by extended families and tightly knit communities—many of these women traversed new social and cultural terrains as they migrated from Guanajuato, Jalisco, and Michoacán through Texas, Kansas, Illinois, Michigan, and Wisconsin. Once in Chicago, they found themselves surrounded not by extended family and longtime associates, but rather by other Latin Americans, immigrants from all over Europe, African Americans, and Filipinos. Settling primarily in three areas—the Near West Side, Packingtown/Back-of-the-Yards, and South Chicago—Mexican women experienced new environments where they were freer to create nontraditional social networks, where they could participate in new forms of recreation and amusement, and where they could work for wages outside the home.

Mexicanas, both rural and urban, brought notions of *mujeridad* with them. *Mujeres decentes*, for instance, were expected to defer to the dominant male figure in their lives, to aspire to and become a wife and mother, and to refrain from work outside the home, which was seen as taking away from her primary roles in the home. Emphasis was drawn away from women's bodies, and modesty and chastity were highly respected. Women's notions shifted and transformed as their travels forced them into new and unfamiliar situations that necessitated new tasks, languages, and labors and that presented new opportunities. Once in Chicago, they encountered the New Woman of the 1920s, who went out socially with men, dressed in current fashions, worked for wages outside the home, and enjoyed movies, dances, and even makeup. This image, including affordable clothing fashions and the rising beauty cultures learned through magazines and Hollywood films, presented clearly conflicting versions of how women should behave even as it offered new freedoms.

These particular freedoms appealed directly to younger women, setting up generational tensions between them and their mothers as each discovered they held very different notions of *mujeridad*. While several of these changes were becoming common in the major cities of Mexico, many of these women first experienced them in the United States and thus understood them to be part of American life. Thus younger women's visions of *mujeridad* reflected U.S. influences more than they did those of their mothers.

Men, on the other hand, appeared to go through a process of "cultural freezing," in which norms that were expected in Mexico became reified after migrating to the United States.[7] Rather than supporting the cultural and social transformation embodied in women's availing themselves of new freedoms, men bemoaned the new freedoms of women in the United States and sought to maintain, recreate, and capture what they believed should be the norms for Mexican women, reflecting their own version of *mujeridad.* Motivated by these gendered expectations then, men often despaired at the freedoms available to American women and by which, they imagined, Mexican women were tempted. They used these threatening freedoms to explain the transformations that their wives, sisters, and daughters underwent in their migration to and settlement in Chicago—that is, these women's "lived regionalities."

Lived Regionalities

As Mexican women lived their lives, they crossed many geographic and existential regions. They carried with them the experiences, memories, and knowledge they gained. As they did, these *mujeres* became literal and figurative embodiments of what I tentatively term lived regionalities. That is, each of the geographic and psychic spaces they lived in, and passed through, became part of their lived regional knowledge—knowledge that shaped the lens through which they experienced and understood subsequent places and spaces in their lives. *Mujeridad* was central to this knowledge, for the regions in which they lived and traveled shaped their perceptions and desires while forcing and creating new situations and opportunities.

Part of understanding the histories of Mexican women involves mapping their lived regionalities, that is, deciphering their migration processes and their settlement and adjustment to illuminate the decisions they made along the way. This is especially critical as the vast majority of studies of Mexicans in the Midwest chronicle the migrations and lives of Mexican men. If women are included at all, they are treated as appendages or as participants in a terrain that, though seemingly gender-neutral, is, in fact, gendered male.

This mapping of Mexicanas' lived regionalities then is an attempt to capture tangible and intangible terrains as they were actually experienced by women themselves. At any given historical moment, the Mexicanas included here were accumulations of the many experiences and the knowledge of the places where they had lived. In this way, the Mexicanas living in Chicago during the 1920s and 1930s helped spin a transnational/multiregional web that extended throughout the midwestern and southwestern United States to parts of northern and central Mexico. For Chicago has stood as the major urban center of the Midwest for most of the twentieth century and has grown into the third-largest concentration of Mexicans in the United States. The centrality of Chicago in the greater Midwest region and Mexicanas' ties to areas along their migration routes—from Mexico and Texas through Kansas City, Detroit, St. Paul, and other Midwestern cities—means that this study necessarily extends beyond the Windy City. In fact, women's experiences require an approach that transcends the Midwest or the Southwest, and that blur Mexico and the United States. The realities of women's lives force such flexibility. Moreover, mapping Mexicanas' lived regionalities highlights the extent to which women experienced fragmented relationships with men as single, widowed, abandoned, or divorced women, many of whom faced the reality of caring for and raising children alone. Although a small number of men came in the 1910s, the 1920s and the 1930s were the first years when Mexicanas came to Chicago, in the midst of vast new changes in mass culture and economic development, and for that reason these years offer a portentous moment through which to understand their newly evolving gender relations.

The challenge of mapping the gendered female experience is complicated by the dearth of information on Mexican women's lives, especially those of individual women, during this era in Chicago. A few left ghost prints of their existence, and the traces that remain must be read against the grain to draw out the textures of their lives. The biographical information about these women comes from their applications to become U.S. citizens. When read as biographical snapshots of these women's lives, rather than as dry government documents, these seemingly dull papers spark to life and make the ghost prints visible. It was very rare for these women to change their citizenship at all. An estimated 2 percent of the Mexican population in Chicago became U.S. citizens and of that, 5 percent were women; thus, these women made up an estimated 0.1 percent of the Mexicans in Chicago.[8] The Mexicanas whose lives are profiled here, then, are truly unusual. Yet they represent what was possible and what in fact did exist in Chicago before World War II.

While only shadows of Mexicanas' lives remain, nevertheless these hints suggest contours of experiences and knowledge that demonstrate that the gendered female narrative of Mexican migration to and settlement in the Midwest differs from that of men. For instance, women's wage labor opportunities were much fewer and more poorly paid than those of men; women faced the physical realities of conceiving and bearing children; women remained the primary care providers for children and were the key figures in supplying a family's daily needs. Moreover, legal and institutional constraints, like regulations on women's travel out of Mexico, ensured that women's lives were tied to fathers, husbands, brothers, or sons.

From migration to settlement, from work to entertainment, the experience of *mujeres* was different from that of Mexican men. Most significant, Mexican women discovered that life in the United States—in spite of its difficulties—provided them with freedoms unavailable in Mexico. Men found that it was these same freedoms that most detracted from life in *el norte*.

Gendered Migrations

The standard narrative of Mexican migration to the Midwest begins near the end of World War I as steel, meatpacking, agriculture, and railroad industries recruited workers for expanding enterprises.[9] That the great majority of these jobs were slated for men is just one indicator of how seemingly gender-neutral information is in fact very gendered; in this case, gendered male. Women's migration into the area was very small, though it did increase dramatically over the course of the 1920s. Throughout the interwar period, however, the number of women remained significantly smaller than that of men.[10] In 1924, for example, there are estimated to have been twenty Mexican men to every Mexican woman.[11]

The 1920 United States census counted 1,141 Mexicans in Chicago. By 1930 the Mexican population had grown to nearly 21,000.[12] In just ten years, then, the net Mexican population had increased by a factor of 17 (1700 percent).[13] The Mexican population of Chicago in 1930 thus represented around 1 percent of the 3 million or so residents.[14] Mexican women represented a much smaller percentage of the overall population of Chicago, thus underscoring how remarkable it is to find any evidence about them at all.

Another element that contributed to the gendering of Mexican migration was that of mobility, or rather the lack of mobility, open to women, especially married women. If a married Mexican woman wanted to travel out of the country either alone or with her children, she was required by the Mexican government to carry written permission from her husband for the trip along with previous confirmation of their relationship.[15] The implications of such restrictions could be pernicious, especially when they hampered a woman's ability to leave the country if her husband had deserted her or if she was attempting to flee an abusive relationship to start a new life in the United States.

Kinship ties often shaped the migratory patterns of Mexican women. Consuelo Medina and David Tapia, for instance, were cousins, born within a month of each other in Irapuato, Michoacán. Consuelo's father, Luz Medina, was the brother of David's mother, Guadalupe Medina. Though it is unclear whether both families traveled or even arrived together in Chicago, the registered births to this kin group indicate that Consuelo's immediate family had lived in Chicago fairly regularly at least from 1925. The extended families registered together at the Mexican Consulate in Chicago in August 1929. In another example, Margarita and Dora Gutiérrez traveled from Guadalajara in the central western state of Jalisco to Chicago with their brother, Xavier.[16] Later they were joined by their widowed mother, Elena Salcedo de Gutiérrez. (Pictured in figure 4.1.) Elena's husband died in 1925 at the age of 58 never having made it to Chicago, and by 1931 Elena lived in Chicago with three of her adult children (her other three children remained in Mexico) and worked as a housekeeper. At the age of 60, Doña Elena filed to change her citizenship, and on November 28, 1940, she became a U.S. citizen.[17] It was that action that provided trace evidence of her existence and that highlighted the centrality of kinship in these migration patterns.

Figure 4.1. Elena Salcedo de Gutiér- rez. U.S. Depart- ment of Labor, Immigration and Naturalization Service. Petition for Naturalization No. 200010, National Archives (NARA), Great Lakes Region, Chicago, Illinois.

Like the Gutiérrez sisters, Fortunato Ramos made most of her journey to Chicago in the company of a man as was customary. She traveled with her husband, Marco.[18] Fortunato left Mexico to live and work in Texas at the age of 18. Through information she gave in her "first papers" (declaration of intention to become a U.S. citizen) and in her "second papers" (petition for naturalization), it is possible to trace her migration process and to note major events in her life along the way. By 1923 she had moved from Hidalgo, Texas, on the Rio Grande bordering Mexico to Lockhart, Texas, a town nearly 300 miles north, near the state capital of Austin. There she married a Tejano, Marco, on November 10, 1923. The couple stayed in Lockhart at least until January 1926, when Fortunato Ramos gave birth to their first child, a daughter, Julia. By 1928 the couple had moved to Chicago, where they had their second child, another daughter, named Eloisa, in March 1928. Eloisa was followed in close succession by four children, all born in Chicago: Juanita in 1930, José in 1931, Elvira in 1934, and Adolfo in 1936. At the end of the 1930s, Fortunato and her family, including her husband Marco, still resided in Chicago. Listed as an unemployed, unskilled laborer, she succeeded in becoming a U.S. citizen like her husband and her six children in April 1940.

Fortunato, like the Gutiérrez sisters and the Medinas, migrated and settled with male family members. Each of these women seemed to embody aspects of *mujeridad* that dictated their roles as wives and mothers. Once in the United States, however, several of these women's situations appeared to have shifted, if only slightly, with women like Fortunato working for wages outside the home and ultimately becoming U.S. citizens. Some *mujeres* were more willing to challenge sociocultural conventions, molding for themselves a freer sense of *mujeridad*. Some, for instance, chose neither to marry nor to have children. Delfina Navarro left her hometown of Guadalajara, Mexico, and entered the United States at Laredo, Texas, when she was just 20 years old. (Pictured in figure 4.2.) Delfina went directly to Chicago, where she remained a single woman with no children until at least the age of 34, when she applied for and received U.S. citizenship.[19] Similarly, Concepción Pérez remained single and childless until she was at least 31 years old when she applied for U.S. citizenship.[20] She, however, traveled much farther and seemed to be even more mobile than these other women. She left her hometown of Mérida in the far southern Mexican state of Yucatán when she was merely 19. Unlike most Mexicans, Concepción came to the United States by ship, traveling across the Gulf of Mexico and up the eastern seaboard to New York City. Nine days after docking, she arrived in Chicago to begin work as a machine operator.[21] It is interesting that when she applied for U.S.

Figure 4.2. Delfina Navarro. U.S. Department of Labor, Immigration and Naturalization Service. Petition for Naturalization No. 195115, National Archives (NARA), Great Lakes Region, Chicago, Illinois.

(T ...pressed so as to cover a portion of the photograph)

citizenship, she changed her name to Caroline, a more common English name (she kept Pérez as her last name). Not only was her journey unconventional, but her choice neither to marry nor have children at a traditionally young age indicated an independence and willingness to avail herself of options—freedoms—in the United States that she did not have in Mexico. Her unmarried status is that much more remarkable when we consider that the pressure to marry, and to be regulated by social institutions, would have been great under the traditional expectations of *mujeridad* and the high ratio of Mexican men to Mexican women, making single Mexican women like Concepción/Caroline a much-sought partner. It is likely too that as a mobile, single, working woman, Concepción's/Caroline's sense of her *mujeridad* included a degree of progressivism that must have included elements of the New American woman.

It is more certain that Celia Hernández enjoyed those new freedoms in the beauty culture of Chicago where she was employed. (Pictured in figure 4.3.) Like Concepción/Caroline, Celia became a U.S. citizen; however, her journey was very different from that of Concepción. Celia was born in November 1908 in the tropical mountains of the state of Guerrero in the capital city of Chilpancingo. After living for a time in Mexico City (176 miles away!), Celia entered the United States legally, walking across the footbridge at Eagle Pass, Texas, on September 10, 1923.

Figure 4.3. Celia Hernández. U.S. Department of Labor, Immigration and Naturalization Service. Petition for Naturalization No. 176592, National Archives (NARA), Great Lakes Region, Chicago, Illinois.

Just 15 years old, she spent the next seven years living predominantly in the United States, and by 1930 she had moved to a small suburb just outside Chicago.[22]

Celia spent her young adulthood in 1930s Chicago as a single woman working in what she termed the beauty culture and in dancing. She continued in these occupations throughout most of the Depression until September 1937. Perhaps she was part of the Latin dance craze that hit Chicago and the nation during the 1930s. (Prominent examples were Alfredo Cano and Bertha "Rosita" Musquiz, performers who donned brilliantly colored costumes and danced traditional Mexican and Spanish numbers to sold-out audiences.[23]) Or more likely Celia participated in the modern dime dancehalls so popular during this period. As was common, young girls were paid to dance with men, keeping a portion of the amount they charged for themselves. With the unequal sex ratios between Mexican women and Mexican men, this form of controlled socializing helped to ensure heterosexual social contacts among Mexicans themselves.[24] Such social regulation would have had the effect of increasing interethnic contacts, but more important, it would have worked to attempt to reduce the numbers of single men and women while reinforcing the desirability of heterosexual social relationships. Being single was often read as a pathology. Among women, being single placed them at risk from predatory men; while single young men were perceived to be at risk for delinquency, crime, and vice.

Regardless of which dancing venue she preferred, Celia continued living her modern *mujeridad* by working for wages outside her home, remaining single and partaking of what she called beauty culture, which included an untraditional focus on a woman's looks and body. She even went to college for a year at the University of Iowa in September 1937 at the age of 29.[25] By June 1938, however, she apparently had returned to Chicago. She remained unmarried at least until she became a U.S. citizen in 1939 at the age of 31.

There were not, however, many like Delfina, Concepción, and Celia, for most Mexican women of their age had married and borne children. In fact, booming birth rates serve as one indicator of a growing Mexican female population. Between May 1929 and May 1930, thirty-five births were recorded with the Mexican Consulate of Chicago.[26] Of those, eighteen had been born in the city. These birth records, though incomplete, also provide a window into the ways families embodied their migrations. Miguel Ortíz López, for instance, was born in Chicago in August 1923, early in the development of Mexican settlements in the area. By June 1925 when sister Consuelo was born, his family was living in Texas. They apparently returned to Chicago within the year, for his brother Andrés, named after his father, was born in June 1926 in Chicago. The López family apparently stayed in Chicago for at least the next three years, during which they welcomed two more little boys into the family.[27] As further evidence, both of female presence and of growing birthrates, slightly more than half the 7,000 Mexicans surveyed in the mid-1930s were under sixteen years old.[28] The extreme youth of the population presented its own set of challenges.

Another, less common angle on the standard narrative of Mexican migration focuses on young men filled with a sense of adventure, who headed *al norte* to try their luck in the various jobs available in the United States during the 1920s. What remains absent from that narrative is the human cost involved for those Mexicanas who joined in the adventure. María Paniagua, for instance, married her husband in her hometown of San Antonio, Texas, against her family's wishes and joined him on the journey north. The couple lived in boxcars in Des Moines, Iowa; Kansas City, Missouri; and finally in Detroit, Michigan, since he worked on the Rock Island Railroad. Along the way, they had children.[29] María's adventure ended, however, when her husband deserted the family in Detroit and María faced caring for and raising the children alone. Initially she worked providing child care and laundry service for other Mexican families in the boxcar camps. The families paid in food for her and the children. During the summer of 1923, María worked in the beet fields with José and Margarita Medina, a couple she knew from the camps in Detroit. After saving enough money for carfare, six months after her husband had left, María and her children moved with the family of Guillermo and Nellie Villalobos to Savannah, Illinois. Shortly thereafter, her brother, already living in Chicago, sent money for her and the children to join him there.[30] Through her own resourcefulness and network of friends and kin, María was able to salvage her situation, but she clearly was struggling, for caseworkers with United Charities visited her regularly with aid and encouragement once she was in Chicago.

María Moreno Corona also found herself in Chicago and deserted by her husband with small children to care for alone. (Pictured in figure 4.4.) She was born in the small, remote, and mountainous town of Arteaga, Mexico, on April 19, 1903.[31] Arteaga lay in the northern state of Coahuila ten miles from the state capital of Saltillo. At some point during her early adulthood, Maria found her way to Saltillo. Just shy of her twenty-second birthday, she traveled from there to the U.S.-Mexico border, crossing legally into the United States over the footbridge at Laredo, Texas. She was eight months pregnant with her first child. Since she had married two years earlier in San Antonio, Texas, it was clearly not her first time coming into and staying in the United States. She made it from Laredo

cover a portion of the photograph)

Figure 4.4. María Corona. U.S. Department of Labor, Immigration and Naturalization Service. Petition for Naturalization No. 196261, National Archives (NARA), Great Lakes Region, Chicago, Illinois.

to San Antonio in time to give birth to Fernando in March 1925. Just over a year later, while still in San Antonio, she gave birth to Amalia in July. By September María had traveled with her newborn daughter and infant son through Texas, Oklahoma, Kansas, Missouri, and Illinois all the way to Chicago.

Once in Chicago, María settled on the Near West Side and worked as a full-time housewife. In May 1928 her second daughter, Aurora, was born, and in May 1930 her second son, Roberto. Sometime during 1930, either just before or right after Roberto was born, María's husband of seven years abandoned her with her four children under the age of five. Somehow she persevered in Chicago through the harshest years of the Great Depression, and by 1937, she had filed her first papers, declaring her intention to become a U.S. citizen. By 1940, shortly after her thirty-seventh birthday, María was sworn in as a U.S. citizen.

María Corona's desertion by her husband, like that of María Paniagua, was not uncommon among Mexican women living in Chicago. Desertion was tied to several factors, including male gender roles and expectations that enabled men to be more mobile (since they did not have primary responsibility for the children), and the lack of legal enforcement that would have made men financially support their wives.[32] According to contemporary social workers in the Chicago area, desertion also took a new turn as women themselves occasionally became deserters. One estimate suggested that "up to one quarter of desertion cases were caused by the wife leaving the children with the husband."[33] Perhaps this was another indicator of their embracing of the "new freedoms" accorded them in the United States, acting as a kind of counter view to women's desertion that implied elements of female agency not accorded by abandonment.

Eva Guerrero also was abandoned, after only three years of marriage.[34] Married at 34, she was considered an older bride during that era, and she had traveled far before marrying. She left her home in Oaxaca at the age of 24 and, after some time in Chiapas, Eva crossed legally as Genoveva L. de Benavídez into the United States at Calexico, California. The assignation of "de Benavídez" suggests she married and took the name of her husband, Benavídez, but there are no details in the records. For thirteen years she lived on the West Coast, not coming to Chicago until May 1937. While in Los Angeles, Eva married Frank Guerrero, a U.S. citizen born in Morenci, Arizona. Eva settled in the town of South Chicago, evidently without her husband, where she worked as a cook.

A few *mujeres* challenged expected trajectories in other ways. Raquel Chávez, for example, was not single, nor was she abandoned—rather, she was a divorced woman.[35] (Pictured in figure 4.5.) Like other women in these narratives, Raquel Chávez's life transgressed many conservative cultural norms. Divorced in her mid-twenties with a young son to raise, she toiled as a factory worker to make financial ends meet. Raquel was born in Torin (also spelled Torim), a small village on the Yaqui River in the Sonoran desert on the Gulf of California. During the Mexican Revolution, several military regiments were stationed in the area. She left in 1919 at the age of 9 (presumably with family), just as an epidemic of yellow fever broke out.[36] After entering the United States lawfully in 1919 at Laredo, Texas, Raquel arrived in Chicago two years later. In September 1930 she married her soon-to-be ex-husband, Manuel Velásquez, and the following year her son, Renato, was born. Just four months into her marriage and a couple of months into her pregnancy, 21-year-old Raquel found her way to one of the Eleanor Association clubs and befriended the secretary of the association, Mrs. Bernice Durkee. Under the auspices of the Eleanor Foundation, the Eleanor Association ran residential clubs for working women and girls, providing them "the opportunity to develop 'the best that was in them' by . . . learning 'to live and work together in healthy cooperation.'"[37] Because the women of Eleanor were primarily single and working (with or without children) in Chicago, Raquel's ties to the association so early into her marriage suggest how short-lived that union must have been. She maintained her link to the Eleanor clubs for at least the

Figure 4.5. Raquel Chávez. U.S. Department of Labor, Immigration and Naturalization Service. Petition for Naturalization No. 214000, National Archives (NARA), Great Lakes Region, Chicago, Illinois.

following ten years, as her friend Bernice became a witness for Raquel's (now known as Rachel) bid to become a U.S. citizen in late 1940.

It is striking how resilient these women were in dealing with the many situations they encountered. While many of them found their lives contoured by the presence of men, they managed to navigate those worlds without the expected male mediator. These women persevered on their own terms. Whether they were abandoned, widowed, divorced, or single, these *mujeres* raised children alone, worked as single women in modern factories, and availed themselves of limited resources to survive. Their resilience is certainly lost in the standard male narrative of migration and settlement of Mexicans in the Midwest. Once in Chicago, the unequal sex ratios between Mexican women and men, along with rising female participation in wage labor, clearly shaped gender relations. The backdrop of emerging mass culture and women's enjoyment of newfound freedoms only exacerbated gender tensions.

Controlling Gender Roles

Both Mexican women and Mexican men struggled with the shifting gender norms and freedoms of the era. Moreover, the explosion of mass culture and its attendant consumerism provided new venues for women and men to identify with American life.[38] For Mexican women, these venues provided new behavior patterns and new symbolic representations of womanhood that transformed visions of *mujeridad* in a variety of ways, including the different valuation of women's work and the creation of fresh spaces for social contact and comportment.[39] These new sites of exchange were further complicated by Mexican women's general welcome of the new freedoms over the objections of Mexican men. Shifting gender behaviors and expectations and generational cleavages erupted throughout the Mexican communities in Chicago. These tensions were typical throughout American society during this period, but Mexican women and men did not seem to be aware of the stresses within the larger society. Rather, they encountered shifting gender norms and expectations concurrent with their adjustments to Chicago, and in that context, they understood them to be part of that adjustment, that is, shifting from the norms they knew in Mexico to those of the United States.[40]

By the mid-1920s nearly a quarter of Chicago's Mexican population was female.[41] Indirect evidence of this growing female population was in advertisements in Chicago's Spanish-language newspapers targeting women. Weekly columns geared toward women began in 1926: one entitled "The Doctor of the Home," the other "The Woman of the Home."[42]

The first mostly carried nutritional information, and the second provided recipes and cooking advice. While acknowledging women's growing presence in the community, such features reinforced their subordinate position.[43] Cook and caregiver were presented as acceptable female roles—both of which were explicitly defined as lying within the home.[44] A man wrote the column on medical advice and a woman provided the recipes. It is interesting that the man's full name, Gustavo Carr, and his credentials were printed in the byline, but only the woman's given name, Maria Luisa, was mentioned—a subtle detail that spoke volumes about the relative respect given to the two writers and ultimately to the readers of the columns. The column of medical advice also attested to the growing professionalization of medical practice.[45] Implicit in having a "doctor of the home" was the notion of a doctor outside the home. If a woman was the amateur doctor of the home, then a man like Gustavo Carr was unmistakably the professional doctor outside the home.

While reinforcing traditional roles for women and opening new possibilities for men, these kinds of columns and advertisements also worked to marginalize the traditional remedies of *curanderas* (female healers) as quack concoctions. Indicative of modernizing trends already underway in Mexico, such reconfigurations also served to reorder traditionally lower-class aspects of women's roles.[46] A trenchant example of this was an advertisement for *Sal de Uvas Picot*. It pictured a young boy paying a male pharmacist for a bottle of this product. The text read "This boy knows what's good. When his mother tries to give him some antiquated, horrible tasting concoction . . . the little boy prefers to. . . . buy himself some delicious *Sal de Uvas Picot* that effectively and gently purges him."[47] Clearly the admonition was to disdain traditional folk remedies in favor of modern pharmaceuticals. The young boy served as the symbolic agent in the implied transformation. The man personified that which was to be embraced.

Alongside efforts to control women's roles was the increasing incorporation of Mexican women into the wage economy of Chicago. Some women entered the wage economy through informal channels. Recall María Paniagua, for instance, who lived in a railroad camp near the Santa Fe tracks and worked for other women in the camp.[48] She helped with child care, cleaning, and laundry while the other women, in turn, provided María with food and a bit of spending money. Some women began working directly for wages outside the home.[49] According to contemporary sociologist Paul Taylor, there were more opportunities for women to work for wages outside the home in Chicago than in the U.S. Southwest, specifically Texas.[50] Nevertheless, employment options open to Mexican women in Chicago were severely limited. Jobs available to them in industry involved what employers termed "typically female" tasks, which often served to reinscribe traditional gender roles.[51] Clotilde Montes, for instance, sewed mattresses at a factory in Chicago.[52] As Mr. Belcher of the Marshall Field Mattress Factory explained, "the [Mexican] women stitch . . . [they] seem to have a natural aptitude with the needle."[53] Such attitudes concentrated Mexican women in low-wage stitching and piecework jobs. Occasionally, however, a Mexican woman worked in a stitching position that was more skilled. Herlinda de la Vega, originally from Guadalajara, Jalisco, Mexico, for instance, was a milliner.[54] (Pictured in figure 4.6.) Like some of the other women profiled in this chapter, she lived her life challenging expected gender norms. When she entered the United States in 1925 at the age of 35, she was unmarried. After coming directly to Chicago, she apparently remained there, working as a milliner until she became a U.S. citizen in 1938. The records seem to show that some of her activities challenging social norms did not remain unnoticed, for by 1953 she had lost her U.S. citizenship and had been deported—"expatriated" for unspecified reasons.

The evidence never clarifies what type of work she performed as a milliner, nor does it suggest how skilled the labor really was. Regardless, Herlinda joined many other Mexican women in stitching. The practice of reserving such employment for Mexican women reified particular

Figure 4.6. Herlinda de la Vega. U.S. Department of Labor, Immigration and Naturalization Service. Petition for Naturalization No. 171129, National Archives (NARA), Great Lakes Region, Chicago, Illinois.

gender roles. Such practices also worked to racially code specific areas of employment as particularly "for Mexican women."[55]

The jobs Mexican women performed paid lower wages than those of Mexican men, a standard upheld by all employers in the area. Such wage inequities betrayed employers' valuing of men's work over women's and may have bolstered hierarchies of authority and power between Mexican men and women.[56] Yet, as historians have discovered elsewhere, earning any wage could also increase a woman's authority in the household.[57] This new authority, coupled with shifting gender norms, opened new freedoms for Mexican women.

New Freedoms

As scholars have shown over the past generation, wage labor provided working women with new freedoms that at once challenged and rein-scribed gender roles. The apparent contradiction spoke to the realities of *mujeridad* in Chicago. Indeed, the very notion of "freedom of women" varied "with the particular situation which each had in mind . . . while the general trend was unmistakably toward acceptance of greater freedom [for women], the amount of freedom thought desirable by individuals was subject to a good deal of variation."[58]

Women experienced new opportunities in heterosexual social commercial activities and redefined notions of family and of female sexuality. Yet these new opportunities also heightened tensions between Mexican women and Mexican men. One Mexican man sought an explanation in strictly practical terms. "In this country," he explained, "everything costs so much that women have to work."[59] A revealing fact is that, as in Mexico, once a woman got married, it was no longer acceptable for her to work outside the home, particularly if she had children. An elderly Mexican woman, reflecting older norms, agreed. "How would you like your wife to work?" she asked, and then explained the impossibilities of such a situation: A woman "can't serve two masters, and one of them has to be your husband."[60]

Many Mexican men seemed threatened and tried either to prevent their wives from working or to control the family monies.[61] Thus, "Mr. Quintero [held] the purse very tightly," forcing Sra. Quintero, who was not working for wages at the time, to ask her husband for money.[62] Some Mexican men, like Raúl DuBois, explicitly associated a woman's freedom to spend her money with being American. "The American woman is freer in the first place," he explained. She "never arranges to regulate how her money is spent," whether she receives that money "from her husband [or] from her work."[63] Another Mexican man agreed, "Mexican men don't like freedom of women. It is all right for the Americans, but not for the Mexicans."[64] Perhaps the sentiments of Mexican men on these new freedoms for women in general highlight their recognition that some Mexican women enjoyed their new autonomy. Younger women expressed pleasure at getting to work outside the home. As one woman explained, "Women like to work here. At home the man is boss, but not while you are at work."[65] Clearly getting out of the house helped to put Mexican women into spaces unregulated by their husbands and sons.

The freedoms associated with U.S. life and the meanings Mexicans attached to those freedoms were fundamentally striated with gendered interpretations. In the minds of Mexican men in Chicago, U.S. women represented a panoply of outrageous behaviors. One Mexican man recounted, "I have an American friend who in his own house can't even . . . order a couple of fried eggs." The man's wife reportedly sent him to a restaurant, telling him that "she did not get married to be a cook for any[one] . . . including her husband."[66] The legal recognition of divorce in the United States was perceived by Mexican men to be another source of women's demise. They considered the reputed ease of divorce to be "nothing but the first step that a woman takes toward her own perdition." Supposedly, divorce allowed women to change husbands so frequently that their lives would become "a succession of 'husbands' only comparable to the lives of those unfortunate ones called prostitutes."[67] Clearly the legacy of Catholic doctrine remained in such views, but perhaps they were also symptoms of the incredible demographic imbalances in Chicago during this period. With so many available men and potential suitors for his wife, a man might worry that she would partake of the new freedoms afforded her. Moreover, his own inability to exert control in his own life or to effectively control his wife (as he believed he had been able to do in Mexico) added to his insecurities. This was particularly true if a man believed that divorce was used by women to "fix" conflicts between them. The U.S. woman, explained another Mexican man, "always has present the recourse of divorce in that it is not seen with horror as with us[;] rather [it is seen] as a medium for fixing difficulties."[68] Perhaps the stigma of divorce added to the number of deserted wives. Women who were devoted Catholics would not have seen divorce as an option, while others would not have wanted to be known as divorced women with its negative social connotations. The ease and commonness of desertion too would have tempered men's desire for divorce. It must surely have been transgressive for Raquel Chávez to divorce just months after her marriage, even before the birth of her baby.

In 1927 Ignacio Sandoval, a Mexican man living on the Near West Side, stated this cultural dissonance succinctly: "here . . . women want to be boss and the poor man has to wash the dishes while the woman goes to the movies."[69] Indeed, mass culture pursuits like films and dances did provide Mexican women with new arenas for individual freedoms and identification with U.S. life. As one young Mexican girl explained, she went to dances and movies, "just like other American girls."[70] Reportedly, upon returning from these events, the young girl "was slapped and beaten by her mother." Maybe the mother depended on her daughter for income, which would explain the outrage with her daughter for "stepping out." Conceivably, interwoven with her outrage were issues of family honor that the young girl was expected to uphold in the oligarchy of the *familia*. It was also likely that the mother held some jealousy for the freedom her daughter had found, a symptom of generational tensions as well.

It was also likely that this mother shared the sentiments of many older Mexicans living in Chicago who disliked the modern dime dances. At one such dance at the Hall of All Nations on Mackinaw Avenue in South Chicago, "girls as young as twelve years [old] . . . were hired to dance with Mexicans." The girls earned five cents of the ten cents they charged per dance.[71] The organizers were jailed for thirty days for running a dance to which minor girls had been encouraged to come and were fined $100 each. Newspaper editors admonished their readers, particularly any who were fathers or mothers, to "maintain the high dignity of the Mexican woman" and prevent her from attending these kinds of dances.[72] Again, the implications here pointed to competing visions of *mujeridad* that, in this case, sliced across gender and generation.

Some of the earliest Mexicana arrivals to the area recalled having strict rules at home to maintain the dignity of young girls. Agapita Flores, for example, came to Chicago with her family in about 1923, and she remembered, "my father was very strict. . . . he wouldn't even let us [go] to the movies . . . nope, no dancing, no movies. . . . that's how it was."[73] Agapita's family had come from Torreón, Mexico, and entered the United States in March 1919 when she was 9 years old. She married her husband, Rubén, in Chicago in 1927 at the age of 17. Two years later, she had a daughter, Ruth. She had her son, Rubén, in 1933. Agapita's daughter, Ruth, who came of age in the early 1940s, not only was allowed to go to the dances but also "would have gone anyways" if her parents had tried to prevent her—a brash transgression/challenge that her mother would not have contemplated only twenty years earlier. As Ruth admitted, "we had a little bit more freedom."

Generational struggles also emerged between fathers and daughters. One father recounted that his daughter had wanted him to buy her a bathing suit so she could join her friends at the beach. He refused, telling her, "You can bathe . . . here at home. I will . . . not buy [you] a bathing suit. You can wait till I am dead and buy it then."[74] One can hear in the father's voice older norms of restraint confronting newer sexual values in which individual sexuality—embodied in the daughter and her bathing suit—held the power of self-definition.[75] Such seemingly headstrong young girls occasionally faced the dire consequences of their choices. Paul Esparza, for instance, murdered his daughter's husband, Thomas Castillo, reportedly because his daughter had married Castillo against her father's wishes at the age of 15. Apparently, the courts sympathized with Esparza's feelings, for he was acquitted of charges only two months later.[76]

These generational cleavages erupted throughout U.S. society during this period with the emergence of mass culture and the rising number of women working in wage labor. Because Mexican women and men encountered these stresses during their adjustments to Chicago, they often perceived the shifting gender and sexual norms to be part of U.S. culture itself. Mexican men in particular revealed their deep frustrations with the unstable terrains of workplace, home, and neighborhood. Mexican women, on the other hand, overwhelmingly spoke hopefully about the changes and opportunities they experienced in Chicago during this period. Indeed, freedom itself seemed to hold meanings structured in gender.[77]

The significance of gender, then, in understanding the lived experiences of Mexicans during the interwar period in Chicago cannot be overstated. Focusing on the lives of individuals clarifies the human dimension of migration and underscores how much Mexican women's lives varied from the standard narratives of Mexican migration to and settlement in the Midwest. Recovering these women's lived regionalities both highlights the textures of their lives and clarifies the extent to which the standard narrative is male-centered.

All these *mujeres* traveled across many geographic and psychic spaces in their journeys to Chicago. They drew from their accumulated lived regionalities—the multiple terrains and experiences of everyday life in many places—to find their way. This concept of lived regionalities, then, offers a tool for understanding the multilayered, interdependent process that shaped women's daily lives. As they encountered and challenged gender norms that often clashed with those of their birthplace, these women embraced new opportunities and challenged traditional gender norms in a variety of ways. The concepts of *mujeridad* and lived regionalities help capture the multiple facets of life as a Mexican woman in Chicago during the interwar period.

The power of these ideas lies beyond their ability to capture the multiplicity of individual *mexicana* experiences. Indeed, lived regionalities pushes beyond region, borders, and the tendency to dichotomize national and international. *Mujeridad* forces an awareness of the social construction of womanhood and its embedment in nation. Together these tools help build a richer understanding of how these Mexicanas in Chicago really lived and made sense of their lives between the world wars.

Notes

1. *Mexico* (Chicago), August 7, 1926, 4.
2. Virginia Sánchez-Korrol, "Women in 19th and 20th Century Latin America and the Caribbean," in *Women in Latin America and the Caribbean: Restoring Women to History,* edited by Marysa Navarro and Virginia Sánchez-Korrol (Bloomington: Indiana University Press, 1999), 82–83.
3. Ibid.
4. *Mexico* (Chicago), August 7, 1926, 4.
5. This, despite the fledgling women's movement growing in Mexico's urban centers. See Anna Macías, *Against All Odds* (Westport, Conn.: Greenwood Press, 1983). The first International Feminist Conference was held in Yucatán, Mexico, in 1916. See Alaíde Foppa, "The First Feminist Congress in Mexico, 1916," *Signs* 5, no. 1 (1977): 192–99; and Emma Pérez, *The Decolonial Imaginary: Writing Chicanas into History* (Bloomington: Indiana University Press, 1999). See also Shirlene Ann Soto, *Emergence of the Modern Mexican Woman, 1910–1940* (Denver, Colo.: Arden Press, 1990).
6. On national apparati trying to define womanhood, see Kim E. Nielsen, *Un-American Womanhood: Antiradicalism, Antifeminism, and the First Red Scare* (Columbus: Ohio State University Press, 2001). On the schisms within "womanhood," see Susan E. Marshall, *Splintered Sisterhood: Gender and Class in the Campaign against Woman Suffrage* (Madison: University of Wisconsin Press, 1997). For a general overview, see *History of Women in the United States: Topically Arranged Articles on the Evolution of Women's History in the United States,* edited by Nancy F. Cott (New York: K. G. Saur, 1992).
7. A scholar who discusses cultural freezing in relation to domestic violence is Yvette Flores-Ortiz, "La Mujer y la Violencia: A Culturally Based Model for the Understanding and Treatment of Domestic Violence in Chicana/Latina Communities," in *Chicana Critical Issues,* edited by Margarita Melville, Tey Diana Rebolledo, Christine Sierra, and Deena González (Berkeley: Third Woman Press, 1993), 169–82; however, the argument that the solidification of norms can occur in relation to other family processes as well appears in Xóchitl Castañeda and Patricia Zavella, "A Hierarchy of Risks: Young Mexicanas' Gendered Notions of Virginity and Transgression," unpublished manuscript, 2004.
8. Data from research I conducted in the naturalization papers of 1906 to 1943 in the Chicago Circuit Court—combing through files of some 45,000 immigrants—I

found several hundred Latina/os, the vast majority of whom were Mexicans, from which I have constructed a preliminary database to extract the aggregate information.

9. The standard narrative of Mexican migration to Chicago and the Midwest can be found in the following works covering most of the twentieth century: Paul S. Taylor, *Mexican Labor in the United States*, vol. 2, *Chicago and the Calumet Region* (Berkeley: University of California Press, 1932); Dennis Valdés, *Al Norte: Agricultural Workers in the Great Lakes Region, 1917–1970* (Austin: University of Texas Press, 1991); Valdés, *Barrios Norteños: St. Paul and Midwestern Mexican Communities in the Twentieth Century* (Austin: University of Texas Press, 2000); and Juan R. García, *Mexicans in the Midwest, 1900–1932* (Tucson: University of Arizona Press, 1996). Zaragosa Vargas's work on Mexicans in Detroit suggests that men of all skill levels and economic backgrounds migrated, as also appears to be the case in Chicago; see Vargas, *Proletarians of the North: A History of Mexican Industrial Workers in Detroit and the Midwest, 1917–1933* (Berkeley: University of California Press, 1993). An older, though still useful, study on the origins of Mexicans in Chicago is Francisco A. Rosales, "Regional Origins of Mexicano Immigrants to Chicago during the 1920s," *Aztlán* 7 (Summer 1976): 187–201.

10. Immigration restrictions and deportation programs would help to equalize or stabilize sex ratios of Mexicans in Chicago, but even into the 1930s numbers remained uneven. On repatriation programs in the United States generally, see Abraham Hoffman, *Unwanted Mexicans in the Great Depression: Repatriation Pressures, 1929–1939* (Tucson: University of Arizona Press, 1974); and Francisco E. Balderrama and Raymond Rodríguez, *Decade of Betrayal: Mexican Repatriation in the 1930s* (Albuquerque: University of New Mexico Press, 1995). On more regional impacts of these programs and of federal legislation, see Emory Bogardus, "Mexican Repatriates," in *Sociology and Social Research, 1933–1934* (Chicago: University of Chicago Press, 1933): 169–76; George C. Kiser and Martha W. Kiser, eds., *Mexican Workers in the United States: Historical and Political Perspectives* (Albuquerque: University of New Mexico Press, 1979); and Louise Año Nuevo Kerr, "The Chicano Experience in Chicago, 1920–1970" (Ph.D. diss., University of Illinois, Chicago, 1976). Some historians have suggested that curtailed immigration allowed Americanization to take hold in the 1930s; see Gilbert Cárdenas, "Los Desarraigados: Chicanos in the Midwestern Region of the United States," *Aztlán* 7 (Summer 1976): 153–86; and Richard A. García, "The Making of the Mexican-American Mind, San Antonio, 1929–1941: A Social and Intellectual History of an Ethnic Community" (Ph.D. diss, University of California, Irvine, 1980).

11. A. E. Jones, "Conditions Surrounding Mexicans in Chicago," M.A. thesis, University of Chicago, 1928; Manuel Bueno, "The Mexican in Chicago," 1924, Ernest Burgess Papers, Special Collections, Regenstein Library, University of Chicago; and Leila Houghteling, *The Income and Standard of Living of Unskilled Laborers in Chicago* (Chicago: University of Chicago Press, 1927).

12. United States Bureau of the Census, *Abstract of the 15th Census of the United States* (Washington, D.C.: United States Government Printing Office, 1933); and Ernest W. Burgess and Charles S. Newcomb, *Census Data of the City of Chicago: 1930* (Chicago: University of Chicago Press, 1933).

13. As Kathleen N. Conzen has suggested, since the population turnover was

disguised in the census snapshots, it would be interesting to consider how many different Mexicans may have experienced life in Chicago during the 1920s. Unfortunately, the scarcity of data does not currently allow for this kind of analysis.

14. In 1910 the population of Cook County was 2,405,233; in 1920, 3,053,017; in 1930, 3,982,123; and in 1940, 4,063,342; *Population Abstract of the United States* (McLean, Va.: Documents Index Incorporated, 1993). Confusion was created by the 1930 census category of Mexican, since some Mexicans were counted as Mexican while others were counted as white—and the lack of information on nativity and gender further hinders estimates of what percentage of the Mexican population in Chicago was female (either foreign-born or native).

15. The Mexican foreign secretary's office issued a directive in 1930 to this effect; see "Dirección General de Aduanas, Informe sobre mujeres que viajan solas," April 3, 1930, Archivo Histórico de la Secretaría de Relaciones Exteriores, Mexico City, D.F., Mexico: IV-169-17. On the mobility of women during armed conflicts in Mexico, see Elizabeth Salas, *Soldaderas in the Mexican Military: Myth and History* (Austin: University of Texas Press, 1990). On women's mobility into and within Chicago, see Joanne J. Meyerowitz, *Women Adrift: Independent Wage Earners in Chicago, 1880–1930* (Chicago: University of Chicago Press, 1988).

16. Margarita was born, in Mexico City. In 1930 she married Charles Fendt, a U.S. citizen by birth, and four years later she had a son, Charles. In that same year she applied for and became a U.S. citizen; National Archives and Records Administration, Great Lakes Region, Chicago Circuit Court, Naturalization Papers, Petition for Naturalization #168225.

17. National Archives and Records Administration, Great Lakes Region, Chicago Circuit Court, Naturalization Papers, Declaration of Intention #132293, Petition for Naturalization #200010.

18. Fortunata/o Ramos—National Archives and Records Administration, Great Lakes Region, Chicago Circuit Court, Naturalization Papers, Petition for Naturalization #198069.

19. National Archives and Records Administration, Great Lakes Region, Chicago Circuit Court, Naturalization Papers, Declaration of Intention #126807, Petition for Naturalization #195115.

20. National Archives and Records Administration, Great Lakes Region, Chicago Circuit Court, Naturalization Papers, Declaration of Intention #193440, Petition for Naturalization #105378.

21. There is no indication of what kind of machine she operated, but the witnesses on her petition for citizenship were both workers in the garment industry, and so it is likely that Concepción was also.

22. National Archives and Records Administration, Great Lakes Region, Chicago Circuit Court, Naturalization Papers, Declaration of Intention #119678, Petition for Naturalization #176592.

23. Rosita donated the costumes she and Alfredo used in their performances throughout the 1930s, '40s, and '50s to the Chicago Historical Society. Like many other young men of his time, Cano left the family ranch in Mexico to work in Chicago in 1922. There he joined cousins who already lived in the city and studied Spanish dance. Rosita was a U.S. citizen, a Mexican born in San Antonio. She and Alfredo met and began their lifelong partnership in 1930. Both Rosita and Alfredo performed in the Spanish and Mexican villages at the 1933 Century of Progress Exposition in Chicago.

24. I discuss this point more fully in chapters 2 and 3 of my book, *Mexican Chicago.*

25. Depositions of two witnesses for her petition to become a U.S. citizen: Adelaide Lasheck Burge, dean of women at University of Iowa in Iowa City, and Herbert Clifford Dorcas, registrar at University of Iowa in Iowa City. National Archives and Records Administration, Great Lakes Region, Chicago Circuit Court, Naturalization Papers, Petition for Naturalization #176502. The question remains, why Iowa? Did she meet people in her first journeys north with whom she maintained contact? The evidence is silent on this.

26. "Registro de Nacimientos en Chicago," Archivo General, 1929, Secretária de Relaciones Exteriores, Mexico City, D.F., Mexico: IV-271–69. The records include the baby's name, sex, date of birth, place of birth, father's name and nationality, and mother's name and nationality. Most of the mother's names are listed, but a few are recorded simply as "Sra. de. . . ."

27. The consulate records indicate Viviano was born in December 1926, but this would have been nearly impossible, since his older brother was supposedly born in June 1926. It is more likely that Viviano was born in December 1927. Either way, two sons were born to the family during that three-year span.

28. Elizabeth Hughes, *Illinois Persons on Relief in 1935: W.P.A. Report 165–54-6018,* Chicago: Works Progress Administration, 1937. The exact percentage was 52.

29. The records do not indicate how many; they merely report that there was more than one child.

30. United Charities case notes, Robert Redfield Papers, Special Collections, Regenstein Library, University of Chicago. Louise Kerr suggested that the growth of Chicago-born children began to affect the Mexican neighborhoods in distinctive ways by the early 1940s, "Chicano Experience," 10. See also Edward J. Baur, "Delinquency among Mexican Boys in South Chicago, 1938," M.A. thesis, University of Chicago, 1938.

31. National Archives and Records Administration, Great Lakes Region, Chicago Circuit Court, Naturalization Papers, Declaration of Intention #126276, Petition for Naturalization #196261.

32. See Marit Melhuus and Kristi Anne Stoler, eds., *Machos, Mistresses, Madonnas: Contesting the Power of the Latin American Gender Imagery* (New York: Verso, 1996). See also David Román, "Tropical Fruit" in Frances R. Aparicio and Susana Chávez-Silverman, *Tropicalizations: Transcultural Representations of Latinidad* (Hanover, N.J.: Dartmouth University Press, 1997): 199–235; Ilán Stavans, "The Latin Phallus," in Antonia Darder and Rodolfo D. Torres, eds., *The Latino Studies Reader: Culture, Economy, and Society* (Malden, Mass.: Blackwell, 1998), 228–39. On Mexican families, see Sylvia Arrom, "Perspectiva sobre la Historia de la Familia en México," in Pilar Gonzalbo Aizpuru, ed., *Familias Novohispanas* (Mexico City: Colegio de México, 1991). On patriarchy in the household, see Elizabeth Dore, "The Holy Family: Imagined Households in Latin American History," in Dore, ed., *Gender Politics in Latin America: Debates in Theory and Practice* (New York: Monthly Review Press, 1997): 101–17.

33. Paul Taylor, *Mexican Labor in the United States: Chicago and the Calumet 7,* No. 2 (Berkeley: University of California Publications in Economics, 1932), 196.

34. National Archives and Records Administration, Great Lakes Region, Chicago Circuit Court, Naturalization Papers, Petition for Naturalization #192395.

35. National Archives and Records Administration, Great Lakes Region, Chicago Circuit Court, Naturalization Papers, Declaration of Intention #138251, Petition for Naturalization #214000. Raquel was only 4'9" and weighed less than one hundred pounds!

36. The epidemic lasted nearly three years and affected both the villagers and the military encampments.

37. Quoted in Jeanne Catherine Lawrence, "Chicago's Eleanor Clubs: Housing Working Women in the Early Twentieth Century," *Perspectives in Vernacular Architecture* 8 (2000): 219.

38. Several excellent monographs trace the impact of mass culture on immigrant women, including Kathy Peiss, *Cheap Amusements: Working Women and Leisure in Turn-of-the-Century New York* (Philadelphia: Temple University Press, 1986); Joanne J. Meyerowitz, *Women Adrift: Independent Wage Earners in Chicago, 1880–1930* (Chicago: University of Chicago Press, 1988). For the impact specifically on Mexican women, see Vicki Ruiz, *From Out of the Shadows* (New York: Oxford University Press, 1998); Ruiz, "'Star Struck': Acculturation, Adolescence, and the Mexican American Woman, 1920–1950," in *Building with Our Hands: New Directions in Chicana Studies,* edited by Adela de la Torre and Beatriz Pesquera (Berkeley: University of California Press, 1993); and Louise Año Nuevo Kerr, "Chicanas in the Great Depression," in *Between Borders: Essays on Mexicana/Chicana History,* edited by Adelaida R. Del Castillo (Encino, Calif.: Floricanto Press, 1990), 257–69.

39. The anthropological literature on gendered spaces is particularly rich and suggestive of analyses that the brevity of this article does not allow. For a general introduction, see Teresa del Valle, ed., *Gendered Anthropology* (London: Routledge, 1993); and Hilda Kuper, "The Language of Sites in the Politics of Space," in *The Anthropology of Space and Place: Locating Culture,* edited by Setha M. Low and Denise Lawrence-Zuñiga (Oxford, UK: Blackwell, 2003), 247–63.

40. Again, most of these changes were beginning in Mexico, particularly in major urban centers, but most of the women who came to Chicago appear not to have experienced them until in the United States.

41. Jones, "Conditions Surrounding Mexicans."

42. *Mexico* (Chicago), May 15, 1926.

43. Louise Kerr explores the reification of traditional gender roles among Mexicans in Chicago during the Depression in "Chicanas in the Great Depression," *Between Borders,* 257–68.

44. For a useful, if dated, historiographic survey of this topic, see Linda Kerber, "Separate Spheres, Female Worlds, Woman's Place: The Rhetoric of Women's History," *Journal of American History* 75, no. 1 (June 1988): 9–39.

45. Maria Elena Rodríguez, "Roman Catholicism, Folk Medicine, and Mexican Institutions," *Purview Southwest* (1991): 15–20.

46. For an in-depth discussion of the practices of *curanderas,* see Robert T. Trotter and Juan Antonio Chavira, *Curanderismo* (Athens: University of Georgia Press, 1981); and Sara M. Campos, "Mexican American Folk Medicine: A Descriptive Study," Ph.D. diss., University of California, Los Angeles, 1984.

47. *Mexico* (Chicago), January 9, 1929.

48. Excerpted from Mary McDowell Settlement House records by Robert Redfield, 1924, Redfield Journal, Robert Redfield Papers.

49. Of the 58 industries and businesses in Chicago that employed Mexicans during this period, 25 employed women. Jones, "Conditions Surrounding Mexicans," 121. See also Peiss, *Cheap Amusements*, and Meyerowitz, *Women Adrift*.

50. Paul Taylor, *Mexican Labor*, 35, 259.

51. Christine Stansell finds similar practices in nineteenth-century New York. Stansell, *City of Women: Sex and Class in New York, 1789–1860* (Urbana: University of Illinois Press, 1986).

52. Immigrant Protective League Papers, Chicago Historical Society, Chicago, Ill.

53. Redfield Journal, Redfield Papers.

54. National Archives and Records Administration, Great Lakes Region, Chicago Circuit Court, Naturalization Papers, Declaration of Intention #110919, Petition for Naturalization #171129.

55. Meyerowitz, *Women Adrift*; and Lizabeth Cohen, *Making a New Deal: Industrial Workers in Chicago, 1919–1939* (New York: Cambridge University Press, 1990).

56. On constructions of Chicano masculinities, see TomásAlmaguer, "Chicano Men: A Cartography of Homosexual Identity and Behavior," in *Men's Lives*, edited by Michael Kimmel and Michael Messner (Boston: Allyn & Bacon, 1995); and Maxine Baca Zinn, "Chicano Men and Masculinity," also in Kimmel and Messner; Annick Prieur, *Mema's House, Mexico City: On Transvestites, Queens, and Machos* (Chicago: University of Chicago Press, 1998).

57. Douglas Monroy, *Rebirth: Mexican Los Angeles from the Great Migration to the Great Depression* (Berkeley: University of California Press, 1999).

58. Taylor, *Mexican Labor*, 195.

59. Ibid., 200.

60. Ibid., 198.

61. Stansell, *City of Women*. See also Vicki Ruiz, *Cannery Women, Cannery Lives: Mexican Women, Unionization, and the California Food Processing Industry, 1930–1950* (Albuquerque: University of New Mexico Press, 1987).

62. Bueno, "Mexican in Chicago," Burgess Papers, Box 187, Folder 4.

63. Raúl DuBois interview, Manuel Gamio Field Notes, Folder 2:5, n.d. but estimated to be around 1927, Gamio Papers, Bancroft Library, Berkeley, Calif.

64. Taylor, *Mexican Labor*, 200.

65. Ibid., 198.

66. Ibid., 200.

67. *Mexico* (Chicago), May 9, 1928, as translated by this author. Clipping in Paul S. Taylor Papers, Box 1, Folder 2, Bancroft Library, University of California, Berkeley.

68. Interview with unnamed Mexican man, undated but estimated to be around 1927, Manuel Gamio Field Notes, Folder 2:5, Gamio Papers.

69. Interview with Ignacio Sandoval, about 30 years old, Gamio Papers, as translated by this author.

70. Madeline Kneberg, "An Informal Study of Broken Homes and Delinquency amongst Mexicans in the City," Winter 1933, Box 133, Folder 4, Burgess Papers.

71. Raymond Nelson, "The Mexicans in South Chicago," Taylor Papers, Box 1, Folder "Mexican Chicago," pp. 14, 33.

72. *Mexico* (Chicago), March 10, 1928.

73. Interview with Agapita Flores and Ruth Rucoba by Jesse Escalante, x/15/1982, as transcribed by this author and Emma Estrada Lukin, Chicago Historical Society, Chicago, Ill. Further information from Agapita's husband's citizenship papers, National Archives and Records Administration, Great Lakes Region, Chicago Circuit Court, Naturalization Papers, Declaration of Intention #106655, Petition of Naturalization #163549.

74. Taylor, *Mexican Labor*, 200.

75. John D'Emilio and Estelle Freedman, *Intimate Matters: A History of Sexuality in America* (New York: Harper and Row, 1988), ch. 10.

76. Chicago Police Department Homicide Reports, vol. 4, Page 30 A 11/8/1925, Illinois Regional Archives Depository, Chicago, Ill.

77. For a powerful analysis of how racism is embedded in the ideology of freedom, see Thomas C. Holt, *The Problem of Freedom: Race, Labor, and Politics in Jamaica and Britain, 1832–1938* (Baltimore: Johns Hopkins University Press, 1992).

CARMEN TERESA WHALEN

5.   *"The Day the Dresses Stopped":*
Puerto Rican Women, the
International Ladies Garment
Workers' Union, and the
1958 Dressmaker's Strike

"The Day the Dresses Stopped" was March 5, 1958. As workers came to New York City's garment center, 200,000 leaflets were handed
out. At 10:00 A.M., sound cars announced, "Calling all dressmakers.
This is a general strike. Leave your machines. Leave your shops. Proceed to Madison Square Garden!" Workers made their way there by the
thousands, packing Seventh Avenue, the cross streets, and moving up
Eighth Avenue. *Justice,* the newspaper of the International Ladies Garment Workers' Union, reported that by the next morning, "Seventh Avenue . . . bloomed with pickets and their signs . . . Word went out that
the strike was 100 percent effective. The billion-dollar-a-year industry
was completely stopped. The historic dressmakers' strike of 1958 was
under way."[1] It was the first major garment strike in twenty-five years.
It halted the production of dresses not only in New York, but also in six
nearby states. An estimated 105,000 members of the ILGWU walked out,
and dressmakers from fifty nonunion shops joined the picket lines. The
Madison Square Garden rally of March 5 drew 28,000 people.[2]

Puerto Rican women were among those who participated in the 1958 strike. After World War II they had come to New York City and entered the garment industry and the ILGWU. Many joined Local 22, the Dressmakers' Union. As they disembarked as part of the first airborne migration, Puerto Rican women arrived at a critical juncture in the history of New York City's garment industry. The industry was about to experience a stage in globalization that included the deskilling of tasks, an increased reliance on contractors, the relocation of jobs to lower-wage areas, and the loss of jobs in the city.[3] The 1958 strike provides a lens through which to explore Puerto Rican women's roles within the union, to investigate how the ILGWU confronted their large-scale incorporation, and to analyze the changing nature of the industry. Mapping the migrations of Puerto Rican women and the garment industry provides a way to rethink the relationships between the ILGWU and Puerto Rican women workers.

Migrations of Puerto Rican Women and the Garment Industry

The migration of Puerto Rican women was intricately intertwined with the garment industry, and as they settled in New York City, their lives and well-being also became intertwined with the International Ladies Garment Workers' Union.[4] Louise Delgado was one Puerto Rican who became a union activist. Born in Guayama, Puerto Rico, she migrated to New York City in 1923 when she was 8 years old, joining her parents and siblings already living in the city. She recalled her arrival: "My mother and father came to get us at the boat and when I came into the apartment, I found my brother in a machine, sewing." Delgado's home life was filled with work: "That machine was going on all day long because if my mother wasn't sewing, I was sewing, my sister was sewing, my brother was sewing, everybody helped out." In 1934 Delgado started working in a garment shop, and she continued in the industry until she retired in 1978. She was not alone. Puerto Rican women became concentrated in New York City's garment industry. Delgado, however, became a union representative—first on the shop floor, as a chairlady or shop steward, then as a member of the executive board, and finally as a business agent with Local 22. In a 1984 interview, Delgado reflected on her years with the ILGWU: "It was a wonderful experience, I wouldn't change it for anything in the world, yeah, I loved it."[5]

After World War II, Puerto Rican women came to New York City as labor migrants, displaced from Puerto Rico's economy. The garment industry of the United States had long gone to Puerto Rico in search of lower-wage workers and tax holidays, and hence higher profits. In that era, policymakers in Puerto Rico and the United States promoted the industrialization of the island, through a series of policies and incentives designed to lure U.S. capital. The garment industry was among the first to take advantage of these policies and relocated to Puerto Rico en masse. As a result, many Puerto Rican women found jobs in the industry. Yet the industrialization program failed to replace the jobs lost in agriculture and agricultural processing. Without sufficient employment, Puerto Rican men and women migrated in search of work; the irony for many of the women was that they found garment jobs in their new destinations as well.[6]

Puerto Rican women found such jobs readily available. New York City's garment industry experienced a boom as a result of postwar conversions and pent-up consumer demand. The war had temporarily slowed the industry's relocation to outlying areas, keeping jobs in the city. Reaching full employment by 1946, jobs in the industry peaked in 1950, with 310,537 workers. Regional employment in women and children's apparel grew from 239,000 to 260,000 between 1947 and 1954.[7] Employers and union representatives complained of labor shortages, especially of skilled workers. In 1947 the general president of the Amalgamated Clothing Workers of America asserted in a letter to the editor of the *New York Times*, "The needle-trade industries alone, both men's and women's, could not only absorb but would welcome thousands as workers."[8] New York City remained the center of the U.S. garment industry, producing 78 percent of unit-priced dresses, 73 percent of coats and suits, 72 percent of blouses, and 68 percent of underwear.[9]

Necessity propelled Louise Delgado and other Puerto Rican women to seek jobs in the garment industry. Like her compatriots, Delgado started in the garment industry with home sewing and then worked in both union and nonunion shops. Delgado's mother was sewing, working at home, as Delgado explained, "because she had so many children." Delgado was one of nine children, five girls and four boys. Her father, who had owned a theater in Puerto Rico, migrated to Philadelphia in 1918 and then to New York City three years later. After working in the Vanderbilt Hotel, he owned a grocery store and later became a self-made accountant, helping other grocery stores and small businesses with tax forms and other paperwork. She recalled, "my father was always in the living room typing, typing, doing all these things." After helping her mother with her home sewing, Delgado went to work in a shop in 1934. Married at 16 years of age, she and her husband separated when their first child was just 18 months old. She explained, "I had to go to work, I had to go to work. So my sister and I decided that what we knew best was sewing by hand, we were going to start that way."[10]

Delgado and her sister's first job was in a factory at Eighth Avenue and 35th Street, hand-sewing children's dresses and becoming members of ILGWU Local 91. She recalled, "So I joined, when I joined the local of the ILGWU, I joined the first one called Local 91, children's dresses. . . . I was very active in the union." She dropped by the local often, took classes, and was interested in the union's activities. She worked in this shop from 1934 until 1942, when her employer opened several shops in Puerto Rico. For Delgado, the impact was immediate and direct: "All the work that we used to do was sent to Puerto Rico. So that's how I lost my job there." She, along with thirty-three African American pressers and sixty operators, mostly Hungarian, lost their work. She, her sister, and one other woman had been the only Latinas. She lamented, "It was a very good shop, . . . and we made very good money."[11] The closing of this shop foreshadowed the growing flight of the garment industry to Puerto Rico and the concomitant loss of jobs in New York City, which would have its greatest impact on Puerto Rican women in the city.

The Delgado sisters' next jobs were in a nonunion shop at 125th Street and Lexington Avenue. Here they worked long hours for low wages. Although she described the boss as "very nice," she added, "I'll never forget, he would pay us two dresses for a quarter." She contrasted the conditions in union and nonunion shops, "The only time I've worked more than five days was when I went to work non-union. I used to work six and a half days, half a day Sunday, to go home with $7 dollars a week." They used this job to learn how to sew by machine and how to make a whole garment. Six months later, they had learned and wanted to return to a union shop in their own neighborhood, El Barrio. They found work in "a very nice shop in 104th Street." Delgado worked in this shop from 1942 until 1958 and considered it a good job. Sewing the complete dress and being paid by the piece, Delgado recalled, "I made very good money because I was a very fast operator and so was my sister." She earned between $150 and $250 per week, and the work was steady, with the shop operating fifty-two weeks of the year.[12]

Indeed, for most Puerto Rican women, organized labor's greatest immediate impact was the better wages and conditions they found in union shops. In 1958 Rosie Flores contrasted the conditions in union and nonunion shops. As she described one of the nonunion shops, it "didn't have any fire escape and the building was a wreck. If it ever caught fire we'd have all been gone." She found the pace of the work stressful: "In the shops that don't have a union it's always a fight to get your work. . . . You have to get there early in the morning and grab for the work. . . . And then you're working fast as you can to get done." She emphasized the difference that the ILGWU made, "Mom and I both are in the union now—that's the International Ladies' Garment Workers' Union—and we get sick pay and holidays and all that. I tell you it's such a difference too. . . . And such a difference in the work, too. Not just getting paid more, but more relaxed." In her union shop, the work was divided among the workers and they were paid a minimum weekly wage regardless of the amount of work. In addition to wages, benefits, and working conditions, the physical atmosphere in the shop differed too. "Well lighted, and clean, and nice machines—they're even painted nice colors. In summer we've got four big fans going, and it's as nice a place as you could find. There's a fire escape right by the window, too." She concluded, "The union makes a big difference, and all the girls go to meetings too. We're glad to belong."[13]

The difference between union and nonunion shops was not the only issue, however. As Puerto Rican women became concentrated in New York City's garment industry, they also became concentrated in particular sectors of the industry, and hence, in particular locals. As early as 1947, the ILGWU had 7,500 Puerto Rican women members and estimated that another 4,000 to 8,000 worked in other small shops.[14] Because of the segmentation of the industry, these women found jobs only in the lowest-skilled and lowest-paid trades. During the 1940s, Puerto Ricans became the "major new source" of labor in undergarments and composed half the labor in the skirt industry. By 1948 Puerto Ricans and African Americans were half the new members in the unit-priced dresses local, and the former became the largest ethnic group in dressmaking, skirts, and blouses. In contrast, Puerto Ricans did not find jobs in the skilled and higher-paid suit trades, nor as cutters and pressers.[15]

The postwar era witnessed the growth of the skirt industry, as women's fashions became more casual and increasingly included separates (skirts and blouses) and sportswear. As the skirt industry expanded, Puerto Rican women filled much of the need for labor. By 1959, 8,000 workers were employed in New York City's skirt and sportswear industry, in 322 shops, averaging 25 workers per shop. Another 1,000 workers were employed in shops connected to the coat and suit industry. Segmentation in the industry was clear and was reflected in the four locals. Puerto Ricans and "other Latin Americans" were almost exclusively in Local 23, Skirtmakers. In 1957 Local 23 had 8,036 members, half were "Latin Americans," mostly Puerto Rican, and almost all were women.

Although declining in numbers, 14 percent of Local 23's members were Eastern European Jews, and another 8 percent were Sephardic Jews. Italians constituted 6 percent of the membership. African Americans had increased to 18 percent, Chinese 4 percent, and the rest were identified as "others." Far fewer Puerto Ricans were found in the pressers and cutters locals. The industry's 500 pressers were divided between Local 48, Italian Cloakmakers, and Local 35, Cloak and Suit Pressers. The Italian local represented a holdover from a previous era of separate-language locals. Local 35 had 422 pressers, all men, and just 60 to 85 "Latin Americans." The disparity in Local 10, Cutters, appeared even greater. In "the most highly skilled craft," just 20 to 30 of 462 men were Puerto Rican, and even here, few were skilled cutters, and most were apprentices.[16] Similarly, segmentation characterized the dressmaking industry, as Puerto Ricans were concentrated in the less-skilled and lower-paid crafts and in shops that made the lower-priced lines.[17]

As Puerto Rican women migrated to New York City and found jobs in the garment industry, the industry itself continued its migrations in search of lower-wage workers and nonunion areas. After World War II, manufacturers resumed relocation of their shops to lower wage areas outside New York City's central garment district. The garment district was located in midtown Manhattan, between Sixth and Ninth Avenues and between Thirty-fifth and Fortieth Streets. Between 1953 and 1961 the proportion of dressmakers working in the garment district decreased by 32 percent. Meanwhile, the number of dressmakers in Harlem, Brooklyn, and the Bronx increased slightly; many of these workers were Puerto Rican and African American women. Wages were lower in these outlying areas, averaging $62.54 a week in contrast to $88.72 in Manhattan in 1961. The garment industry was also relocating to other areas in the Northeast, especially to Pennsylvania, where wages were even lower, averaging between $46.55 and $47.20 a week. Moreover, the wage gap was increasing, as Manhattan's wages rose by 33 percent and those for the Northeast in general and Pennsylvania in particular rose by only 16 and 15 percent, respectively.[18] Puerto Rican women became concentrated in precisely those sectors of the garment industry that were first affected by deskilling, contracting, and relocation. This segmentation shaped the incorporation of Puerto Rican women into the ILGWU.

The migrations of the garment industry and of Puerto Rican women had their impact on the ILGWU. Puerto Rican women were displaced from Puerto Rico's economy, migrated in search of work, and found it in the garment industry in New York City and elsewhere. But even within the city, garment jobs were relocating. Delgado, for example, initially worked in the garment district, at Eighth Avenue and 35th Street, but she went to a nonunion shop at 125th Street and Lexington Avenue, and then to a union shop in East Harlem at 104th Street. Many Puerto Rican women became members of the ILGWU just by virtue of working in union shops. They benefited from the better working conditions and wages there. The extent to which Puerto Rican women became active union members or leaders depended on the union's response to the rapid increase in Puerto Rican members and to its response to change in the garment industry. The challenge for the ILGWU became not only dealing with the rapid increase in Puerto Rican women members, but also dealing with the industry's relocation to areas beyond the garment district that employed Puerto Rican women, as well as to Pennsylvania.

Joining Local 22

Puerto Rican women did not enter garment shops without incident. In 1942 when Louise Delgado and her sister got their jobs in a Local 22 shop, they were the first two Puerto Ricans and they were not welcomed. Delgado recalled: "When we sat down to work, the girls stopped because they didn't want any Puerto Ricans working in the shop." The other workers called in the business agent, Joseph Piscitello. Neighborhood tensions between Italians and Puerto Ricans had spilled onto the shop floor. Second Avenue had become a boundary between Italians and Puerto Ricans in East Harlem, and violence erupted as Italian residents tried to prevent Puerto Ricans from using a newly built swimming pool. Delgado made her case to Piscitello, "I'm also an American, I tell him, 'I'm more American citizen than some of these people are,' that they didn't even know how to speak English, you know. And what happened? He gave them hell, he gave them hell, all right?" Delgado recounted, "He told them that this was America, that no matter what was happening around the neighborhood, you know, it had nothing to do with the shop, that this was a union shop and the union was for everybody, not just for a certain race or nationality. So we sat down and we started working." Reminiscing, she described Piscitello, "This manager over here was Italian, he was an old time Socialist, the most wonderful person you ever came to know. . . . He believed that to help the poor. . . . And he belonged to every kind of organization and every kind of club there was in East Harlem in order to help out, no matter if they were Italian, or they were Black, or they were Hispanics. . . . He was that type of a man, he was a wonderful person." Although Delgado confronted racial tensions in the neighborhood and on the shop floor, the union's response and her own political commitments fostered her activism in ILGWU Local 22. She had already been involved with a strike and picketing. When she got married, her husband was an upholsterer, "There was a big strike and he had to go all the way upstate and that's how come I learned about the, about picketing, because I used to go and help him."[19]

Just a few days after her coworkers had protested her arrival in the shop, a very different incident sent Delgado on her way to becoming the shop's union representative. When one of the workers made a mistake on a dress, the boss "started screaming at her and threw the dress on her face." Delgado figured, "If he's going to do it to her today, tomorrow he'll do it to me." She stopped the shop by turning off the electricity. Realizing that the women were nervous, since this had never happened before, and many were related to the boss, Delgado insisted, "Look, he threw the dress in your face, and after all, we're not animals over here, we're women, you know, he can't treat us like that just because he happens to be the boss." The workers turned to their business agent, but when they returned to work the following day, the employer had locked them out. They took their case to the impartial chairman for negotiation and resolution. The employer was fined, and the workers returned to the shop. A few weeks later at a shop meeting, Delgado was elected chairlady. She recalled, "That's when everything started." As chairlady, she was the workers' representative on the shop floor and their liaison to the union. She served for fifteen years, from 1942 to 1957, and then became a business agent with Local 22.[20]

Delgado was part of the shifting racial composition in the garment industry and the ILGWU. During her tenure in the shop, more Puerto Rican women joined her and her sister, responding to the help-wanted sign posted downstairs. The twenty-eight operators were Puerto Rican, Italian, Cuban, and Jamaican women. She recalled, "It was very diversified, you know, the type of people there, and we got along fine."[21] Dressmakers Union Local 22 was one of four locals involved in the manufacturing of dresses, which was affiliated with the Joint Board of Waist and Dressmakers Union of Greater New York. These four locals—Dressmakers Union Local 22, Italian Dressmakers Union Local 89, Dress Pressers Local 60, and the dress division of Amalgamated Cutters Local 10—reflected the nature of racial change. In 1953 these locals had 61,000 members, and 80 percent were women. By far the largest were Italian Dressmakers Union Local 89, with more than 29,000 members, and Dressmakers Union Local 22, with 25,800 members. Local 89 was a "language local" established in 1919 to incorporate Italian-speaking immigrants. In the aftermath of the general strike of 1933, Local 89 grew to 39,500 members, and Local

22 grew to 30,300 members, 70 percent of whom were Jewish. The most dramatic racial change took place in Local 22. As the Jewish membership aged and retired, Puerto Ricans and African Americans took their places. Between 1945 and 1953, Jewish membership declined from 63 to 51 percent, Puerto Rican membership doubled from 8 to 16 percent, and African American membership held steady at 15 percent.[22]

Tensions surrounded these shifts and created a leadership gap between the old-timers, Jewish and Italian, and the newcomers, Puerto Rican and African American. Writing in 1953, Will Herberg thought that the tensions accompanying these "drastic changes" had "manifested themselves first in the shops, and then in the union." For Herberg, the ethnic attitude of employers played a secondary role, as "it is primarily a question of the relation of the 'old-timers' (Jews and Italians) to the 'newcomers' (Negroes and Latin Americans) in the shops." In the shops, where so much "depended on connections and goodwill," Puerto Ricans and African Americans "continually came up against the ethnic 'clannishness' of the better established groups." Herberg emphasized union prohibitions against discrimination but conceded the continuing impact: "Overt discrimination, such as is well known in other industries and other parts of the country, is rigorously banned by the union and very few cases have been rumored. But that impediments and handicaps, rooted in ethnic prejudice, do exist there can be no doubt." Similarly, he added, "'Racial' prejudice is regarded as a high crime in the union ethic, and no one will confess to it. But it is by no means absent from the shops, as all observers testify."[23]

In moving from the shop floor to the union hall, Herberg found, "The prejudices and tensions manifested in the shops are greatly inhibited, but do not altogether disappear, in the union hall." Herberg was most concerned by "the crisis of leadership," which he saw as "basically a reflection of the cleavage between two membership generations." He did not see the issue as one where "the old-timers are deliberately keeping the ethnic newcomers down," nor did he accept that there was a "natural lag of leadership replacement." In 1953, Local 22 elected 80 people, including a general manager, 26 business agents, 29 executive board members, and 24 delegates to the ILGWU convention. Of those elected, 78 percent were Jewish, a proportion significantly higher than their 51 percent of the membership. On the other hand, "Latin Americans," overwhelmingly Puerto Rican, were underrepresented, constituting 9 percent of those elected and 16 percent of the membership. Similarly, African Americans were 10 percent of those elected and 15 percent of the membership. Herberg concluded, "The discrepancy is obvious."[24]

Despite this leadership gap, Local 22 sought to organize its Spanish-speaking members into internal groups as early as 1934. The local also appointed Spanish-speaking organizers and offered educational, cultural, and recreational programs.[25] Delgado participated in the "Spanish" group. Saby Nehama, the head of Local 22's Education Department, ran the group, which met the first Tuesday of every month. A Sephardic Jew and fluent in Spanish, he explained current events in the industry, personnel benefits, and other topics. There were citizenship and English classes. The group was also "very, very social," taking trips to Puerto Rico and Florida, and more locally to Tanglewood, in Lenox, Massachusetts, for concerts. They had dancing classes with costumes for performances, boat rides, and Christmas parties as well. Delgado reminisced, "Then everybody was young and everybody, you know, was interested, interested in the union."[26] In 1957, Local 22's minutes revealed the importance that it attributed to the education program, "Brother Jo Mazur, Educational Director, reported that in line with our educational policy of drawing more members into the union activities, he was reporting that there was being organized a Spanish Chorus which already had about fifty enrollees. He expressed the hope that this would build up into a fine organization of active members."[27]

In addition to involving Puerto Rican members, Local 22 sought connections to the broader Puerto Rican community. Throughout 1957, Local 22 made frequent contributions to Puerto Rican organizations and events. For example, the executive board bought tickets for the "Testimonial Dinner to Judge Manuel A. Gomez, first Puerto Rican to be appointed a Magistrate in New York," and for a concert by Puerto Rican violinist José Figueroa, sponsored by the Council of Spanish-American Organizations. The local supported the Spanish-language newspapers *El Diario de Nueva York* and *La Prensa,* as well as the New York Puerto Rico Scholarship Fund, "whose purpose is to assist Puerto Ricans who are worthy to give them the benefits of higher educational facilities."[28] Charles Zimmerman, manager of Local 22 and vice president of the ILGWU, served on New York City's Committee on Puerto Rican Affairs and on others that addressed issues confronting the Puerto Rican community. Previously skeptical of broader community activities, Nehama stepped in for Zimmerman in August 1957, and he "completely changed his mind," because "he has had a chance to study at first hand both the great usefulness of these organizations and the high esteem in which Zimmerman's leadership was held by these bodies. . . . He has acquired a national reputation in the field of labor, civil rights and numerous other struggles for equality and social justice."[29] Zimmerman was also elected chairman of the Civil Rights Committee of the AFL-CIO at a conference called "to consider ways and means of eliminating discrimination within the trade union movement."[30]

Local 22 also addressed a range of issues of importance to Puerto Rican workers in New York City, including civil rights and rent control. With the reminder that "the struggle for civil rights is going on not only in the South, but in other sections of the country," the executive board discussed municipal legislation against discrimination in housing and "the staff was urged to concentrate on stimulating an intensive drive among the workers in the shops."[31] In February 1957, Gus Tyler, political director of the ILGWU wrote, "thanking Local 22 for their great interest in the fight to continue rent controls in New York with particular mention of the fine job accomplished by Jo Mazur in planning Local 22's drive on this issue."[32] The activism continued. The following month, Mazur went to Albany "to fight against rent increases" and reported, "The Trade Union Council of the Liberal Party had two buses of people who helped get the message of strengthening rent control. We were more or less the only labor people there and it was a worthwhile venture." Mazur also testified in Albany "to pass legislation to protect the consumer when he buys on installments. We have found that many of our members have been cheated, and defrauded by unscrupulous merchants. Wage garnishes and long payments usually followed."[33] These were issues affecting not only union members, but the broader Puerto Rican working-class community.

As Local 22 worked to organize Puerto Rican and other workers, Delgado became involved in the union's organizing drives during the 1940s and 1950s. Called on to help organize shops during the busiest months of April through July, she recalled, "So I used to go out leaving a job [where she would have made] $150, $175 a week to get paid $75 a week [by the union], get up at five o'clock in the morning till ten o'clock at night, every single day for three, four months." She described the organizers' activities: "We used to go and picket, go inside and pull everybody out. . . . Go and visit the homes, make the girls sign cards, convince them, convince them." Working with Nehama and a group of ten to fifteen regulars, she recounted their success: "We organized half of Harlem and half of the South Bronx."[34]

In 1957 Delgado left her shop to become a business agent with Local 22, a full-time employee of the union. Initially, she was reluctant to leave her shop, her position as chairlady, and what she considered a very good job. She made her decision during a trip to Puerto Rico with the Spanish group the same year. She recalled: "We went down over there because we were thinking about starting a union in Puerto Rico and we went over there and we made a very great impact." The impact on Delgado proved significant as well. Joseph Monserrat of the Migration Division of Puerto Rico's Department of Labor took her aside: "Look, Louise, in the Bronx they need someone that speaks both languages. They're going to have a big strike and when the strike goes on they're gonna try and see how many shops will be able to come in." When she questioned her own abilities, he reassured her. "It's exactly the same thing that you do in the shop now. You take care of all the problems of your shop and you try to settle [the piecework pay for] garments and . . . [a]ll you need to be a business agent is common sense." Apparently, her dedication to the work sufficiently outweighed the pay cut involved, from between $150 and $175 to $99 dollars a week.[35]

In appointing Delgado business agent, Local 22's executive board members revealed a certain urgency. She replaced Marie Calera, who Delgado described as "cubana mexicana."[36] Board members praised Calera's contributions, with Zimmerman stating that she "as a Rank and File Executive Board member, as a Convention delegate, and now as a Business Agent, had done a wonderful job." Nehama agreed, adding, "In all the ten years of her working with him and the organization he never heard of any complaint by any member as to the way she did her job. Both in her work as a Business Agent and in the Spanish section, Marie did a very fine job. It will be very difficult to replace her."[37] Delgado made "a recommendation to the Executive Board of a Spanish speaking business agent to replace Marie Calera," and Zimmerman agreed. "It is necessary to make this appointment immediately . . . to have a Spanish speaking Business Agent for this district." Nehama consulted "with the active Spanish speaking members" and "submitted the recommendation of Sister Louise Delgado for appointment to the staff."[38] At the Executive Board meeting, "Zimmerman praised Sister Delgado as an active and conscientious Executive Board member." Similarly, Nehama noted her dedication: "there was never an occasion when Sister Delgado was absent when there was work to be done or any activity to be taken on by the Spanish group. He assured the Board that he was confident that the Board would be proud of Sister Delgado and find her a good officer." Her appointment was approved with a unanimous vote.[39] Delgado became one of very few Puerto Rican women working full-time for the union, though their representation was increasing among "chairladies" on the shop floors, at least in some locals.[40]

The urgency to appoint a Spanish-speaking business agent came, in part, from the continued increase in Puerto Rican members and from

Local 22's commitment to involve those new members. Between 1953 and 1956, membership in Local 22 decreased from 25,506 to 23,191. While the proportion of Jewish members declined from 51 to 47 percent, "Spanish" members increased from 17 to 20 percent. In 1956 alone, there were 596 new "Spanish" members and another 163 who were reinstated. The membership was overwhelmingly female, 88 percent.[41] In May 1957 Zimmerman challenged the negative portrayals of Puerto Ricans in New York City. Speaking at a general membership meeting, he noted, "There is a great deal of discussion about the problems of the Puerto Ricans and the Puerto Rican invasion here." He countered, "In all the discussions that are going on there is one important point missed and that is the contribution that the Puerto Ricans are making to New York as a labor force for the garment trades. . . . They are contributing to the economy of our city and help to maintain a big industry in our city." Turning to their role in the union, Zimmerman insisted, "They are just as good union people and just as good workers as any group of workers that came into our industry. . . . The newcomers who have come to our midst are retaining the spirit of the organization." He called for "proper housing" and "better schooling" for the newcomers, so "Then you will have no problem with the Puerto Ricans, Negroes, Jews, or anybody else."[42]

There was perhaps another, related, reason for the urgency in appointing a Spanish-speaking business agent—there were already signs of trouble in the industry. At the same general meeting, the union addressed the relocation of garment jobs to Pennsylvania. Zimmerman reported, "We have a fight in Pennsylvania to increase the rates and to close the gap between what is paid there and the rates in New York." While employers "distributed circulars to the workers [in Pennsylvania] saying that all the New York unions want is to get the work back to New York and to deprive them of employment," the union prevailed and the workers were "convinced that the Union was fighting for them to get them higher pay and get the rates to which they are entitled." He noted, "Our agreement is expiring at the end of this year and pretty soon we will have to sit down and negotiate."[43] Those negotiations would not go smoothly.

The 1958 Dressmaker's Strike

As their contract approached expiration on January 31, 1958, the ILGWU began preparing for a strike. On January 8 at "an overflow meeting of Dressmakers' Local 22," Zimmerman reported on the lack of movement toward a settlement, and "in a rousing voice vote, the dressmakers, at their Manhattan Center meeting, authorized strike action should this become necessary in order to win the demands made by the union."[44] The union's demands included a 15 percent wage increase, a $10 increase in guaranteed weekly minimum earnings, additional paid holidays, and improvements in overtime pay. It had been five years since the last wage adjustment, and the cost of living had continued to rise. The union also demanded the establishment of a severance pay fund and stricter contract enforcement procedures, as well as the use of a union label. In addition to "economic demands" and "a series of contract changes designed to strengthen enforcement," there was "a third category of requests dealing with special problems, such as non-unionized shops."[45] The 1958 strike became a key moment in the ILGWU's responses to its Puerto Rican members and to changes in the garment industry.

The union's demands addressed the changing nature of the industry, including relocation. The union addressed relocation by involving its Eastern, Out-of-Town, and Northeast departments and by organizing in seven states. As *Justice* reported, "For the first time in the dressmakers history, shop leaders from Pennsylvania, New Jersey and other states where contractors work for New York jobbers rallied together with chairmen and chairladies of New York City's dress shops."[46] They sought to decrease disparities in wages and working conditions, to improve those conditions in other areas, to eliminate competition between workers, and perhaps to reduce employers' incentives to relocate. When shops did relocate, the union wanted severance pay for displaced workers. As ILGWU president David Dubinsky asserted, "We want severance pay to protect our people against those employers who pick up their money bags and run out of this industry, leaving thousands of our members unemployed and stranded. They must be made to meet their responsibility."[47] On February 26, the dress strike was authorized by a unanimous vote of shop chairpersons from seven states—Pennsylvania, New York, New Jersey, Massachusetts, Connecticut, Rhode Island, and Delaware.[48]

The union's demands also addressed the industry's increased reliance on contracting shops, which relied heavily on Puerto Rican and African American women workers in metropolitan New York. During this era, the industry had three types of employers: manufacturers, who handled all aspects of garment production from manufacturing to selling garments; jobbers, who bought materials, designed garments, and sold them but did not do any production or assembly; and contractors, who did only assembly work. Between 1953 and 1961, dress shops operated by manufacturers and jobbers decreased by 22 percent, while those operated by contractors decreased by less than 1 percent. As a result, the proportion of dress workers in contracting shops increased from 69 to 79 percent. This shift toward contracting shops meant lower wages for workers. Workers in shops operated by manufacturers and jobbers earned 1.6 times as much as their counterparts in contracting shops.[49] Those involved in the strike revealed the impact of these trends in their industry. Of the workers involved, 22,499 were employed by 736 manufacturers and jobbers. Substantially more—64,300—were employed by 1,550 contractors. Of those contractors, 633 employed 29,800 workers outside New York City.[50]

Lower wages, contracting shops, and relocation were all connected to one another and to another change in the industry—the deskilling of work and the increase in section work. Delgado explained: "They started setting up work in Pennsylvania because the mines were closing up and some of these jobbers decided, 'Let's take the work over there.' Because over there they could work much cheaper than the girls over here in New York." For Delgado, the relocation coincided with the increase in section work, "When they started out . . . since they didn't know how to sew, so they started taking the garment and breaking it up. The girls, some of the girls would just make darts, some of the girls would just make sleeves, some would just set the sleeves, some of the girls would make the collars, some of the girls would make the skirts, some of the girls would just make the waistline, you had zipper setters, you know, so totally different. . . . Assembly line, that's the way things went." She emphasized the difference with New York City, "No, we never had section piece work in New York. The girls didn't wanna work . . . they refused to make . . . they wouldn't work it. Their pride was hurt if they were set down in a shop and worked section. All they knew was how to work complete garment." She conceded, however, that section work was taking hold in sportswear and in the cheaper lines in New York City.[51]

The union was affected by these changes and sought to counter them with its demands. *Justice* invoked the union's legacy in these struggles. In addition to fighting for higher wages and shorter work days, the union had struggled "to establish the jobber as the factor responsible for rates in the contracting shops" and "to spread their union to wherever the work goes, so that workers should not have to compete and bid against other workers."[52] In the present context, Dubinsky proclaimed, "we are one union in one industry, fighting for one agreement so that all can enjoy the same benefits." "One industry, one union, one contract," became a strike slogan.[53] By February 24, strikes were already in place against seventeen New York jobbers of contracting shops in Pennsylvania and other outlying areas. Although covered by the original contract, these jobbers refused to abide by the one-month extension, and the union sought to hold them accountable while sending the message that the union was ready to take action. The increase in contracting and relocation made contract enforcement a central demand. Dubinsky asserted, "Our chief interest is to get an agreement through which the workers in this industry will receive what they are entitled to get, and that they will get it not only on the paper of a contract, but in their pay envelopes." He hoped the use of a union label would facilitate organizing and strengthen accountability.[54]

The morning of March 5 became "the day the dresses stopped." Despite an extension to February 28 and a union concession on economic demands from an estimated 22 to 15 percent of the overall payroll, no agreement was reached as employers stood at a 5 percent increase in overall payroll and just a 3 percent increase in wages.[55] The battle lines were drawn. With Madison Square Garden set up for that evening's boxing matches, the ring became the speakers' platform, as "one after another, the managers of the four Dress Joint Board locals and other speakers came to the microphone to stress the urgency of the union's demands." The huge banners above the platform read "On with the strike! On to victory!" The speakers reflected the diversity of the workers, "First Vice Pres. Antonini capped his oration with moving words in Italian. Saby Nehama addressed the Spanish-speaking workers in their tongue. Maida Springer added to the accepted vocabulary of the industry by insisting that enforcement provisions of the new agreement must be strong enough to block any 'kunkel-munkel' business." Springer, an Afro-Panamanian woman, had become a business agent for Local 22 in 1947 and represented the American Federation of Labor (AFL) in its international efforts, especially in Africa. The audience was also described as diverse. "Dressmakers of all crafts, ages, creeds, and national origins listened intently to union leaders' calls for all-out, unflagging activity, capped by three-shift picket lines at all shops, to ensure victory for just demands of workers."[56]

The strike's success would depend on the active participation of all the union's members, and Puerto Ricans responded to the call. In February Nehama described "the response to the request for volunteers from among the Spanish workers to serve on the various strike committees" as "overwhelming and particularly gratifying to him." He added that "this will give us a wonderful opportunity to bring these newer elements closer to the Union."[57] At its height, the strike involved 105,000 dressmakers in seven states. These workers included 15,000 from shops that had withdrawn from employers' associations and 2,000 New York shipping clerks. In the city 22,000 dressmakers struck more than 700 jobber and manufacturing firms, and another 35,000 struck more than 900 contracting shops. Beyond New York City, 30,000 workers struck more than 600 contracting shops. On the other side were five associations, three representing jobbers and two representing contractors.[58]

Not having conducted a general strike in twenty-five years, the old-timers found themselves confronting a variety of new circumstances. Zimmerman remarked, "During the last strike we had in 1933, we were able to get halls to house all the strikers, but now none of these halls were obtainable." As a result, "our strike halls this time would be the streets of the garment center." They organized a three-platoon system, with each shop chairperson organizing the shop into three groups, one to picket from 8:00 to 11:30, the next from 11:30 to 3:00, and the last from 3:00 to "6:00 or 6:30, as long as necessary." "Flying squads" filled in at night and on Sundays. Zimmerman was struck by "the spirit of our strikers, it was real discipline." With life on the streets and three shifts of pickets, Zimmerman "walked through the picket lines and saw many of our members shivering in the cold." He arranged for coffee and 25,000 raincoats, with "ILGWU 1958 Strike" imprinted on them. For communication, the union put each business agent in charge of each district to maintain contact with the shop chairs and turned to daily television and radio reports. For Zimmerman, "The splendid response of our entire membership and the splendid conduct of all the members on the picket line and the responsibility each and every member felt . . . won the admiration of the entire community, not to say only of the labor movement."[59]

In the end Local 22 celebrated the scope of the strike, the victories, and the participation of Puerto Rican women workers. Proclaiming "Strike Won!" in its headline for March 15, 1958, *Justice* celebrated new collective agreements that "provide gains exceeding any embodied in previous contracts." The strike, for most of those involved, had lasted just five days. Economic gains included an 8 percent wage increase, overtime pay after seven hours a day in a thirty-five-hour workweek, and six and a half paid holidays that pieceworkers would now receive along with weekly workers, who had already been receiving them. Minimum wage scales were raised by approximately 10 percent, bringing the lowest minimum to $1.21 an hour or $42.50 per week. Revealing the preexisting regional disparities in wages, "the impact of the higher minimum rates will be felt chiefly among some workers outside of New York City." With victory in the demand for severance pay, the union's Health and Welfare Fund became the Health, Welfare, and Severance Fund. Employers would contribute an amount equal to 0.5 percent of their payroll to a severance-pay fund. After the fund accumulated for two years, "workers left stranded by firms going out of business" would receive one week's pay for each year that they were employed "by the departing firm."[60] Hence, the union addressed regional disparities in wages and the impact that runaway shops had on workers. The union also won the right to use a union label in garments and asserted, "Adoption of a garment industry union label now becomes a major ILGWU goal."[61]

Addressing changes in the garment industry, especially the growing use of contractors, the union sought to increase jobbers' accountability. The union was concerned that "some jobbers have held temporary contractors in such a state of uncertainty" and that the uncertainty was "transferred to their workers." Hoping to bring greater stability to the industry, the union wanted to increase the number of permanently registered contractors and decrease the number of temporary registrations. In addition, jobbers were prohibited from sending more work to contractors than they could complete, and contractors were prohibited from sending work to other contractors, or subcontracting. In a key provision, jobbers were held ultimately responsible for paying piece rates to workers, if contractors did not pay the settled, or decided-upon, price. Finally, jobbers who sent work to nonunion shops or to nonunion cutters would have to pay damages "offsetting the advantages gained and covering the losses sustained by workers and the union." The union concluded, "Thus, an important extension of the concept of jobbers' responsibility for the workers he employs either directly through inside shops or indirectly through contractor shops has been won."[62]

After the strike, union leaders praised the members' unity and solidarity, often in language that stressed the relations between the old-timers and the newcomers. *Justice* celebrated the unity and diversity of the picket line in words and photographs. "Thousands also heard the sound of the picket line, and many were impressed with the inspiring brotherhood of the sidewalk. . . . There was no recognition of race or religious differences, and the hope of the strikers broke out in words and chants and songs of many languages. It was refreshing for oldtimers, it was inspiring for newcomers."[63] At the March 11 ratification meeting, Vice President Moe Falikman, manager of Cutters Local 10 and chairman of the strike picket committee, "expressed pride over the effectiveness of the picket lines" and "of the manner in which the picket line had become the meeting place for old-timers and newcomers sharing a timeless ILGWU tradition." Zimmerman went a step farther. For Zimmerman, the picket line built unity: "On the sidewalk, where the force of the battle against chiseling and for a better life for the garment workers was carried on," he told the enthusiastic audience, "neither race nor color nor creed nor nationality of origin mattered. Many languages were spoken on the picket line, for ours is a union of many origins. . . . But regardless of the language, the meaning was the same: a hope for a better life, not only economically, but also one that would be rid of the prejudices and fears that divide human beings. Indeed, . . . the picket line is one of the most potent instruments for uniting them."[64]

Zimmerman revealed, however, that some had doubted the Puerto Ricans' roles: "Whatever the doubts may have been of the response of our new element to a call for a general strike, they certainly gave a very convincing demonstration by their determination and militant behavior."[65] According to Zimmerman, "Many of the old timers were under the impression, well, we knew how to fight and we did know. . . . But they weren't sure of those who were never in a strike. . . . And there was doubt and many thought how will the old timers, how will the newcomers behave." The doubts seemed to intensify because of the proportion of women. "You know a large portion of our membership was never in a general strike, since 1933, 25 years, there is a big turnover especially in an organization where the great majority are women."[66] Any lingering doubts about "the response of our new element to a call for a general strike," were presumably laid to rest with the success of the strike, and for many, with a continuation of the ILGWU's legacy. "The strike lessons in solidarity, in unity of purpose, will long remain an inspiration for all workers. The spirit and idealism that sustained the dressmakers in 10 major strikes during the period from 1909 to 1933, blossomed again with the same vigor after 25 strikeless years."[67]

While the doubts dissipated, a hefty dose of paternalism remained. Zimmerman commented, "I think the old timers established a certain precedent, they set the pace, they showed in the past how to picket and how to strike and how to fight for conditions and I think that the newcomers in our Union absorbed fully the spirit of the old timers and it was one army marching on the picket line." In essence, he portrayed Puerto Rican newcomers as blank slates, ignoring their histories of international socialism, labor activism, and political activity in Puerto Rico and in the United States. Instead, Puerto Ricans supposedly absorbed their activism from the old-timers. Still, Zimmerman acknowledged the role of Puerto Rican workers at the general membership meeting: "Saturday morning it was biting cold as all of you know, I saw many of our members, especially many of our Puerto Rican members, brought their children with them on the picket lines. That was a fine spirit of responsibility that we have from our new members."[68]

Local 22's rhetoric blended remnants of international socialism with paternalism, and gender doubtless contributed to the persistence of the latter. In addition to grappling with the changing racial composition of its membership, the union continued to grapple with the shifting gender composition. Although noting that 80 percent of dressmakers were women, the union made repeated references to "the wives and daughters of millions of union members." In the campaign for a union label, the union emphasized women's roles as wives and responsible consumers. Dubinsky argued, "The wives and daughters of millions of union members buy the garments we make, and they are entitled to know which garments are made under decent conditions. The union label will tell them."[69] Similarly, *Justice* asserted the hope that the label would "enable millions of wives of unionists and American women in general to identify dresses made under higher and healthier union conditions, as distinguished from any that may be made in hideaway, substandard, nonunion plants."[70]

Even as the union declared victory and embraced the newcomers, the struggles continued. Within one week, the strike was brought to "a full and successful conclusion" for 90 percent of the strikers. The union hoped that a settlement would be reached in Pennsylvania and anticipated that less than 3,000 would remain on picket lines "in a fight against a small group of die-hard, anti-union jobbers."[71] Pickets continued in Pennsylvania, as well as in Harlem and the Bronx, where Puerto Rican women workers continued their activism in their own neighborhoods. *Justice* announced victory in the Pennsylvania strike on April 15, 1958, but the campaign to organize additional shops and enforce the newly won contract waged on.[72] Zimmerman called for continued solidarity: "Now the big problem before us is with the same spirit that our members showed on the picket line, the same alertness that they have shown on the picket line now, they should show also in the shops, and together, the leadership and the membership should be alert to enforce this agreement and we will have a good Union, a good membership, and good conditions in our shop."[73]

Louise Delgado's work was not finished either; she was assigned to the Bronx.[74] "In view of the influx of new people into the union, most of them Spanish speaking and most of them in the Bronx," Zimmerman recommended Delgado, adding, "She will bring experience and ability to that post and would be extremely helpful in this situation." Underscoring the challenge, Zimmerman reported, "As far as Pennsylvania is concerned, there are still eleven jobbers out on strike and these are the toughest ones against whom the Harlem and Bronx strikes are still in progress." Yet he also noted the successes. "As a result of the strike, we have organized so far 50 non-union jobbers, some have been in business and out of union contracts for about thirty years, and 86 contractors, some in every borough. We must see to it that conditions are enforced immediately and that they get into the habit of recognizing and living up to the agreement."[75] Delgado remembered the strike and the subsequent organizing work as a success, recalling that during "the big strike," they organized seventy-five shops, of which fifty were predominantly Spanish-speaking. She continued working in the Bronx for the next ten years, visiting the shops, solving problems, settling prices, and appointing committees. "I loved it, I loved every minute of it. I love serving, I love serving people."[76]

Conclusions

The 1958 strike provides a lens through which to view the ILGWU's response to the changing nature of the garment industry and to rethink the relationship between the ILGWU and Puerto Rican women. Here, as elsewhere, I posit an earlier development of globalization than do some other scholars, by focusing on the industry's relocation to Puerto Rico in the late 1940s.[77] In the 1958 strike, the union was aware of and sought to address the underlying dynamics in the industry, especially contracting and relocation, as well as the critical issues of jobbers' accountability and contract enforcement. The victories of 1958 only temporarily obscured these underlying dynamics, which continued to reshape and devastate the garment industry. The contract could not halt the increase in reliance on contractors nor the industry's continued flight to low-wage areas. Contract enforcement remained a never-ending challenge as a result. The union's efforts to level the playing field by spreading "their union to wherever the work goes" became increasingly difficult as the industry became ever more mobile and moved to ever farther destinations.[78]

Largely overlooking the early impact of globalization, the few scholars who have explored the relationship between Puerto Rican women and the ILGWU in the post–World War II era have leveled harsh criticisms against the union. In 1974 Herbert Hill, the labor secretary for the NAACP, linked "powerlessness within the union and economic exploitation." He asserted, "Ironically, those labor unions which in the past were important vehicles for improving the economic condition of workers now use their power to prevent the entry of certain groups of workers into the labor market or to lock these groups permanently in unrewarding menial and unskilled job categories."[79] Similarly, other critics, focusing on the leadership gap and the lowering of wages in the industry that coincided with the increasing proportion of workers who were Puerto Rican and African American, conclude that the ILGWU discriminated against these groups.[80] Segmentation within the industry played a critical role in shaping Puerto Ricans' and African Americans' incorporation into the union, and it is unlikely that the union could have reshaped the industry's historic segmentation by race, ethnicity, and gender. It is similarly unlikely that the union could have halted the industry's "race to the bottom," as employers set contractors to competing against each other for the lowest costs and went global in their search for the lowest wages. At the very least, the ILGWU's early responses to globalization and the union's relationship to Puerto Rican women deserve a fuller exploration. This chapter is a first step in this direction.

In addition, these critics treat the ILGWU in isolation, neglecting the larger context that sought to define Puerto Ricans' place in New York City and in the United States in general. Along with remnants of international socialism and paternalism, the ILGWU's rhetoric drew on civil-rights discourse. Another lesson from the strike that concerned the problem of civil rights, Zimmerman explained, was "the bigots who are carrying on fights say you cannot have desegregation in housing because people cannot live together, you can't have negroes and whites live together. I think we have shown a lesson, that our membership consisting of many different racial origins, of different colors, of different tongues, people speak Italian, Jewish, Spanish, and English and various other tongues, negroes and whites, Puerto Ricans and other Latin American countries, those who were born here and those who were born in Europe, whether it is in Italy or Eastern Europe, they all marched together, one army, it was one family, striking for good conditions and striking for a better life." Zimmerman proclaimed, "We are fighting against bigots."[81] This public stance by a union leader put the ILGWU far in advance of other unions, and the larger New York City community as well, at a time when *West Side Story* portrayed Puerto Ricans as gang members and newspapers decried the "Puerto Rican problem." Still, questions remain about how this played out in other locals and how it would all play out as New York's garment industry faced devastation in the years to come.

Finally, harsh criticisms of the ILGWU have, perhaps inadvertently, overshadowed Puerto Rican women's plight as the industry was devastated and have also obscured Puerto Rican women's union activism. Indeed, this sector of the industry was among the first to flee New York City for lower wage areas, including Puerto Rico. As contracting and relocation increased, it was the union's newcomers, Puerto Rican women, who became displaced workers. At the same time, a unilateral, negative portrayal of the ILGWU renders invisible those Puerto Rican women who became activists on the shop floor and beyond. Before, during, and after the 1958 strike, Local 22 sought to increase their participation. Louise Delgado was one of those women, and as a union activist, she too was aware of and concerned about the changing nature of the garment industry. She lamented, "The ILGWU was very concerned about the shops that were moving. . . . they tried to convince Washington DC what was happening. . . . But at that time, they didn't pay any attention to us because, after all, it would only hit us, you know, the dress industry, it didn't hit anybody else. Now you hear everybody screaming."[82] Her words and her migration—from Puerto Rico to New York City, between nonunion and union garment shops, and through the ranks of the Local 22—reveal what can be gained by revisiting the union's responses to globalization and Puerto Rican women's roles within the union.

Notes

1. "The Day the Dresses Stopped," *Justice*, March 15, 1958, pp. 4, 13.
2. "Dress Union Out in 7–State Strike; Peace Hopes High," *New York Times*, March 6, 1958, p. 1.
3. On the causes of the postwar migration, including the role of the garment industry, see Carmen Teresa Whalen, *From Puerto Rico to Philadelphia: Puerto Rican Workers and Postwar Economies* (Philadelphia: Temple University Press, 2001); and on the impact of globalization, see Whalen, "Sweatshops Here and There: The Garment Industry, Latinas, and Labor Migrations," *International Labor and Working-Class History* 61 (Spring 2002): 45–68.
4. On the pre–World War II history of Puerto Rican women in New York City's garment industry, see Altagracia Ortiz, "'*En la aguja y el pedal eché la hiel'*: Puerto Rican Women in the Garment Industry of New York City, 1920–1980," in *Puerto Rican Women and Work: Bridges in Transnational Labor*, edited by Altagracia Ortiz (Philadelphia: Temple University Press, 1996), 55–81; and Virginia Sánchez Korrol, *From Colonia to Community: The History of Puerto Ricans in New York City, 1917–1948*, 2d ed. (Berkeley: University of California Press, 1994).
5. Louise Delgado, interview by Celia Alvarez, and Blanca Vásquez, August 15, 1984, and February 17 & 22, 1985, transcript, pp. 9–11, 37, Puerto Rican Pioneras Oral History Archives, Center for Puerto Rican Studies, Hunter College, City University of New York. See also the important publications related to this oral history project, Rina Benmayor, Ana Jurabe, Blanca Vázquez Erazo, and Celia Alvarez, "Stories to Live By: Continuity and Change in Three Generations of Puerto Rican Women," *Oral History Review* 16 (Fall 1988): 1–46; and Rina Benmayor, Ana Jurabe, Celia Alvarez, and Blanca Vázquez, *Stories to Live By: Continuity and Change in Three Generations of Puerto Rican Women* (New York: Centro de Estudios Puertorriqueños Working Paper Series, 1987).
6. Whalen, *From Puerto Rico to Philadelphia*.

7. Saskia Sassen-Koob, "Changing Composition and Labor Market Location of Hispanic Immigrants in New York City, 1960–1980," in *Hispanics in the U.S. Economy,* edited by George J. Borjas and Marta Tienda (Orlando, Fla.: Academic Press, 1985); and Roy B. Helfgott, "Women's and Children's Apparel," *Made in New York: Case Studies in Metropolitan Manufacturing,* edited by Max Hall (Cambridge, Mass.: Harvard University Press, 1959).

8. Jacob S. Potofsky, "Proposal for Immigration," *New York Times,* February 19, 1947, p. 24.

9. Robert Laurentz, "Racial/Ethnic Conflict in the New York City Garment Industry, 1933–1980" (Ph.D. diss., State University of New York at Binghamton, 1980), 248.

10. Delgado interview, 10, 13, 15.

11. Ibid., 15, 67.

12. Ibid., 110, 68, 16, 21, 22.

13. Rosie Flores quoted in Dan Wakefield, *Island in the City: Puerto Ricans in New York* (New York, 1957), 199, 195, 198.

14. "Puerto Rico Seeks to Curb Migration," *New York Times,* February 23, 1947, p. 20.

15. Helfgott, "Women's and Children's Apparel," 94–95.

16. Roy B. Helfgott, "Puerto Rican Integration in the Skirt Industry in New York City," *Discrimination and Low Incomes: Social and Economic Discrimination against Minority Groups in Relation to Low Income in New York State* (Albany: State of New York: Interdepartmental Committee on Low Incomes, 1959), 254, 276.

17. Will Herberg, "The Old-Timers and the Newcomers: Ethnic Group Relations in a Needle Trades Union," *Journal of Social Sciences* 9 (Summer 1953), 15.

18. Laurentz, "Racial/Ethnic Conflict," 254–58.

19. Delgado interview, 17–18, 102, 112, 26.

20. Ibid., 18–20, 103–4.

21. Ibid., 25.

22. "Others" increased slightly, accounting for the remainder of the membership. While Local 22's total membership had declined slightly, by 2 percent, during this period, Local 89's membership had declined by 23 percent (Herberg, "Old-Timers," 13–14).

23. Herberg, 14–18.

24. Ibid.

25. Ibid., 16.

26. Delgado interview, 73, 75–77.

27. Minutes of the Executive Board Meeting, Dressmakers Union Local 22, ILGWU, April 2, 1957, Executive Board Minutes Collection 5780/036, Box 2, Kheel Center for Labor-Management Documentation and Archives, M.P. Catherwood Library, Cornell University (hereafter Kheel).

28. Minutes of the Executive Board Meeting, Dressmakers Union Local 22, ILGWU, August 20, 1957, November 12, 1957, February 19, 1957, Collection 5780/036, Box 2, Kheel.

29. Minutes of the Executive Board Meeting, Dressmakers Union Local 22, ILGWU, August 20, 1957, Executive Board Minutes Collection 5780/036, Box 2, Kheel.

30. Minutes of the Executive Board Meeting, Dressmakers Union Local 22, ILGWU, June 4, 1957, Executive Board Minutes Collection 5780/036, Box 2, 1943–1958, Kheel.

31. Minutes of the Executive Board Meeting, Dressmakers Union Local 22, ILGWU, August 20, 1957, Executive Board Minutes Collection 5780/036, Box 2, Kheel.

32. Minutes of the Executive Board Meeting, Dressmakers Union Local 22, ILGWU, February 19, 1957, Executive Board Minutes Collection 5780/036, Box 2, Kheel.

33. Minutes of the Executive Board Meeting, Dressmakers Union Local 22, ILGWU, March 5, 1957, Executive Board Minutes Collection 5780/036, Box 2, Kheel.

34. Delgado interview, 27.

35. Ibid., 29–31.

36. Ibid., 35.

37. Minutes of the Executive Board Meeting, Dressmakers Union Local 22, ILGWU, January 8, 1957, Executive Board Minutes Collection 5780/036, Box 2, Kheel.

38. Minutes of Organization Committee Meeting, Dressmakers Union Local 22, ILGWU, March 13, 1957, Executive Board Minutes Collection 5780/036, Box 2, Kheel.

39. Minutes of the Executive Board Meeting, Dressmakers Union Local 22, ILGWU, March 18, 1957, Executive Board Minutes Collection 5780/036, Box 2, Kheel.

40. Helfgott, "Puerto Rican Integration."

41. Minutes of the Executive Board Meeting, Dressmakers Union Local 22, ILGWU, January 8, 1957, Executive Board Minutes Collection 5780/036, Box 2, Kheel.

42. General Membership Meeting Minutes, Dressmakers Union Local 22, ILGWU, May 14, 1957, Executive Board Minutes Collection 5780/036, Box 2, Kheel.

43. Ibid.

44. "Resume N.Y. Talks on Dress Renewal As Deadline Nears," *Justice*, January 15, 1958, p. 4.

45. "105,000 in 7-State Dress Strike," *Justice*, March 1, 1958, p. 2; and Minutes of the General Executive Board of the ILGWU, May 12–15, 1958, 2, Executive Board Minutes Collection 5780/016, Box 7, Kheel.

46. "Dubinsky Victory Forecast Hailed by Shop Chairmen," *Justice*, March 1, 1958, p. 2.

47. "Dubinsky Victory Forecast," p. 2.

48. "105,000 in 7-State Dress Strike," p. 2.

49. Laurentz, "Racial/Ethnic Conflict," 252–53.

50. "Negotiations Collapse after 3-Month Talks," *Justice*, March 1, 1958, p. 8.

51. Delgado interview, 113–15.

52. "Spirit of the Dressmakers," *Justice*, March 1, 1958, p. 6.

53. "Chairmen Hail Victory Now," *Justice*, March 1, 1958, p. 8.

54. "Dubinsky Victory Forecast," p. 2.

55. "105,000 in 7–State Dress Strike," p. 2.

56. "Day the Dresses Stopped," pp. 4, 5. See Maida Springer, "We Did Change Some Attitudes," in *Rocking the Boat: Union Women's Voices, 1915–1975*, edited by Brigid O'Farrell and Joyce L. Kornbluh (New Brunswick, NJ: Rutgers University Press, 1996), 84–109.

57. Minutes of the Executive Board Meeting, Dressmakers Union Local 22, ILGWU, February 25, 1958, 3, Executive Board Minutes Collection 5780/036, Box 2, Kheel.

58. "105,000 in Seven States Were Out at Strike's Peak," *Justice,* March 15, 1958, p. 6. See also Minutes of the General Executive Board of the ILGWU, May 12–15, 1958, 2, Executive Board Minutes Collection 5780/016, Box 7, Kheel.

59. Minutes of the Executive Board Meeting, Dressmakers Union Local 22, ILGWU, March 18, 1958; and General Membership Meeting Minutes, Dressmakers Union Local 22, ILGWU, March 20, 1958, Executive Board Minutes Collection 5780/036, Box 2, Kheel.

60. "Terms of the Settlement," *Justice,* March 15, 1958, p. 2.

61. "Terms of the Settlement," p. 13.

62. "Terms of the Settlement," pp. 3, 13. Despite the gains, there was a concession. At the ratification meeting on March 11 at Manhattan Center, Dubinsky explained, "In order to win on a more important point—jobbers' responsibility for payment of wages in contractors' shops—we gave up something else. That's collective bargaining."—"We Have Won More Than Ever in Our History." *Justice,* March 15, 1958, p. 7.

63. "On the Line," *Justice,* March 15, 1958, p. 8.

64. "Ratification of the Pact," *Justice,* March 15, 1958, p. 12.

65. Minutes of the Executive Board Meeting, Dressmakers Union Local 22, ILGWU, March 18, 1958, 3, Executive Board Minutes Collection 5780/036, Box 2, Kheel.

66. General Membership Meeting Minutes, Dressmakers Union Local 22, ILGWU, March 20, 1958, 7, 20.

67. "An Historic Strike," *Justice,* March 15, 1958, p. 3.

68. General Membership Meeting Minutes, Dressmakers Union Local 22, ILGWU, March 20, 1958, 7, 20, Executive Board Minutes Collection 5780/036, Box 2, Kheel.

69. "Dubinsky Victory Forecast," p. 2.

70. "Terms of the Settlement," p. 3.

71. "Penna. Contractors Reaching Agreement," *Justice,* March 15, 1958, p. 3.

72. "Penna. Strike Won! Anti-Union Forces Defeated," *Justice,* April 15, 1958, p. 1.

73. General Membership Meeting Minutes, Dressmakers Union Local 22, ILGWU, March 20, 1958, 21–22, Executive Board Minutes Collection 5780/036, Box 2, Kheel.

74. Minutes of the Executive Board Meeting, Dressmakers Union Local 22, ILGWU, April 1, 1958, Executive Board Minutes Collection 5780/036, Box 2, Kheel.

75. Minutes of the Executive Board Meeting, Dressmakers Union Local 22, ILGWU, May 8, 1958, Executive Board Minutes Collection 5780/036, Box 2, Kheel.

76. Delgado interview, 30, 32.

77. See Whalen, *From Puerto Rico to Philadelphia,* and Whalen, "Sweatshops Here and There."

78. "Spirit of the Dressmakers," p. 6.

79. Herbert Hill, "Guardians of the Sweatshops: The Trade Unions, Racism, and the Garment Industry," *Puerto Rico and Puerto Ricans: Studies in History and Society,* edited by Adalberto Lopez and James Petras (New York: Halsted Press, 1974), 404, 399.

80. Altagracia Ortiz, "Puerto Ricans in the Garment Industry of New York City, 1920–1960," in *Labor Divided: Race and Ethnicity in United States Labor Struggles, 1835–1960,* edited by Robert Asher and Charles Stephenson (Albany: State University of New York Press, 1990), 105–25; and Laurentz, "Racial/Ethnic Conflict."

81. General Membership Meeting Minutes, Dressmakers Union Local 22, ILGWU, March 20, 1958, 20–21, Executive Board Minutes Collection 5780/036, Box 2, Kheel.

82. Delgado interview, 66.

PART III

Political Spaces

ELIZABETH SALAS

6.   *"The Floating Borderlands":*
Identity, Farmwork, and
Políticas *in Washington State*

Despite a history that includes Spanish explorers and Mexican pioneers, Chicanas in the northwestern border state of Washington have developed an identity around twentieth-century migratory farmwork.[1] The atrocious conditions they faced in farmwork are a common memory in their personal stories and a traditional rallying point in their politics. Despite this commonality, Mexican American women in the state legislature have not always united their community around this aspect of their identity because of competing agendas. Because Hispanic politicians are under little electoral pressure to work together for "Mexican" farmworkers, they have often responded to issues more important to powerful constituencies that demand an American identity, reflected by more acceptable labels such as Mexican American or Hispanic.

Spanish Colonists in the Floating Borderlands

While Spanish explorations in the eighteenth century and "pioneer" women in the nineteenth are parts of the historical record, much of the memory of Chicanas in Washington revolves around historical and current issues relating to farmworkers. On the other hand, educated, upwardly mobile women are often identified as Hispanic, a label that can link them to the state's early Spanish colonial past, whether they are aware of it or not. Most of the early Hispanic history of these far northern Spanish borderlands is associated with water, floating ships, and colonizing men. There was never any overland connection between this frontier and those farther south, even as near as California—thus the appropriateness of the paradoxical phrase "floating borderlands" applied to the region by some Hispanic poets.[2] Ironically for Hispanic women who might seek a white colonial heritage, males predominated in the Spanish imperial exploration of the Pacific Northwest, since women, white or otherwise, did not accompany them on the voyages and brief settlements of the 1770s. But native women played a role that could allow later mestiza Chicanas to identify with indigenous elements of this early history.

Indeed, the ordinary seamen who served in the expeditions were often of mixed ancestry, while the officers tended to be Spanish. Thus, the *mestizaje* of earlier borderlands floated up the Pacific Coast on Spain's ships, belying the story of purely European exploration imagined by those who would whiten their ancestry. The naval base for Spanish explorations was the port of San Blas, Nayarit, within what is now Mexico; Juan Pérez (1774), Bruno de Hezeta and Juan Francisco de la Bodega ye Quadra (1775), and Ignacio de Artega and Bodega ye Quadra (1779) led the initial expeditions. First contact took place when Haida canoes discovered the foreign ship *Santiago* commanded by Pérez. Indigenous peoples interpreted these first vessels as floating fish but soon realized that people were on board. Native women often were the first to initiate contact with the mestizo and mulatto sailors, leading eventually to further interbreeding among these peoples of many borderlands.[3]

Spain hoped to join these frontiers across the seas by establishing migratory links between them. As if to symbolize the connections of this new map, a native woman traded a bird sculpture to a sailor on the *Santiago,* a sculpture that now resides in a museum in Madrid. In fact, Spanish expeditions took between five and twenty-five children, many of them girls, to the missions of California for conversion and Hispanization with the idea that they would return to the Pacific Northwest to further Catholic missionary work and secure the new border region. Spain then attempted to anchor this floating borderland with a colony on what is now the boundary between the United States and Canada. In 1792 the Spanish established a two-year garrison of soldiers on Vancouver Island and another outpost at Neah Bay on the Olympic Peninsula. The Spanish settlements consisted of about eighty male colonists of mixed ancestry, including Peruvian Indians. The arrival of the latter further complicated the migratory map established for "Hispanics" as long ago as the colonial era.[4]

Despite the absence of native, mestiza, or mulatta women among the arriving Spanish imperial ships, the *mestizaje* that might manifest itself in Chicana identity had begun in Spanish-occupied territories to the south and continued in the Northwest. Any offspring from unions between the occupying colonial men and indigenous women became part of already established tribal groups in the Pacific Northwest, thus establishing an identifiable link between these peoples and Chicanas to come. Though Spain's attempt at settlement proved transitory—the last contingent of twenty soldiers left the Nootka outpost in 1795—it provided a historical basis for later Hispanic identification with the region. By 1819 Spain had relinquished its claim on the Pacific Northwest, and by 1821 the Spanish colonials of New Spain had achieved independence and reidentified as Mexicans, eventually contributing to the floating identity of Chicanas and Hispanics in the northwestern borderlands.[5]

Mexican Women in Territorial Washington

Nineteenth-century Mexican pioneers in the Washington Territory can provide today's "Mexican American" women with an identity linking them to the time of Anglo American settlement. During the 1860s, Mexican men, women, and children migrated into Washington during gold rushes into the Pacific Northwest and Western Canada, but they stayed only for short periods. For example, Rosario Romero, a woman from Sonora, settled in Yakima with her husband for a few years during that decade. She is considered the founder of sheepherding in the region. According to historian Erasmo Gamboa, the family of Sebastián and Carmelita Colón represented the first permanent Mexican residents. They had come seeking gold and established a mule train business in Walla Walla in the 1870s. The couple also started a business making and selling tamales primarily to non-Mexicans; consequently, he became known as the "Hot Tamale King of the Northwest." Well into 1905, one could find "Carmelita and Sebastian welcoming customers to their Mexican restaurant, near the corner of 4th and Alder in downtown Walla Walla." But the descendants of the Colón family left Washington during the 1950s.[6] This pioneer Mexican presence in early Washington forms a wispy connection for Mexican American *políticas* who might identify with the early Americanization of the Evergreen State.

Mexican Farmworkers at the Canadian Border

Mexican American women's history in Washington is, however, mostly a twentieth-century experience. In early and mid-century, migration into farmwork would be an experience that many Mexicans throughout the United States shared. Biographies written by women in farmwork, such as Jessie De La Cruz, Elva Treviño Hart, Frances Esquibel Tywoniak, and María Elena Lucas, suggest that identification as a farmworker is a core element in Chicana identity, in Washington as much as elsewhere. But because of the faint ties to the Spanish and pioneer periods, the memory of migratory farmwork is a more important aspect of that identity in the Northwest than in the Southwest. Moreover, in contrast to the Midwest experience, there was little early movement in the Pacific Northwest from farm labor to industrial jobs. Farming and retaining a close connection to the land remained the aspirations of the first immigrants. One of the first Mexican female settlers, Mrs. Geraldo Cárdenas, came with her husband and family in 1913. The Cárdenas family had left Zacatecas in 1911, traveled to Idaho, and was lured to Bellingham, Washington, near the Canadian border. The U & I Sugar Cane Company promised land for people willing to farm sugar beets. The family tried to farm in Bellingham but gave up because of too much rain and the unsuitability of the land for sugar beets. The Cárdenas then moved to the Yakima Valley to do farmwork, remaining part of the countryside.[7]

Many ethnic Mexicans were attracted to the Pacific Northwest specifically to do farmwork, though government and railroad policies augmented this pattern of migration. As a result, by World War II migration commenced into the rural parts of the state and established permanent Mexican farmworker settlements, unlike the temporary mining camps of the nineteenth century. An earlier labor force of Native Americans, Euro Americans, and Asians either left farm labor for better jobs, or in the case of the latter were forced out by exclusion acts. The connection between Mexican immigrants and farmwork was reaffirmed by the Bracero Program between the United States and Mexico. Mexican guest workers called braceros came into the Pacific Northwest from 1942 to 1964. The all-male labor force worked mostly directly in agriculture but also on the railroads through which many arrived, switching to farm labor after arriving. Women left behind in Mexico would send letters to their men and expected letters in return. By sending letters Mexican women reaffirmed their importance in the memories of their migrant husbands in Washington. One woman, Esperanza Fernández Bautista, wrote a letter to a Mexican government official on November 20, 1945, asking for information about her husband. In Spanish she inquired, "I am sorry to bother you, but I am writing to find out about my husband who left here [Mexico City] contracted as a bracero. His name is Fausto Fernández Ramírez, number 28–0003. At first he wrote to me from the Northern Pacific roundhouse in Tacoma, Washington. I am wondering if he is ill or suffered some tragedy." When a Mexican bracero died, his wife would receive a death benefit of $150. In one case, Urbano Martínez lost his life in Washington State, his wife was paid the government death benefit, and he was buried at Tacoma's Oakwood Cemetery.[8] Railroad companies, for cost-saving reasons, did not want to send the bodies of dead workers back to Mexico and pushed for local burials, literally making Mexican migrants one with this northern borderland.

Farmwork was also one of the few jobs that Mexican women could get, a situation that often separated them from their husbands even in Washington. Refugia (Cuca) Partida, for example, picked tomatoes and cherries at a Walla Walla labor camp while her husband Hilario worked alongside braceros and African Americans as a section hand in a Pasco railyard in 1954. For five years, they lived separately while her mother took care of their daughter Gloria. Hilario recalled: "It was hard for us men, you know, living in the bunk cars (boxcars), with 100-degree heat outside and us having to cook inside on a wood stove. . . . Once a week, we got to go by rail to visit our families."[9] The separations caused by migratory work, and its gendered inequities, continued as families and individuals floated from place to place within the state.

An extraordinary surge of farmworkers came from central Mexico in the aftermath of World War II. While some farmworker families would stay in Washington, others would consider their stay a temporary one. Contrasting examples of migratory movements are the experiences of Esperanza García and Marcella Samora. Esperanza García was born in the state of San Luis Potosí, Mexico. At the age of 13 she traveled alone across the border, bringing with her a cage of roosters and wary of the Texas Rangers whom her family had told her to fear. She stayed for a while in Edinburg, Texas, working as a maid from 7 A.M. to 5 P.M. for $2.50 a week. Though married in 1923 to an irrigation-canal watchman, she and her sons migrated to the Northwest for farmwork. The family learned that there were jobs and possibly a fortune in Washington, recalling the lure for the Mexican gold miners of the previous century. Starting off on March 8, 1945, Esperanza journeyed to the Yakima Valley. Forty persons in seven families traveled by truck the 2,200 miles from Edinburg to Yakima. The trip lasted eleven days. After the truck broke down in Pasco, another truck hauled them the remaining 75 miles to the Yakima Valley.

Esperanza recalled the misery of farmwork: "I felt so alone, because my husband had stayed in Texas. Although my sons tried to console me, I wanted to cry; there were no houses only tents to live in. Everything looked strange, cold, dust everywhere, and then a woman that arrived earlier told me, 'Why did you come, there is no work here?'"[10] Tragedy struck when her eldest son died suddenly. Yet his death brought a kind of redemption for Esperanza, for she determined to stay in Washington to be close to her deceased son, now buried in the state's soil. His memory ended her migration.

On the other hand, Marcella Samora was born into a farmworker family in the state of Washington. She met and married Abraham Quintanilla when he was stationed as a soldier at Ft. Lewis, just outside Seattle. She left Washington to travel with her husband to Texas, where they had more opportunities outside of farmwork. Abraham and Marcella Quintanilla's daughter Selena would become a Tejana singing sensation whose meteoric rise and tragic death would be chronicled in the popular film *Selena*, the movie that made Jennifer López a star. Through such cases, farmwork can be viewed as a key element in the movements of ethnic Mexicans across state and national borders, into distant lands, and back again. Unlike their colonial predecessors, they traveled overland by car, truck, or bus in the twentieth century. It is the memory of farmwork that links ethnic Mexicans across the map between the Pacific Northwest, the Midwest, and the Southwest. The memories of those migrations exist in all these regions but are especially salient in Washington State, so far from Mexico and so close to Canada.[11]

Mothers played a significant role in nurturing their daughters to expect more from life than to stay in rural areas and settle for low-paying jobs in farmwork. Probably the best-known mother-daughter farmworker story from the 1940s is that of Irene and Antonia (Nenita) Castañeda. Irene moved from Texas to Washington and her daughter, Antonia, moved back to Texas and had considerable success as a Chicana scholar and activist. The Castañeda family left Crystal City, Texas, to settle in Toppenish, Washington, after World War II. Irene, born and raised in Texas, recalled that "Mexicans had neither voice nor vote. . . . the women who cleaned house for the white people got their meals outside, or else there was no food." Irene didn't want to stay in Crystal City, and she "had to fight with cloak and sword" to get out of that town. She "begged God with open arms" to help her leave the town, which she said was "so ignorant, so wretched, full of taverns, full of filth."[12] In her case, being a farmworker in Washington was better than being one in Texas, where she vowed never to return. Irene showed that ethnic Mexican women had the determination to seek opportunities in distant lands; they could also instill in their daughters a Chicana identity formulated on fighting for family welfare and social justice.

The Castañeda family left Crystal City for work picking asparagus, corn, fruits, and hops in Washington. The family left on March 13, 1946, and arrived in Toppenish five days later. Initial housing consisted of "rows of shacks without doors" and no heat; some growers provided only tents. (Washington still has some of the worst housing for farmworkers in the country.) Irene described how the weather was "colder than the dickens" and how hard it was to fire up wood stoves using wet wood. Irene recalled that when she worked in the hops, the women were paid 75 cents an hour, while the men were paid 85 cents an hour. The gender inequities of farm labor persisted from border to border.[13]

Irene's notions of discipline and fearless womanhood took hold on her daughter, as Antonia recalls traveling from Texas to work in the fields of Washington:

> "Andale, trepate, no tengas miedo," my mother said, urging me to hop onto the back of the flatbed truck where my brother Jorge was perched, ready to pull three-year-old me into the troca enlonada that would take us al norte, to los trabajos."Andale, subete, ya nos vamos pa'l norte," she repeated, as she helped me onto the splintery floorboard of the tarp-covered truck we rode with five other families from the Rio Grande Valley of South Tejas to the Yakima Valley. . . . Under reclaimed desert skies, rows of fields, patches, orchards, vineyards and hop yards stretched before us, waiting for our contracted bodies: cotton, spinach, potato, beet, tomato, melon, hop, cucumber, lettuce, beans, asparagus, berries, apple, grape, peach, plum, lemon and cherry. Walking, bending, crouching, straddling, crawling, dragging, climbing, stretching, lugging sacks, pails, baskets, boxes and crates, and wielding knives, hoes, cutting forks, and shears, we worked from March through October.[14]

Through the values learned from her mother in migratory labor, Antonia finally left the fields, attended the University of Washington, earned a Ph.D. from Stanford, and became a history professor at St. Mary's University in San Antonio. Her identity as an educated upwardly mobile Chicana was firmly established on her experience in the fields of the northwestern borderland.

Such a shift in identity was not guaranteed, as can be seen in a story by a Chicana journalist who combined her own familial memories of farm labor with those of a seemingly unchanging ethnic Mexican family still migrating between Texas and Washington. From July 7, 1991, to July 5, 1992, reporter Isabel Valle of the *Walla Walla Union Bulletin* ran a series of articles about migrant farmworkers, Raúl and María Elena Martínez, and their family. Valle herself had grandparents who were migrant workers, and her parents, living in San Antonio, also recalled working in the fields. When she began living with the Martínez family for the purposes of her article, she would get up very early in the day to help María Elena in the kitchen. All day long Valle "had to wash, cook, and clean and tend to the children" and "was not to talk back to any of the men, even when I disagreed with them, and I was not to air my opinions." She contrasted this continuation of traditional women's identity with her own professional identity created and claimed from memories of her father telling her, "you have to get a good education and get into a good career so you can stand on your own two feet."[15]

Valle described a very circumscribed life for a migrant mother. After waking up at 3 A.M. to make breakfast and lunch, including many flour tortillas, she awakened the family at 4 A.M. Then she would take the children to a day-care center or a neighbor's house for the day; school-age children would also be dropped off, to be taken to school later. By 4:30 she would be driven to the fields with the other workers. Fieldwork completed by 1 or 2 P.M., the women returned home to heat up lunch, after which housework commenced. The children would return at 4 P.M. and have to be picked up. She then made dinner, including another stack of flour tortillas. After dinner she had to prepare the children for the next day, do kitchen chores, and act as a hostess if other workers came by to her house. Bedtime for her would be at 10 P.M., with just five hours to sleep before the new day. Migrant women are taught to believe that housework is a woman's responsibility "and that men do not lift a finger to help," as to do so would be "unmanly." María Elena Martínez, who had three married daughters and four daughters-in-law, felt proud that they were all workers and homemakers: "son amas de casa [they're homemakers] and that's the way Raúl wanted them raised. And they all take care of their husbands real well."[16] Thus, a rural, working-class ethnic Mexican identity persisted in 1990s Washington even as some women developed college-educated and middle-class perceptions of themselves.

An important experience that would help expand the self-identity of Chicanas was their increasing participation in politics, a participation that nevertheless recalled their oppressive lives around farmwork. The Martínez family's migratory experiences between their home base in La Grulla, Texas, to Pasco and Walla Walla, Washington, provided reporter Valle a personal example of political subordination. She recalled an occasion in Texas when she was invited to a home where a political candidate was going to speak. She was told by the male candidate that the women were in the kitchen, and she should go there. Valle said she found political discussions more interesting than going to the kitchen and exchanging food recipes, but after "disapproving stares" from the men, she retreated. The struggle for Chicana identity manifested itself in this story of gender dynamics in the oppressive culture of ethnic Mexican migratory farmwork. Such stories caused many Chicanas to remember that subordination and build the fortitude necessary to change their lives politically, whether in Texas or Washington.[17]

The brutal nature of migratory life for women can be garnered from the reports of registered nurse Margaret Caicedo of the Walla Walla Family Medical Center. She thought that the women of farmworker families faced many difficulties and even abuse within the home: "I know of three families . . . where girls are taken out of school to serve as housekeepers and child care providers. In one family, a 14–year-old niece was brought over here from Mexico to purposely take care of the family of eight and the house, . . . men will convince their wives that they have no other option but to stay in the situation that they are in, and many times the women feel they have nowhere to go. The woman has a lot of kids, she has no papers, and she has very limited English skills, so she feels she can't get out. . . . Also, the husbands will get themselves legalized—but they won't do that for their wives." Caicedo said that "women were treated like slaves" in many of the cases that she worked on in the Walla Walla health center.[18]

The most common thread through the many stories written about farmworkers was the contrast between the suffering that the women endured and their daughters' glowing dreams of furthering their education. Many of the young women related their deep desire to stop doing farmwork and to excel in school. In 1988 Janie Gutiérrez, a high school student in Pasco, attended the State Leadership Conference at Central Washington University in Ellensburg. She commented: "I work in the fields. I see weeds in my sleep. I dream about them. My back hurts. I'm doing it, but I want to do something in this world. . . . Some kids have to go to work when they are only 9. That's not a life. Kids miss out on a lot. . . . I want to be my own boss, have my own business. I want to stay as far away from the fields as I can. . . . Many of our parents left Mexico for us. My grandpa calls my mom and begs her to come back. But she says, 'Dad, I can't go back.' I'm thankful my mom is doing it. I have it and I'm going to keep it."[19] Like her nineteenth-century predecessors, Janie sought to become an entrepreneur. Janie Gutiérrez's burgeoning Mexican American identity floated between nations, occupations, and generations.

The harsh experiences that young women faced in migratory farm-work in the 1940s were echoed in the 1990s. In 1999 Bernice García was a student at Davis High School in Yakima when she wrote short stories from her memories as a farmworker. In "Routine" she writes the follow-ing: "My name woke me up along with some shoving. It was time to go to work. My eyelids couldn't open, my body was tired and not ready to go. My mom talks of how if we hurry and work hard, we'll get home earlier. Earlier I thought, earlier is never early enough. My sister was always more into it than I was. . . . After we heard the tractors in the morning we got up and picked cherries. The day finally ended and we were overjoyed, my sister and I. On the way home there was usually always a stop to DQ for ice cream." García conveys the child's view of her very hard life as a farmworker. Her experiences are recounted in another insightful and heart-wrenching short essay: "We used to have races, my sister and me. We'd run up and down the fields and sometimes we'd slip and fall, but we'd keep going because this was our break from carrying the bucket on our backs."[20] This story is poignant in that it depicts apparent violations of child labor laws. Curiously, because García narrates her stories from the perspective of a student, they obscure the fact that 86 percent of mi-grant youth in the 1990s still did not finish high school in Washington.[21] Clearly, upward mobility was limited for girls with such poor education; their identities were also more likely restricted by tradition.

Of similar background, though successful despite the odds in educa-tion and occupation, was Sister María de Jesus Ybarra. A nun for more than thirty years, Sister María was born in Texas to migrant farmwork-ers who settled in Yakima. Of their thirteen children, four girls became nuns, and one son became a priest. In 1988 she was counselor, Hispanic consultant, and program administrator for the Education Center of the Catholic Diocese of Yakima. At the time, 60 percent of the 52,000 Catho-lics in the diocese were Mexicans. Perhaps because of her own family's success, Sister María tended unfortunately to blame the farmworkers for their situation: "Our Hispanic community lacks education. Many drop out because parents encourage them to work in the fields. . . . Our people do not vote."[22] She referred to her community as Hispanic, a label that gained currency by the conservative 1980s, but clearly she recognized her roots among farmworkers as well as Spanish Catholic missionaries. Sister María was naturally thankful she had not been restricted to migrant work. On a redemptive note, she said that if she had not become a nun, she would have become a politician and addressed the lack of political power among Mexican Americans, especially farmworkers.

Identity, Farmwork, and Políticas

A major reason Chicanas became activists was that they saw daily the impact of farmwork on their communities. On drives outside their towns and cities, they continued to witness the heartbreaking reality of men, women, and children working in the fields through sun and rain. Among the most vulnerable and exploited workers in Washington, what these people experienced in the fields, exposed to pesticides and unhealthy working conditions, affected not only them but also subsequent generations. One would expect such a sight would politically galvanize the ethnic Mexican community from a sense of its shared cultural and social identity as farmworkers or descendants of farmworkers.

From the beginning of electoral participation in Seattle, ethnic Mexican politics was rooted in farm labor despite individual political behavior. Moving from farmwork to city life, two Chicanas campaigned for the Seattle City Council. Stella Ortega and Yolanda Alaniz ran for positions. Both women had been farmworkers as children and identified with the Chicano movement. They consequently argued for better jobs, higher wages, and bilingual education and against discrimination and racial profiling. Born into a family of migrants in Texas in the 1950s, Ortega attended the University of Houston where she fought for the rights of farmworkers and students. In Seattle she worked for El Centro de la Raza, a settlement house that provided various legal, social, and job-related services for Latinos. She worked there for seven years and was noted for developing one of the best and most comprehensive social delivery systems in Seattle. It is significant that she also participated in the American Indian Movement for enforcement of treaty rights on the Nisqually River in Washington and at Wounded Knee in South Dakota. Evidently, she identified with the indigenous heritage of ethnic Mexicans in Washington. Nevertheless, this Chicana failed to win election to the Seattle City Council.[23]

Yolanda Alaniz, another longtime activist, also ran for the city council. She had earned the nickname "Seattle's favorite firebrand and organizer" because of her tireless efforts to address social injustice. Born to farmworkers, as a child she moved from Brownsville, Texas, to Sunnyside, Washington, in 1956. The Yakima Valley of Eastern Washington is often called the "Mississippi of the Northwest" because of the harshness of race relations and farm labor. Alaniz recalled the dangers of farmwork for children in the incident when she and her sister Louise had saved their brother Ramón from drowning after he fell into an irrigation ditch. Raised a political activist, though only 6 years old Alaniz, as the eldest daughter, walked beside her mother and role model, Ninfa, on the picket lines.[24]

Deeply identifying with her mestiza heritage and migrant background, Yolanda Alaniz nonetheless represents the migrant child's desire to leave farmwork and go to school. Despite working in the fields during the day, Yolanda recalled her fierce determination to stay up late at night studying to finish high school and go on to college. At the University of Washington she became a Brown Beret and joined MEChA (El Movimiento Estudiantil Chicano de Aztlán). She was critical of the United Farm Workers led by César Chávez for its failure to incorporate Mexicano nationals into the union. She was part of the Chicana backlash against MEChA, which despite its revolutionary nationalist rhetoric was very conservative when it came to gender relations. MEChA leaders maintained that Chicanas were engaging in adultery, so Yolanda wrote an essay called, "In Defense of Adultery." When Chicanos refused to help her organize a campus union for lowly paid workers, Yolanda decided to leave Chicano organizations and join the Freedom Socialist Party in 1976. Considering the working class the mover for change, the group embraced the rights of women, people of color, lesbians, and gays. Yolanda became a major spokesperson for Radical Women, a branch of the party. In 1991 she ran for a seat on the Seattle City Council and garnered 18 percent of the vote. Yolanda spent thirty years as one of the most radical activists in Seattle, but in 1995 she decided to move to Los Angeles. What drove her was an incredible anger over her childhood experiences as a farmworker the core of her Chicana activist identity.[25]

Dora Sánchez Treviño, who had many jobs as a sugar-beet farmworker, teacher's aide, bureaucrat, Democratic organizer, and labor activist, was born in Texas in 1947. Dora moved to Quincy, Washington, at the age of 15 in order to help her older brother take care of his household. But she resented the familial machismo that gave her brother so much power. She noted that men also had too much power and privilege as workers in the packing sheds: "In the potato sheds the women were always put on the conveyer belts to sort the potatoes, and it was constant and rapid work. And the men never worked on the belts but would be paid between ten and twenty-five cents more an hour. The excuse was that men did heavier work, but their work was lot slower and they had periods of rest in between loading the potatoes onto trains or whatever. Women rarely received any breaks during the day and the less pay was what really bothered me. Also, women stood on their feet all day, and if any woman needed a bathroom break they had to wait for someone to take their place on the belt line." By 1963 the entire farmworker family had moved to Quincy where Dora's mother, Ignacia, went to the city hall to register to vote, which she had always stressed was important. But the city clerk gave Ignacia a hard time and denied her the right stating that "she was not fluent in English."[26] She had voted in Texas, but denial of the franchise in Washington was so devastating that Ignacia never did register in Quincy. Dora held on to this memory, became a Chicana activist, and became among the first to sit on a city council in Washington, serving in 1978 on the Quincy City Council, where her mere presence at that time redeemed her heritage in farmwork.

An activist Chicana image was understandably difficult to maintain among politicians who had to win office, but such an image was possible with some constituencies. Moderate to conservative middle-class constituencies, Anglo and Mexican American alike, could react negatively to perceived radicalism. In 1989 an advocate for farmworkers, Luisa Torres, was appointed to the Pasco City Council, but when she ran for election she lost. Her advocacy did not go well with Pasco's conservative white population. On the other hand, relying on blue-collar Mexican American voters, in 1997 Clara Jiménez ran for the Toppenish City Council and won. She grew up a farmworker with a strong desire to become a history teacher and an activist. She said, "I just decided I was going to be a councilwoman and showed them I could do it running a good, clean campaign." She relied on a local Spanish-language newspaper to spread her message to the large ethnic Mexican community on the east side of Toppenish. Also contrary to expectations, Becky Díaz, an activist in Bellingham, a town in Whatcom County close to the border with Canada, ran for the school board in 1997 and won with a large crossover vote from liberal Anglo American supporters. She was active in the Whatcom Hispanic Organization, which had programs that specifically targeted educational services for farm labor camps. She identified herself as a housewife who equated elected office with taking care of the educational and community needs of a household. This appeal to traditional family values effectively countered any perception that she might be radical. Her greatest fear was that Mexican American children without a proper education would not be able to compete in American society. Regardless of ethnic label, these candidates obviously related to the heritage of Mexican farmwork in Washington.[27]

In the 1990s the top three Mexican American politicians in Washington State were significantly all women, and two had been farmworkers as children. The three were Democratic state senator Margarita López Prentice of the 11th district in Seattle, Republican state representative Mary Skinner of the 14th district in Yakima, and Democratic state rep-

resentative Phyllis Gutiérrez Kenney of the 46th district in Seattle. Although several Chicana politicians have taken up farmworkers' issues
over the last forty years, the most visible leaders in the Washington legislature have not been united on those issues. They have been divided
by many factors, including personality and party, but especially by the
need to address the particular issues of the voting constituents of their
districts, not only those of the poorest, usually nonvoting, members of
their own ethnic group.

Born in the early 1930s, Margarita López grew up in California, the
daughter of Mexican immigrants. Before going into politics, she worked
as a registered nurse for forty-six years. Reflecting a new *mestizaje,* she
married William C. Prentice, who played a major role in her political
education, for he was a lifelong New Deal Democratic activist. She first
served as a member of the Renton School Board before running as a state
representative and then as a state senator. Her husband Bill was often
remembered traveling with Margarita, bringing along his big corn cooker
to political events and never failing to remember the ice and cooking
utensils. The couple was cleverly engaging in gender role reversal to win
over female voters. A key aspect of her campaigns for office initially involved supporting farmworker legislation for better housing and pesticide
controls. But as she grew more powerful as a state senator, she distanced
herself from Mexican American causes, especially advocacy on behalf
of farmworkers. In 1992 she had stated, "Hispanics in Washington state
must unify and become more politically active . . .," and she had run
in favor of better housing for migrants. But by 1997 she commented to
a reporter, "Why should we require roofs that withstand snow? All it
does is raise costs." Seeking a broader Democratic, urban, middle-class
political base, Prentice began promoting the labor union rights of professors, students, and nurses, apparently forgetting the migratory work she
had never experienced personally. Migrants, moreover, often resident or
illegal aliens, were not a voting constituency who could reward a politician's efforts. Never having labeled herself a Chicana, Prentice seemed
increasingly comfortable with a Hispanic or even an Anglo designation,
with her married name.[28]

By 2005 Mary Skinner was serving in her fifth term as a Republican
state representative. Born into a migrant family, she worked as a junior
high school teacher, became a community volunteer, and served as a
member of the Washington State Board of Education. Illustrating how
the new *mestizaje* could also lead to political assimilation, her marriage to a Euro American Republican decidedly influenced her views in
a conservative direction. The 14th district that she represented could

have benefited from a politician dedicated to the rights of farmworkers, who made up a sizable portion of the population, but unfortunately not much of the electorate. The main agricultural products of the 14th district were tree fruit, grapes, and wines; fruit packaging and processing were related industries in the district; light manufacturing and tourism added some diversity to the local economy. In the 2000 election she received 15,401 votes or 66 percent from the mainly Republican electorate. Though somewhat concerned with the individual educational advancement of Mexican Americans, Skinner generally did not address their other issues, especially farmwork, since much of her political support came from growers.[29] While she proudly proclaimed her farmworker youth, her adult convictions as a Republican and a friend of growers were more pronounced. Skinner thus kept her Mexican migrant past a memory as she developed a Mexican American identity based more on her assimilated political views and class values.

On the other hand, Phyllis (Felipa) Gutiérrez Kenney, a Democrat, remained a strong advocate for Mexican Americans in both rural and urban communities. Her parents came from Mexico in 1919 and worked as migrant farmworkers. Phyllis, the sixth of eight children, was born in Hardin, Montana, in 1936. Her father helped to organize the sugar-beet workers in Montana during 1936–1937, but by 1942 the family had moved to Washington. She grew up in the Yakima Valley, Wapato, and Toppenish. In Wapato she entered the first grade knowing only Spanish. Allergic to the pesticides applied to hops, Phyllis suffered when she worked in the fields. She remembered that there were no bathroom facilities where she picked asparagus for seventy-five cents an hour. A friend died after falling off a plank and into an irrigation ditch, and her brother died of pneumonia aggravated by poor housing. Snow would come into the cracks of their house, and the windows would break. Her family would cover the windows with blankets, but their living quarters remained very cold. It was from these memories that Phyllis became and remained a strong advocate for farmworkers, especially helping their children attend college.[30]

With her first husband, a Mexican American, Phyllis had ten children. The family would pick grapes, prunes, and other fruits in the Tri-Cities area on the weekends to make extra money. She took the surname of her second husband, Larry Kenney, a Euro American and a former president of the Washington Labor Council, whose views successfully corresponded with those of her community. The ethnically mixed couple moved to North Seattle in 1976, where for a time she owned a small fashion shop called Felipa's. She drew the inspiration to own a business from her widowed mother, who owned a Mexican restaurant (an industry, as we have seen, established by nineteenth-century Mexican pioneers). It took her mother, a former farmworker, a long time to learn English. She was fond of saying, "I can do it. I'm going to do it." When Kenny opened her retail store, she wanted a loan, but bank officials seemed lukewarm at best. The bank officer told her to put it on her or her husband's credit card. This episode spurred Kenney to sit on committees that dealt with women as small business owners.[31] Though a businesswoman, Kenney never forgot her identity as a farmworker. She pushed for migrant day-care, health care, and educational programs for rural families, students, minorities, and workers.

Kenney made the move from activist for farmworker and women's rights to Democratic politician in 1996 at the age of 60, when she ran for the position of Washington secretary of state. She wanted to live out her parents' values of helping the community. While she did not win the election, she was appointed state representative for the 46th district in Seattle in 1997. As a state representative, Kenney became a tireless force behind educational advancement for the children of Mexican farmworkers. She wrote legislation that allowed students without U.S. citizenship, but with a long residency in Washington, to pay in-state fees at public colleges, rather than the much higher fees charged nonresidents. Though she did not call herself Chicana, with the increasingly conservative electorates of the new millennium, her actions were in keeping with the politics of earlier Chicana activists.[32]

On occasion Prentice, Kenney, and Skinner clashed with each other over issues related to farmwork. Prentice and Skinner seemed to give themselves more credibility because they had always run and been elected to office. Kenney, on the other hand, was seen as an outsider who was first appointed to office and then ran in a safe Democratic district. At times it seemed that the antifarmworker legislation proposed by Prentice was meant to insult Kenney rather than actually harm farmworkers because the bills never had a chance of passage in the legislature. But Kenney adamantly pursued promigrant legislation regardless of whether the two other Mexican American women joined her. Despite memories of farmwork and the visible realities of that labor all about them, these politicians took individual positions on that issue and did not join in common cause on this critical aspect of ethnic Mexican life in Washington. Indeed, as Hispanic women like Prentice and Skinner became more upwardly mobile, they distanced themselves from the working-class aspects of their heritage.

Nevertheless, for some young up-and-coming Chicanas, their political heritage remained centered on farmworker issues. Alma Sánchez came from San Isidro, Michoacán, to Washington in 1988 when she was five years old. In an interview in 2001, she said if she had remained in her village, she would probably be getting ready to marry. Sometimes she felt like the Mexican movie character la India María, who was "ni de aquí ni de allá" (neither here nor there). She contrasted her life in Michoacán with her experience in Washington by saying "here, you've basically got it made—with determination and a lot of hard work." While at Cashmere High School, she was elected associate student body secretary, Spanish Club president, and Concert Choir treasurer; she was also a soccer player and significantly a representative on the Migrant Education Program's State Advisory Committee. She lamented that her mother had not attended the fifth grade in San Isidro because she could not afford the school uniform. She wished that her school teachers in Washington "would know the story of all of us because I think they would respect us more if they knew we had to come all the way from Mexico, then learn English, while our parents were working in the fields."[33] It is interesting that Alma Sánchez's incipient political activities reflected not only her Mexican heritage, and her American present, but also her desire to help farmworkers like her parents.

Another young woman, Alex Narváez, a MEChA activist, became the first Chicana to win election as president of the Associated Students of the University of Washington in 2002–2003. She cited as her political education trips with her parents to Olympia and eastern Washington to aid the migrants: "my parents always made a point to go show their support." In a display of solidarity with her community, Narváez strongly backed Rep. Kenney's legislation in favor of in-state college fees for undocumented workers in Washington. Although the Chicano movement had supposedly ended in the late 1970s, young women continued to identify with its emphasis on their Mexican heritage, including the indigenous past, farmwork, and radical reform.[34]

As we have seen, the history and identity politics of ethnic Mexican women in the border state of Washington has a floating quality about it, in its migratory, multiregional, transnational, and interracial aspects. The history includes the distinctive explorations of imperial Spain that contribute to a Hispanic identity. The history of racial intermixing in the colonies adds to the Chicana identity. The nineteenth-century history of Mexican women who pioneered on the Washington frontier contributes to a Mexican American identity focused on Americanization. It is, however, the twentieth-century history of farm labor that has had its greatest impact on the identity politics of Chicanas in the state. Though sometimes minimized as a result of competing constituencies, the memory and continuing presence of migrant work has forced the most assimilated of *políticas* to recognize its significance to the identity of the ethnic Mexican community of Washington State.

Notes

1. The leading historian of farm labor in the state is University of Washington professor Erasmo Gamboa. His works include "A History of the Chicano People and the Development of Agriculture in the Yakima Valley" (M.A. thesis, University of Washington, 1973); "Under the Thumb of Agriculture: Bracero and Mexican American Workers in the Pacific Northwest, 1940–1950" (Ph.D. dissertation, University of Washington, 1984) and *Mexican Labor and World War II: Braceros in the Pacific Northwest, 1942–1947* (Seattle: University of Washington Press, 1990).

2. I borrow the phrase "floating borderlands" from University of Washington professor Lauro Flores's anthology *"The Floating Borderlands": Twenty-Five Years of U.S. Hispanic Literature* (Seattle: University of Washington Press, 1998). Flores quotes from a Juan Felipe Herrera poem: "tonight we shall eat the assumptions of ourselves, of our house and where we are going. Tonight we shall embark on the Floating Borderlands towards our liberation" (p. 3). Flores also uses the metaphors "New Navigators of the Floating Borderlands" and "Calabash cousins," as labels for Chicanos/as living in Washington.

3. Tomas Bartoli, *The Malaspina Expedition at Nootka, in Spain and the North Pacific Coast: Essays in Recognition of the Bicentennial of the Malaspina Expedition, 1791–1792*, edited by Robin Inglis (Vancouver, B.C.: Vancouver Maritime Museum, 1992), 88, 92–95.

4. Ibid.; see also David J. Weber, *Bárbaros: Spaniards and Their Savages in the Age of Enlightenment* (New Haven, Conn.: Yale University Press, 2005), 27–29, 236.

5. Bartoli, 88, 92–95.

6. Gamboa, "History of the Chicano People," 36, 38.

7. Ibid.; Fran Leeper Buss, *Forged under the Sun/Forjada bajo el Sol: The Life of Maria Elena Lucas* (Ann Arbor: University of Michigan Press, 1993); Elva Treviño Hart, *Barefoot Heart: Stories of a Migrant Child* (Tempe, Ariz.: Bilingual Press/Editorial Bilingüe, 1999); Gary Soto, *Jessie De La Cruz: A Profile of a United Farm Worker* (New York: Persea Books, 2000); and Frances Esquibel Tywoniak and Mario T. García, *Migrant Daughter: Coming of Age As a Mexican American Woman* (Berkeley: University of California Press, 2000).

8. Conversations with Erasmo Gamboa, January 2004.

9. Ibid.

10. Ibid.; "García" is a pseudonym.

11. Joe Nick Patoski, *Selena: Como la Flor* (Boston: Little, Brown, 1996), 4.

12. Irene Castañeda, "Crónica personal de Cristal, primera parte" and "segunda parte," in *Literatura chicana: Texto y contexto*, edited by Antonia Castañeda Shular, Tomás Ybarra-Frausto, and Joseph Sommers (Englewood Cliffs, N.J.: Prentice-Hall, 1972), 27–29, 243–49.

13. Ibid.

14. Antonia I. Castañeda, "Que Se Pudieran Defender (So You Could Defend Yourselves): Chicanas, Regional History, and National Discourses," in *Frontiers* 22 (no. 3, 2001): 127, 129.

15. Isabel Valle, *Fields of Toil: A Migrant Family's Journey* (Pullman: Washington State University Press, 1994), 205–11.

16. Ibid.

17. Ibid.

18. Ibid.

19. Bob Marvel, "They're Leaving the Fields Behind and 'Going for It,'" *La Voz*, April 1988, p. 10.

20. Bernice García, "Routine," in *With My Hands Full/Con Mis Manos Llenas*, edited by Jim Bodeen (Yakima, Wash.: Blue Begonia Press, 1999), 175–76.

21. Valle, 39.

22. Maria Medina, "Family, Faith and Tradition: The Stories of Three Women," *La Voz*, April 1988, pp. 12–13.

23. Elizabeth Salas, "Mexican-American Women Politicians in Seattle," in *More Voices, New Stories: King County, Washington's First 150 Years*, edited by Mary C. Wright (Seattle: King County Landmarks & Heritage Commission, 2002), 218–20.

24. Yolanda Alaniz and Megan Cornish, "The Chicano Struggle: A Racial or a National Movement?" *Freedom Socialist*, September–November 1986.

25. Ibid; and Yolanda Alaniz and Nellie Wong, eds., *Voices of Color* (Seattle: Red Letter Press, 1999).

26. Jerry García. "A Chicana in Northern Aztlán: Dora Sánchez Treviño," in *Women in Pacific Northwest History*, edited by Karen J. Blair (Seattle: University of Washington Press, 1988), 212.

27. Salas, 218–20.

28. "Farm Worker Protection Bill Sponsored by Rep. Prentice," *La Voz*, March 1991, April 1992; "Legislature OKs Tents, 'Shanty Towns' for Farm Workers: State Senator Margarita Prentice Leads Effort for 'Segregated Housing': Latinos, Others, Want Gov. Locke to Veto It," *La Voz*, May 1997; *La Voz*, April 1992 and December 1997; and J. Patrick Coolican, "William C. Prentice, New Deal Democrat, Dies at 71," *Seattle Times*, May 27, 2003.

29. Salas, 217–18.

30. Ibid., 225–27.

31. Ibid.; Phyllis Gutiérrez Kenney, comments at the Washington State Business Symposium, North Seattle Community College, June 30, 2003.

32. Randy Trick, "Undocumented Students to Pay Resident Tuition," *Daily* (University of Washington), May 8, 2003.

33. *Migrant Education News* (Washington Office of the Superintendent of Public Instruction), April 2001.

34. Anne Kim, "Alex Narváez Raised to Reform," *Daily*, May 13, 2002.

MARISELA R. CHÁVEZ

7. *Pilgrimage to the Homeland:*
California Chicanas and
International Women's Year,
Mexico City, 1975

In the early months of 1975, Celia Herrera Rodríguez, a reentry student at California State University, Sacramento, regularly attended Communist Party meetings held in northern California. At one of the meetings, she heard about and was intrigued by the forthcoming International Women's Year Conference, to be held in Mexico City in June. With few financial resources, but determined to attend, she called Frances Romero, a friend of hers in Fresno active with El Teatro Campesino (a theater group affiliated with the United Farm Workers Union, headed by César Chávez and Dolores Huerta), and asked if she wanted to attend. The two women gathered their welfare and financial aid monies (Rodríguez was the mother of two young children, and both women were students) and hitchhiked from Fresno to the U.S.–Mexico border. From there, they walked to the bus station in Tijuana, Baja California, and took a bus destined for Mexico City. When they arrived in the city two days later, the two women had a total of four dollars left to their names. They found their way to Rodríguez's mother-in-law's house. During their stay, they took the bus from the house in a working-class area to the Tribune at the Medical Center. In order to eat, Rodriguez, an artist, sold her sketches at the conference. In fact, that is how the women managed to make enough money for their trip back to California. Although the circumstances were challenging, Rodríguez recalled that one of the reasons she wanted to attend the conference was precisely because it was in Mexico: "Well, because I really felt that I knew nothing about Mexico and that yet it was home. There was something there that was almost like a spiritual feeling to it that I wanted to go."[1]

Rodríguez and Romero joined thousands of women and men, both official government representatives and unofficial participants, when they descended upon Mexico City for the United Nations–sponsored International Women's Year (IWY) Conference and Tribune. The U.N. IWY represented the culmination of more than thirty years of work by women organizing internationally and within the United Nations. Although women had called for an international conference immediately after World War I, as well as at the first session of the U.N. Commission on the Status of Women in 1946, it was not until 1972 that the U.N. General Assembly approved an International Women's Year.[2] Then, in December 1974, the U.N. General Assembly approved the IWY program itself as well as the conference to open on June 19, 1975, in Mexico City. The IWY Conference, which was for official government representatives, however, differed from the Tribune. From previous world conferences, U.N. officials knew that many unofficial participants would come to Mexico City. The officials therefore also planned a separate public meeting, called the Tribune, organized by and in cooperation with several nongovernmental organizations (NGOs) affiliated with the U.N., thus reserving the IWY Conference for official government representatives.

Among the thousands of women who attended the IWY Tribune, between two and three hundred Mexican American women from across the United States arrived in Mexico City for their first international women's conference of any sort.[3] Participation in the meeting was a significant step for Chicanas. As a group, they attempted to make the transition from struggling for recognition on a national stage to struggling for it on an international stage. In addition, they attempted to make political connections with Mexican women transnationally.

The IWY Conference represented another phase in the ongoing development of Chicana feminist consciousness in several ways. The IWY Conference occurred four years after the first national Chicana conference, La Conferencia de Mujeres por La Raza, held in Houston, Texas. Although conflicts arose at the Houston conference over the place of feminist concerns within the context of the Chicano movement, and half the women eventually left the meeting in protest, the resolutions it passed placed these concerns in the public eye.[4] In this manner, the

Houston conference became a significant step in voicing Chicana feminist ideologies in the United States.

Through an analysis of the experiences of Chicanas from California at the IWY Tribune, their expectations, and the implications of their attendance, this article examines four interrelated developments that affected Chicana identity and political formation, especially as a result of their participation in the 1975 IWY Tribune. First, by traveling to this conference, that is, without the accompaniment of men, the participants defied their traditional gender roles as helpmates within the movement. Second, Chicanas attended an international women's meeting as representatives from an imagined Chicano nation. As such, they acted as public figures for a movement typically defined only by males. Third, because Chicanas at the Tribune both influenced and were influenced by women from all over the world, their participation at the event transcended the U.S.–Mexico border that usually determined Chicano and Chicana ethnic and cultural identity. Fourth, Chicana experiences challenged how they conceived of themselves as members of an oppressed minority group in the United States when they had to come to terms with their own privilege as Americans in relation to Third World women.[5]

The Chicana/o Movement

For more than nine years, women in the Chicano movement had struggled to craft their own identity within the milieu of Chicano nationalism in the United States. The movement, a quest for power based on a common Mexican American identity, spanned the mid-1960s through the late 1970s. Although accurately identified as a social movement, the development was not seminal, but rather part of a long trajectory of Mexican activism in the United States. Chicano cultural nationalism, or Chicanismo, emerged as an identity based on a claim to the nation of Aztlán, the mythical homeland of the Aztecs, believed to be north of Mexico City.[6] Conveniently, the U.S. Southwest was to the north and thus allowed Chicanos to claim that Aztlán's true location was in a region that had once been Mexican territory. Such claims allowed Chicanos to emphasize primordial roots in U.S. territory, thereby declaring their legitimate place and rights as true Americans. As such, Chicanos also asserted their rights as members of the culturally defined, imagined nation-state of Aztlán. Historian Ernesto Chávez defines cultural nationalism as a "culturally constructed ideological movement for the attainment and maintenance of autonomy, cohesion and individuality for an ethnic group deemed by its members to constitute an actual or potential nation."[7] Aztlán became the Chicano potential nation. While the proposed methods for attaining that nation varied, cultural nationalists sought self-determination, defined what it meant to be Chicano, and held strong anti-U.S. beliefs. During this time, Chicanismo could be explained through five major terms: *la raza* (the race, or the people), *la huelga* (the strike, in reference to the UFW struggle on behalf of farmworkers), *carnalismo* (brotherhood), as well as *Chicano* (a new self-defined identity), and *Aztlán.* Beyond this common language, however, the Chicano movement was made up of a great diversity of individuals with different goals and strategies. These included establishing a variety of newspapers and journals and founding political, community, academic, and women's organizations. Chicano cultural nationalism also set forth an embrace of Mexican culture, extolling deep pride in Mexican history, and ultimately set in motion a great renaissance in Chicano artistic and literary expression.[8]

Amid a political and cultural ideology that celebrated indigenous roots, rejected assimilation, and glorified masculinist traditions, Chicanas defined their own experiences and political and cultural ideologies, including resistance to gender discrimination. They formed student support and political groups such as Las Hijas de Cuauhtémoc (the Daughters of Cuauhtémoc), established at California State University, Long Beach, in the late 1960s, and the Comisión Femenil Mexicana Nacional (the National Mexican Women's Commission) in 1970, a political and economic advocacy group that still exists today; they also established newspapers such as *La Razón Mestiza* devoted to Chicana and Latina issues. During this period, Chicanas grappled with the difficulty of merging cultural nationalism with feminism and integrating what were deemed women's issues such as reproductive rights, sexism, child care, welfare reform, and equality in leadership as core issues within the Chicano movement as a whole. Chicana feminists, like the movimiento itself, did not constitute a unified political or ideological front. They also met consistent and sometimes harsh resistance from both men and other women activists in the movement.

Those Mexican American women who attended the IWY Tribune ultimately engaged the process of identity formation on a new level, an international one. They expected to have a natural bond with Third World women, especially Mexican women. At this critical moment, however, Chicanas who attended the Tribune had to come to terms with the fact that culturally they were American, as much as or more than they were Mexican. Despite this shocking realization, for most, attendance at the conference also validated the struggle they waged at home. They came away from the Tribune with a more global understanding of women's oppression and their own place in world politics.

Chicanas' experiences in networking and collaborating with women from around the world radically changed neither their beliefs nor their organizing strategies back home. Experiences in Mexico City, however, galvanized these Mexican American women to act locally and nationally in light of their newfound international bonds. Their experiences also coincided with other transformations in the Chicano movement itself. The mid-1970s witnessed a shift in the orientation of Chicana/o activist ideology. Questions of transnational solidarity and identification with Mexicans in Mexico arose as well as the establishment of networks with other Latino/a and other ethnic/racial groups. The IWY Conference also laid the groundwork for the U.S. International Women's Year Conference held in Houston, Texas, in 1977. In Houston, members of the Comisión Femenil Mexicana Nacional who had attended the IWY Tribune began to organize for what they believed was the proper representation for all U.S. Latinas and eventually built strong coalitions that culminated in the majority at the Texas meeting passing the Minority Women's Plank.

The Historical Context of International Feminism

Although Chicano and women's studies have proliferated in the historical literature over the past two decades, few address the international connections among activists that have arisen since World War II. As historian Leila Rupp wrote in 1997, "historians in general seem to have clung so tenaciously to topics defined by the nation-state that international organizations of any kind have been left to the political scientists."[9] Yet it was due to decades of organizing and lobbying by women active in international politics that women's equality with men became part of the U.N. charter of 1945, and a year later the U.N. Commission on the Status of Women was founded. Rupp argues that this first wave of activism "links the pre-1945 international women's movement to what might otherwise seem the 'emergence' of such a movement in the 1970s."[10]

Scholars in the fields of international relations, women's history, sociology, and political science agree that the 1975 U.N. conference in Mexico City, which launched the "Decade of Women" and established the foundation for subsequent world conferences in 1980 and 1985, provided a base for the formation of international feminist networks, especially through the establishment of the International Women's Tribune Center. The 1975 U.N. conference also became the stage that revealed a struggle between First and Third World women over the intersections of economics and women's issues. A major fissure in an international consensus on feminism and women's rights appeared as those from the

First World stressed equal rights while their counterparts from the Third World stressed the impact of economics and colonialism.[11]

Despite these conflicts, most scholars agree that through its initiation and support of women's conferences, the United Nations has been instrumental in fomenting international feminism. From the formation of the Commission on the Status of Women in 1947 to the most recent U.N.-sponsored women's world conference in Beijing in 1995, the establishment of transnational networks has been a fundamental step in movements for equality worldwide. In addition, the consciousness-raising effects on women at each world conference, specifically Mexico City, allowed female participants to perceive the roots and effects of their social, economic, and cultural oppression.[12]

The Road to Mexico City

Like Celia Herrera Rodríguez, Chicanas found out about the U.N. conference from networks established among women activists across California. Those who attended tended to be interested in feminist issues and involved in organizations concerned with such matters. For some, pure excitement, curiosity, and optimism about changing the world propelled them to participate in the first international women's conference. Yolanda López, at the time a master's student in fine arts at the University of California, San Diego, and newsletter editor for the Chicano Federation in San Diego, remembered: "I was . . . bright eyed and bushy tailed. I thought there was going to be great stuff. We'd go there and meet Mexican women and meet other women and change the situation for women. We thought, at least I did, that we would go down there and be part of the great audience there and actually begin to, you know, make policy for the U.N. regarding women."[13]

Other women viewed the conference in less idealistic terms. More informed about the processes of the IWY Conference itself, these women traveled to Mexico City because they did not believe the U.S. government would appoint people like themselves as official delegates. "I knew there was going to be a conference and I made up my mind—I was going to be a member," recalled Connie Pardo, a member of the Comisión Femenil in Los Angeles and a longtime activist. "We could only be members of the . . . non-governmental [meeting], because you know, our government wasn't going to pick on somebody like me with my background. . . . So we went."[14]

In addition to general excitement and issues of representation, that the conference was scheduled in Mexico City intrigued many Chicanas. To attend such a meeting in the Mexican capital merged two basic values held by Chicanas interested in women's issues. First, they would meet and connect with women from the world over, expecting to share a common sisterhood. They especially believed that Mexico City would allow them to connect with Mexican feminists and to establish common ground in their respective struggles. Sandra Serrano Sewell, at the time a homemaker and member of the Comisión Femenil, stated, "We thought, oh, yeah, we're Mexican Americans. . . . we're going to find all this natural connections, you know, and sort of like a romantic view that was quickly dispelled."[15]

Second, Mexico constituted part of their cultural and spiritual roots. To be sure, many Chicanas would not have attended had the conference taken place in Europe, Asia, or any other distant land. Mexico City was a close geographical destination, and most Chicanas who attended either spoke Spanish or at least had a rudimentary understanding of it. They could therefore easily navigate the city once they arrived and did not need translators. Although many of them took issue with the masculinist aspects of Chicano nationalism, their experiences in the movement led them to believe in Mexico as a homeland. Dorinda Moreno from Concilio Mujeres, a San Francisco–based organization, avowed, "Raza women should not be invisible, since this conference is going to be held in our motherland. This was the Mestiza's continent, from Alaska to the Patagonia, and she should be the most known."[16] Such views resemble the later analysis of literary critic Sheila Contreras, who finds that for activists of both sexes, "The tie to Mexico is filial—one of kinship, blood ties, and a shared history of conquest and oppression. The idea of Mexico exudes comfort; it feels like *home*. When you are on *this* side that is."[17] Pinpointing the classic conundrum of their identity itself, Contreras identifies nostalgia for the homeland of Mexico as occurring only within the borders of United States. Upon travel to Mexico, most Chicanas and Chicanos, like those who attended the conference, realize that expectations of home or kinship do not always materialize.

The Chicanas who attended the Mexico City conference were relatively privileged and included college and graduate students, businesswomen, political activists, artists, and writers. Their ages ranged from the late teens to early sixties. They had the financial resources or the ability to attain the funding for travel; and most were educated beyond high school and worked as professionals or aspired to such careers. If they were not formally educated, most Chicanas who attended brought years of experience in community work and organizing.

Although Chicanas from throughout the United States attended the

IWY Conference, it is unsurprising that the largest numbers of them came from California and Texas, where most Mexican American political activity was occurring. Most women who traveled to the conference were already politically engaged and attended in groups and as delegates of their respective organizations, including the Organización Chicana from the University of California, Los Angeles, the Comisión Femenil Mexicana Nacional, Poder Femenino, the Chicana Service Action Center, La Raza Unida Party, and the Chicano Federation in San Diego. From Texas, the most visible and the largest group of women represented La Raza Unida Party, the Chicano third party.[18] Approximately 100 to 150 California Chicanas traveled to Mexico City.[19]

Attending the Tribune required a certain dedication to activism and a commitment of time and resources. Chicanas organized to fund their transportation, arrange for child care, and make the other necessary arrangements to travel to Mexico City. Many Chicana students obtained funding from their student body governments or used their financial aid or welfare funds. For example, the Organización Chicana of the University of California, Los Angeles, obtained funds from both the student government and the Chicano Studies Research Center, so that a group of six women could attend. In return, the women promised to document their experiences with slides, videotape, and audiotape and through the pamphlets and handouts they would collect at the conference.[20] Chicanas who were not students or who did not have this avenue of fundraising, like Celia Herrera Rodríguez and Frances Romero, saved their own earnings to attend. Women who were members of the Comisión Femenil, many of whom were young professionals, as well as those who did not work for pay outside the home, financed their own travel.[21]

The IWY Tribune

The IWY Tribune took place at the Convention Hall of the National Medical Center of Mexico City, across town from the official IWY Conference. Because this dual IWY conference was the first of its kind, most women had no idea what to expect upon arrival in the city. Although the Tribune occurred simultaneously with the official conference, participants of the Tribune had no prospect of addressing the official meeting, at which 1,300 delegates from 130 countries assembled to discuss a World Plan of Action, already drafted by the Secretariat of the United Nations.[22] The World Plan of Action, which was adopted by national delegations to the official conference, proposed guidelines for both government and nongovernment groups to promote the goals of equality, development, and peace. In addition, the official meeting adopted the Declaration of Mexico, which is best known for equating Zionism with racism, which the United States, Israel, and Canada opposed.[23]

Most of the arriving Chicanas assumed that there would be one conference, which everyone who had traveled to Mexico City would be able to attend in order to propose resolutions and changes to the World Plan of Action. Most were shocked to find that they were not able to enter the official U.N. conference and could attend only the Tribune. In fact, many of the Chicanas did not know that the Tribune was not the official U.N. conference. As one Chicana attendee stated, "most of the women who were there as observers or individuals were sort of in awe of the whole bigger question and the official UN stuff."[24]

The Tribune, organized by Mildred Persinger and Rosalind Harris, both from the United States and appointed by the U.N. Commission on the Status of Women, was financially backed with $225,000 from more than twelve sources, including the Ford Foundation, John D. Rockefeller III, the Gulf Oil Corporation, the Government of Norway, and the Canadian International Development Agency.[25] A total of 2,500 representatives of NGOs, along with another 2,500 or so independent women, attended the Tribune. Of the 5,000 participants at the IWY Tribune, one-third came from Latin America, one-third from North America, and one-third from Europe, with eighty-two countries represented.[26]

Attendees at the IWY Tribune included leaders of local and national women's organizations, individual legislators, judges, lawyers, female educators, members of professional associations, provocateurs (individuals hired by governments or groups to purposely disrupt the gathering), and members of the media.[27] From the United States, women represented a diversity of groups, including the League of Women Voters, the International Lesbian Caucus, Baha'i International, the American Association of University Women, Amnesty International, the YWCA, the World Population Society, trade unions, and International Planned Parenthood.[28] Chicanas represented approximately 5 to 10 percent of the participants.[29]

Harris and Persinger had planned a structured program of twenty-five Tribune sessions organized in concert with the themes of the IWY, including the family, peace and disarmament, women in public life, women at work, education, law and the status of women, and health and nutrition. *Xilonen*, the Tribune newspaper, reflected this format in its daily calendar. After a group of American feminists took over a meeting at the U.S. Embassy on June 21, 1975, to complain about what they thought was too rigid a conference structure, the organizers added a lunchtime "global speak-out" and informal "rap sessions" to the daily agenda.[30] In addition to these two added events, by the fifth day of the conference the posted sessions in *Xilonen* more than tripled, with presentations scheduled at least every half-hour from 9:00 A.M. to 9:30 P.M. Accordingly, over the span of twelve days, women at the Tribune could attend more than 300 presentations as diverse as "Women across Cultures," "U.S. Coalition for Life," and "National Committee of Household Workers/Trade Unions Africa."[31] Chicanas appeared on the agenda after the change in structure: On June 24, they led a session entitled "Mujeres Chicanas del Partido Raza Unida" (Chicana Women from the Raza Unida Party) and on June 26, a session entitled "National Chicana Coalition."[32]

Political Fault Lines

At both the official conference and the Tribune, a central question emerged that paralleled the struggle Chicana feminists faced at home: What was to come first, national liberation and world economic justice, or women's rights? In the Chicano movement, women had faced a similar question: Chicano liberation first or Chicana liberation? For many women participating in both the Tribune and official conferences, the battle lines were drawn between those who came from First World countries, who stressed women's rights, and those who came from Third World countries, who stressed national liberation and economic justice.[33] Despite the fact that many Chicanas who attended the Tribune stressed liberation for themselves at home as part and parcel of the liberation of Chicanos as a whole, at the meeting, they found themselves aligning with Third World women, who stressed that women's equality could not come about without a change in the world economic order, or in other words, a redistribution of the world's wealth.

At the Tribune the conflict between economic development and women's rights became personal as women from the United States became targets for anti-American sentiments. For example, at one of the informal "speak-outs" at the Tribune, a woman from India, identifying herself as a resident of a developing nation, couched American mainstream feminism as the "psychological liberation of Western women." She went on to say, "If you American ladies paid more attention to the imperialist economic policies of your government, women throughout the world would not have to worry about such unfashionable problems as starvation and homelessness."[34]

Many U.S. women of color, including Chicanas, found themselves in the uncomfortable and ironic situation of being labeled Americans, but desiring greater political alignment with Third World women. This dilemma caused many women of color to refine their views. They continued to voice political ideologies more in line with those from Third World nations. For example, the delegation from the Texas Raza Unida Party, one of the few Chicana groups to hold a panel session at the Tribune, described the situation of Chicanas in the terms of internal colonialism as well as gender discrimination.[35] Internal colonialism for them meant that they saw the process by which they became Mexican Americans as one of conquest and colonization of Mexico by the United States. Thus, like those who lived in colonized nations, Chicanos and Chicanas lived as second-class citizens in their own land.[36]

The divisions at the Tribune did not stop at the conflict between rich and poor nations, for the contingent from the United States had its own internal divisions. Three separate disagreements surfaced. First, many women, especially women of color from the United States, did not feel that their country's official delegation adequately represented them. Second, these women of color felt that high-profile U.S. feminists at the Tribune did not speak for them. Third, many women at the Tribune felt that U.S. feminists were trying to monopolize the conference with their views.

These fault lines materialized in Mexico City because of the nature of the conference. The IWY Tribune served as a tangible representation of the world on a slightly more manageable level. For the fourteen days of the event, women from across the globe met each other in one central location and on a smaller scale so that particular national issues also came to light. When women from different regions of the United States met in a central location, tensions that already existed between mainstream feminists and Chicanas rose to the surface.

Many encounters between Chicanas and Euro-American feminists struck a familiar chord of disharmony. To Chicanas, mainstream feminists insisted on a gender-only agenda and positioned themselves as all-knowing on global and feminist issues. This type of contact occurred at two distinct levels: between Chicanas and the official U.S. delegation to the U.N. conference, and between Chicanas and mainstream Euro-American feminists at the Tribune.

Chicana relations with the official U.S. delegation to the U.N. Conference were tenuous, at best. Like many other U.S. women of color at the Tribune, Chicanas felt that "their" national delegation to the official IWY Conference did not represent their views. Because the official delegation was made up of forty-three people appointed by U.S. Secretary of State Henry Kissinger, Chicanas took issue with its makeup and political standpoint. The delegation had two chairpersons, Daniel Parker, head of the Agency for International Development, and Patricia Hutar, U.S. representative to the U.N. Economic and Social Council's Commission on the Status of Women and former vice chair of the Republican Party.[37] Yolanda López, a Chicana Tribune attendee from San Diego, California, later wrote, "The U.S. delegation was in a sense a true representation of U.S. policy and our international posture—but in no way is it a true representation of American women."[38] Bea Vásquez Robinson, a Chicana from San Jose, California, wrote, "The IWY Conference in Mexico City once again exemplified too few (and too white) making decisions for too many. Our country's delegation was a farce. Women were appointed with little or no regard given to their knowledge of and expertise in the problems facing the doubly oppressed women in this country. Their backgrounds could in no way give them any insight into the concerns and issues of the minority or poor woman. They represented as usual the white, middle- and upper-class woman. Even the token minority was representative of that class."[39]

In the estimation of Chicanas, the U.S. delegation consisted of women, and one man, who served the interests of the government. As minority women who believed that the unjust lot of their people rested in large part on the action (or inaction) of the U.S. government, they obviously did not feel that these delegates could ever represent their views. Chicanas also believed that middle-class women on the official delegation could not represent them because, regardless of professional status in the United States, these Chicanas still viewed themselves as working-class women of color.

As a result, Chicanas began to organize on two fronts. First, to voice their discontent with the Tribune and the official U.S. delegation, Chicanas joined with African American and Latin American women under the name the Coalition of Unrepresented Women (CUW). The women in the group drafted a set of demands in which they protested the makeup of the U.S. delegation and voiced their frustration with the organization of the Tribune itself. At a press conference held by the official U.S. delegation on June 21, the coalition disrupted the meeting and called for the primacy of issues of race and class in regard to any feminist position. In this sense, many U.S. women of color concurred with the position of Third World women that economic equality needed to be addressed.[40]

The Coalition of Unrepresented Women demanded that minority women be "given immediate and equal representation on the United States delegation on the Presidential Advisory Commission on International Women's Year" and that the United States delegation "admit

182 of MARISELA R. CHÁVEZ

to and correct the political, economic, and social injustices that pre-vail in the United States." To be able to voice their political views, the CUW also wanted a time slot for a panel presentation where they could "expose and discuss the issues of racism, discrimination, economic exploitation, human rights and the oppression of women in the United States and throughout the world" and a conference room open at all times equipped with translation services and a public address system to discuss the same issues.[41]

The demands made by the CUW echoed sentiments in a call to action issued by Latin American women for a meeting at the Tribune to discuss issues of class, race, economic independence, and sexual repression. According to these women, the Tribune should have been discussing economics and their relationship to women's daily experiences, which they saw as more of an issue than any feminist ideologies. They thus called for a more profound discussion of the issues and needs of women worldwide that would result in "concrete and permanent action." They also supported "structural changes on an internal and international level to propagate an effective transformation of the woman's condition in all social groups."[42] Mainstream U.S. feminists, however, saw this position as antifeminist because they feared that emphasizing economics or race would ultimately make those issues take precedence over gender. Thus, many times, women who called attention to race and economics were accused of being the enemy, or the puppet of men. In some cases, they were correct in that some delegates were in fact speaking the party lines of male leaders.

According to U.S. mainstream feminists, economics was a male paradigm. For example, Carole De Saram stated, "The true issues, the problems of women, are being forgotten here. Instead this conference is concentrating on political issues that represent the male mentality. The direction here is not coming from women, it's coming from men."[43] For women like De Saram, it seemed that there could be no merger between political and economic issues and the "problems of women." By trying to separate women's issues from economic or political issues, supporters of De Saram's position focused only on issues of gender, which stemmed from an inherent belief in universal sisterhood—gender issues or problems were the most important, or the only issues for women of the world. This view permeated even press coverage of the meetings. Barbara Cady, a reporter for the *Los Angeles Times,* wrote "Unfortunately, far too few women attending the United Nations International Women's Year Conference in Mexico City had come primarily as females. . . . In fact, their femaleness often seemed completely irrelevant to their intentions."[44]

As evident from these statements, a classic component of the women's movement in general played itself out at the Tribune. De Saram, Cady, Friedan, and others assumed that women could, in essence, check their race, ethnicity, class, nationality, and language at the door and assume positions only as females. De Saram and Cady, for example, could not understand how any woman could fail to concentrate solely on women's issues and thus considered all women who did not agree with their line of reasoning as obviously led by men. They positioned themselves as the true representatives of all women and criticized the others as antifeminist or as puppets of men. While it has been documented that many female representatives of national governments at the conference did, indeed, participate as "spokesmen" for their governments and many times aired opinions that privileged economics at the expense of women's individual rights, U.S. mainstream feminists did not, and possibly could not, differentiate between these women and their compatriots who called for attention to the intersections of race, class, and gender. In this way, mainstream U.S. feminists engaged in what Angela Gilliam calls "sexualism," an ideology that focuses on sex and sexuality at the expense of economics and politics.[45] By emphasizing gender oppression to judge all women in measuring their commitment to women, mainstream U.S. feminists insulted Chicana and African American participants at IWY by accusing them of being antifeminists. It did not occur to mainstream feminists that Chicana, African American, and Third World women did not have the privilege of a solely gendered perspective because of the salience of race and class in their lives.

The second level of organizing occurred solely within Chicana circles at the Tribune. With concerns similar to those of the Coalition of Unrepresented Women, Chicanas met as a group under the name the National Chicana Coalition. Bea Vásquez Robinson, from northern California, who organized the meeting, wrote, "It was very spontaneous," she recalled. "I was really disgusted with the whole conference." At the meeting, approximately 250 to 300 Chicanas raised their complaints with the Tribune and the official U.S. delegation, and as a result, the National Chicana Coalition formed several groups to address these issues. At a meeting of the U.S. delegation at the Tribune, Chicanas forced their way to the podium and articulated their complaints and demands. After this takeover the National Chicana Coalition received an audience with the U.S. delegation.[46] As a result of this meeting and the actions of the Coalition of Unrepresented Women, some Chicanas believed they effected changes in the World Plan of Action. For example, Ada Peña, a Chicana from Texas, echoed the sentiments of many California Chicanas when she stated, "In some of the amendments to it, the Plan reflects our input, like when they mention involvement or discrimination referring to women of minority groups, blacks or women of an ethnic background."[47]

Class and race also came to the fore as women of color took issue with U.S. feminist superstars at the Tribune, such as Betty Friedan and Gloria Steinem, who became the voice of American women for the media. A longstanding refrain, Chicanas felt that mainstream feminists voiced the concerns of middle-class Euro-American women. As Ada Peña put it, "Personally, I do not feel that Betty Friedan represents the women's movement in the United States. I feel she has made many inroads, but she has projected the middle-class white woman. Her presentation to the Tribune came as middle-class white women and made no mention of minorities."[48]

An example of what may have angered Peña occurred at one of the many press conferences held by Friedan. Friedan, who, like Steinem, was one of the few women at the Tribune to command the media's attention, protested that she welcomed the separate organizations of African American and Chicana women, but her comments revealed a general ignorance about such organizations and women of color in the United States: Although black women and Chicanas had founded separate organizations in the late 1960s, Friedan called the groups new. She stated that the women's movement had been the only social movement to survive from the 1960s to the 1970s and then stated, "but now, there is a new development of a separate Chicano feminist women group and black feminist and they are increasingly uniting in the old raw women's movement which is so very large now that you cannot possibly look at it in terms of one organization alone."[49] Yet Friedan's comments reflect that she saw the roles of Chicana and African American women's organizations as late arrivals to the women's movement, sharing the same agenda. Chicanas therefore saw Friedan as misinformed and, indeed, dangerous because she presented her misinformation as truth to an international audience. It was one thing to be ignored by the official delegation, a government-appointed one, but to be ignored by women who professed to be speaking for all women reinforced the disillusionment Chicanas had already felt at home.

Chicanas and International Realizations

Through their participation at the Tribune, Chicanas gained three insights on international feminism. First, listening to and meeting women from all over the world gave them the sense that women's oppression was universal. Second, they realized their relative nearsightedness in regard to their struggle in the United States and in doing so, some realized the multiplicity of women's issues in different areas of the world. Finally, meeting so many women actively engaged in bettering women's lives validated their own activism.

As Chicanas conversed with women from around the world at the panels and presentations, they began to think more globally about common issues. They began to feel a bond with international women on the basis of gender and began to transcend national and ethnic identity. Yet this bond differed from the universalist approach they had often heard from mainstream U.S. feminists. While Chicanas came to believe that discrimination and oppression against women were universal phenomena, they held fast to the belief that race, class, and ethnicity had definite and tangible effects on how these phenomena affected the women of the world, including themselves. Their experiences at the Tribune therefore solidified their beliefs.

For many of the California Chicanas who attended, the realizations about women's oppression called into question their ideological stance on what it meant to be a Chicana. For most Chicanas who attended the Tribune, having that identity meant that you believed in social, economic, and political justice for Chicanas *and* Chicanos. In other words, they were part of a larger struggle. At the conference, they came to see that they had to question their beliefs not only in regard to gender but also in regard to the so-called Chicano movement itself. For example, general Tribune panels addressed topics such as attitude formation and socialization process, law and the status of women, population and development with a focus on women and children, women at work, and the family.[50] In a 2002 interview, Corinne Sánchez remembered that the larger panels made her "realize the things I was experiencing—barriers, discrimination— . . . were not barrio at all, they were universal."[51] Reflecting on the conversations and interactions she had with Latin American women at the Tribune and how they affected her, Celia Herrera Rodríguez said that she realized that "It was not just North America and that we as Chicanas were part of a huge, big history and big struggle and I think that was clear. . . . we had our issues that resonated, that had place, that had purpose, that had a history. I think all that became manifested within that milieu of all of those women."[52]

In addition, Chicanas came to see that issues of gender in their own struggle could not be appendages, but had to take center stage together with racial, ethnic, and class discrimination. A presentation that had a great impact on the Mexican American women was by Domitila Barrios de Chungara, a Bolivian tin miner's wife and organizer against her country's repressive government, who had been jailed for her activities. In Mexico City, Barrios de Chungara spoke of her experiences and thoughts about feminism, which linked the issue of women's oppression to economics and social justice. The only goal was not equal rights for women, she claimed. She instead argued for a women's liberation that included "women being respected as human beings, who can solve problems and participate in everything. . . . a liberation that means our opinion is respected at home and outside the home."[53] For Yolanda López, Barrios de Chungara's presentation "just totally imbued me with the idea that dealing with gender was the next frontier as far as how we were going to revolutionize, not only our society, but also our political agenda."[54]

Although experiences in the Chicano movement had shown these women that gender had to be addressed, the Tribune gave them many visible examples of other women who were on the same path. This opened a whole new world for Chicanas, who at the meetings realized that they had been almost insular in their own struggles. In addition, the Latin American participants inspired the Chicana activists and broadened their struggle. Because many of the struggles of these international women seemed more drastic because of the repressive governments they faced, Chicanas gained a sense of hope in their country, one that at least practiced its democratic ideals to some extent. They therefore felt inspired that they might be able to work and achieve what they wanted at home.

The second presentation that strongly influenced Chicanas at the conference was given by Chilean women and took place on June 26. It was what happened at the panel, rather than what was said, made the impact on Chicanas. During a discussion on Mexican women, Anna Nieto Gómez recalled, "troops came into [the room], it was an oval room. And we were in the middle, so troops with rifles, infantry, came around and raised the rifles and they told us that the meeting was over and that we had to leave immediately or else we'd get arrested."[55] For women like Nieto Gómez, this experience was important in two ways. First, she realized that living in the United States protected her from being apprehended by the military, and that her political activities, however antigovernment or antiestablishment, did not necessarily put her in danger of being arrested and incarcerated. Second, she realized the degree of commitment of women in countries like Chile, who actually did put themselves on the line because of what they believed. "The rights that we were exercising to protest the wrongs in the United States," Nieto Gomez explained, "weren't even rights that people had in a lot of countries, women didn't have."[56]

The lack of rights in other countries made Nieto Gómez and the other Chicanas who attended the meetings realize that they had to come to terms with their identities as American citizens and all the privileges that came along with this status. Although police brutality, police and FBI infiltration, false arrests, and general harassment had plagued the Chicano movement, Mexican Americans, except those serving in Vietnam, never had to face the prospect of egregious torture or the possibility of military arrest for their antigovernment actions. Therefore, while Chicanas may have expected to find natural connections and bonds with other Third World women, they never expected to appreciate the privilege of U.S. citizenship.

American identity, however, also brought with it the unexpected experience of being associated with Euro-American feminists such as Betty Friedan and with the United States government. At odds with the picture of American women that Friedan painted, and adamant about educating others at the IWY Tribune about themselves as Chicanas, these women became de facto ambassadors for their people as a whole. In explaining their own identity, Chicanas gained affinity with other Third World women. Corinne Sánchez explained: "So our whole banner was, we're fighting oppression, we're fighting for self-determination and we call this Chicano. We are not Mexican Americans."[57] Although some Chicanas may not have felt themselves representatives of the United States, they became so in the sense that they provided an alternative view of the country to other women.

In other circumstances, however, being identified as Americans caused negative reactions and challenges from Third World women. As Nieto Gómez remembered, the "first thing that we always confronted was when they met us, they met us as Americans, people of the United States, and [asked] what were we doing about United States foreign policy."[58] Most Mexican American women attending the meetings saw U.S. foreign policy in a negative light because of their experiences and views on the Vietnam War, the high percentage of Mexican American men who died in the conflict, and the repression exerted on antiwar protesters by law enforcement. Many of the women they met in Mexico City had other foreign policy concerns, especially the need for economic aid. Besides the U.S. neglect of economic aid for many Third World countries, the attempted Americanization of those nations also gave rise to antagonism. For Chicanas, it proved ironic that they were held responsible for U.S. foreign policy decisions, when they themselves felt that they were struggling against very similar policies.

Although attendance at the meetings does not seem to have radically altered belief systems, conference participation reinforced Chicana views on the importance of gender in their own country and gave them a broader perspective on how their struggle fit into the world. Connie Pardo, who was in her mid-forties when she attended the meetings, remembered: "It fit my sense of internationalism where women are concerned and it fit my sense of internationalism vis-à-vis the class struggle."[59] The Tribune gave many proof that they were not alone in their struggle.

While their perspectives became more global and more complex, the world Chicanas returned to after the 1975 International Women's Year Conference had not changed. In 1977 the Comisión Femenil expanded its reach into the national political arena after the gathering in Mexico City. The 1977 National Women's Conference, held in Houston, Texas, was the U.S. effort to recognize the International Decade of Women sponsored by the United Nations. Bolstered by the U.N. Plan of Action that was passed in Mexico City, nations across the world were to enact their own visions.

Because Chicanas, especially from California, felt disenfranchised at the 1975 meetings in Mexico City because of the separation between the official U.N. Conference and the Tribune, women from the Comisión Femenil made a point of becoming involved in the National Women's Conference in Houston. The conference in Houston was scheduled from November 18 through November 21, 1977, prior to which each state held its own preconference meeting. California's meeting, which 6,500 women attended, was held from June 17 through June 19 in Los Angeles.[60] At this meeting, the California women elected their delegates for Houston, totaling 96. Of these, 19, or almost 20 percent, were of Spanish surname and 4 were members of the Comisión Femenil.[61] In late August the Comisión Femenil had begun its planning for travel and participation. In October the organization planned a general membership meeting to discuss the Houston event and to disseminate logistical information. In addition, the October meeting would address possible Chicana resolutions to propose or support in Houston, as well as consider what general role the Comisión Femenil would play.[62]

As a result of this planning, at the Houston conference the Comisión Femenil was 1 of 4 Latina organizations with official display booths out of a total of 158 booths.[63] Staffed daily by Comisión Femenil members, the booth provided a brochure published by the organization that gave basic information about the group, established a message center for Latinas, and provided a calendar of events specifically for them at the conference. The brochure, entitled *La Mujer: International Women's Year 1977*, articulated Comisión Femenil's vision of itself. Highlighting the historic nature of the conference and of Latina participation, the brochure went on to say that the comisión supported "all women's issues" and the "National Plan of Action." But in supporting these aims, the Comisión Femenil also wanted to "insure the input of Hispanic women and their concerns." The brochure highlighted the three Latinas who sat on the national planning committee and the Latina vice chair to the California delegation, Grace Montañez Davis, a Comisión Femenil member and also deputy mayor of Los Angeles. The brochure concluded by articulating a notion of sisterhood. It stated, "During these four days, as the national focus is upon us, let us show the cariños [caring], support and lasting unity that we have for one another. Las Mujeres de California [the women of California]."[64]

As a testament to the Comisión Femenil's proactive stance and co-alition building at the Houston conference, the president of the national organization at the time, Sandra Serrano Sewell, stood on stage on the last day with Ana María Perera of the National Association of Cuban Women and Celeste Benítez, senator from Puerto Rico and chair of the Puerto Rican delegation, to present the Hispanic women's plank as part of the Minority Women's Plank to the entire gathering. The latter plank was the only resolution to be passed by the conference unanimously.[65] The Minority Women's Plank represented work by Latina, African American, Asian American, and Native American women. Serrano Sewell recollected the Comisión Femenil's position at the conference, "we were a much more sophisticated organization by that time and, you know, knew how to flex our weight, and knew how to intimidate, and knew how to articulate. And so our sophistication level had just grown so much that we were able to change—the part of changing the minority women's plank."[66] As Comisión Femenil reported in its conference newsletter, "The unity demonstrated among all minority women was unprecedented. Even Bella Abzug, presiding officer, was inspired to comment that the unity among all the minority women was the most impressive ever at a feminist convention."[67] These actions resulted in the Comisión Femenil's becoming recognized as the national organization representative of Mexican American women.[68]

In an ongoing effort for more visibility for the organization, as well as for Chicanas in general, the Comisión Femenil continued to attend international conferences. In 1980 members attended the International Women's Conference in Copenhagen, this time as a nongovernmental organization affiliated with the United Nations, which allowed the organization to hold an official panel session and to set up an official booth to distribute information. Once again, the Comisión Femenil published a newsletter for the conference.[69] Serrano Sewell remembered about Copenhagen: "And when you have a booth, and when you print information, and when you have things to hand out, and when you put together your fact sheets and when you do all those things you make other women aware of who you are. My belief is that when we were in Mexico City we were probably—other women thought we were just Mexicans. And so, you're just in a different ballgame."[70]

Conclusion

In 1975 when California Chicanas traveled to Mexico City for the first International Women's Conference, most arrived with a political ideology framed by cultural nationalism and a U.S.-specific awareness of racial, economic, political, and gendered oppression. Within the Chicano movement, they had attempted to amalgamate cultural nationalism and feminism and had forged various methods of achieving this goal, such as working within existing organizations, founding periodicals, and establishing Chicana specific organizations, such as the Comisión Femenil Mexicana Nacional. In Mexico City, Chicanas took their struggle into an international realm. In the milieu of the meetings in Mexico itself, in their interactions with women from across the world, and in the information they received, these women began to recognize their U.S. American identity. Thus, while they began to understand the global nature of women's oppression, and their own place in world politics, their attendance at the U.N. meetings also confirmed that their struggle at home was important. Their experiences revealed that they could think of themselves as part of a worldwide movement of women while they worked on issues at home. By 1977 many of the attendees at the meetings in Mexico City worked to ensure their representation at the women's conference in Houston, the U.S. program for International Women's Year. Realizing the strength of coalition building, Chicanas worked with other U.S. women of color to pass the Minority Women's Plank at the conference. In addition, the Comisión Femenil Mexicana Nacional became a nongovernmental organization affiliated with the United Nations and thus maintained an international presence at the subsequent conference for International Women's Year in Copenhagen. Chicana experiences and the Chicano/a movement itself have been categorized as local, regional, and insular. Yet Chicanas who attended the first International Women's Year Conference and Tribune in Mexico City defy that categorization, and study of their experiences thus opens broader geopolitical directions for the investigation of Chicana lives.

Notes

1. Celia Herrera Rodríguez, interview by author, October 10, 2002, Oakland, Calif.

2. See Leila J. Rupp, *Worlds of Women: The Making of an International Women's Movement* (Princeton, N.J.: Princeton University Press, 1997); Virginia R. Allan, Margaret E. Galey, and Mildred E. Persinger, "World Conference of International Women's Year," in *Women, Politics, and the United Nations*, edited by Anne Winslow (Westport, Conn.: Greenwood Press, 1995), 29; and Estelle B. Freedman, *No Turning Back: The History of Feminism and the Future of Women* (New York: Ballantine Books, 2002), 107.

3. For a discussion of foreign travel by activists in the Chicano movement, see Elizabeth Martínez, *De Colores Means All of Us: Latina Views for a Multi-Colored Century* (Cambridge, Mass.: South End Press, 1997).

4. Vicki L. Ruiz, *From Out of the Shadows: Mexican Women in Twentieth-Century America* (New York: Oxford University Press, 1998), 108.

5. I use the term *Third World*, following the work of Cheryl Johnson-Odim, to mean the following: to identify "underdeveloped" and "overexploited geopolitical entities," such as nations and regions; and to identify those who live in or come from said nations and regions. I use the term *women of color* to identify non-European and non-Euro-American women who believed that race, gender, and class directly had a negative impact on their lives. "Women of color" is to be used with its appropriate national signifier, such as U.S. women of color. See Cheryl Johnson-Odim, "Common Themes, Different Contexts: Third World Women and Feminism," in *Third World Women and the Politics of Feminism*, edited by Chandra Talpade Mohanty, Ann Ruso, and Lourdes Torres (Bloomington: Indiana University Press, 1991).

6. On Aztlán, see John R. Chávez, *The Lost Land: The Chicano Image of the Southwest* (Albuquerque: University of New Mexico Press, 1984).

7. Ernesto Chávez, *Mi Raza Primero: Nationalism, Identity, and Insurgency in the Chicano Movement in Los Angeles, 1966–1978* (Berkeley: University of California Press, 2002).

8. Ernesto Chávez, "Creating Aztlán: The Chicano Movement in Los Angeles, 1966–1978" (Ph.D. diss., University of California, Los Angeles, 1994), 3–5; also see Chávez, *Mi Raza Primero*.

9. Rupp, *Worlds of Women*, 4. For a discussion of the effects of Chicana/o politics on foreign policy, see Lorena Oropeza, "La Batalla Está Aquí: Chicanos Oppose the War in Vietnam" (Ph.D. diss., Cornell University, 1996).

10. Rupp, *Worlds of Women*, 223–24, specific quotation on 224; Margaret E. Galey, "Promoting Nondiscrimination against Women: The UN Commission on the Status of Women," *International Studies Quarterly* 23 (June 1979): 275. Galey identifies 1947 as the founding year of the Commission on the Status of Women.

11. See Jane S. Jaquette, "Losing the Battle/Winning the War: International Politics, Women's Issues, and the 1980 Mid-Decade Conference," in Winslow, *Women, Politics, and the United Nations*, 45–49; Estelle B. Freedman, *No Turning Back: The History of Feminism and the Future of Women* (New York: Ballantine, 2002), especially ch. 5; Johnson-Odim, "Common Themes," and Angela

Gilliam, "Women's Equality and National Liberation," both in Mohanty, Ruso, and Torres, *Third World Women*; as well as Ruth Rosen, *The World Split Open: How the Modern Women's Movement Changed America* (New York: Penguin Books, 2000), epilogue.

12. See Allan, Galey, and Persinger, "World Conference," 29, 34–39; Jaquette, "Losing the Battle/Winning the War," 56; and Margaret E. Galey, "The Nairobi Conference: The Powerless Majority," *Political Science* 19 (Spring 1986): 255–65.

13. Yolanda M López, interview by author, March 15, 2002, Los Angeles, Calif.

14. Connie Pardo, interview by author, March 29, 2002, Los Angeles, Calif.

15. Sandra Serrano Sewell, interview by author, March 14, 2002, Los Angeles, Calif.

16. "Announcements," *Women's New Journal* (June 1975): 11.

17. Sheila Marie Contreras, "Blood Lines: Modernism, Indigenismo, and the Construction of Chicana/o Identity" (Ph.D. diss., University of Texas at Austin, 1998), 193, emphasis in original.

18. Organización Chicana of UCLA was a student group; the Comisión Femenil Mexicana Nacional was a political and economic empowerment organization for Chicanas; Poder Femenino was a chapter of the Comisión Femenil; La Raza Unida Party was the Chicano third party; and the Chicano Federation was a community organization in San Diego, California.

19. The exact number of Chicanas who attended is impossible to ascertain. I have arrived at this number from a review of oral history interviews and what Chicanas have written about the conference, especially Bea Vásquez Robinson, "Are We Racist? Are We Sexist?" *Agenda* (Winter 1976): 23–24.

20. Barbara Cady, "Women's Year Conference in 3 Rings," *Los Angeles Times*, July 9, 1975, sec. 4, p. 9; Adelaida R. Del Castillo to Roberto Cabello, January 16, 1976, Año Internacional de la Mujer Mexicana Collection, Chicano Studies Research Library, University of California, Los Angeles.

21. Serrano Sewell interview.

22. Judy Klemesrud, "Scrappy, Unofficial Women's Parley Sets Pace," *New York Times*, June 29, 1975, p. 1.

23. Margaret E. Galey, "The Nairobi Conference," 256; Judy Klemesrud, "International Women's Year World Conference Opening in Mexico," *New York Times*, June 19, 1975, p. 1.

24. Klemesrud, "International," p. 1.

25. Cady, "Women's Year Conference in 3 Rings," p. 1.

26. The number of participants that sources report attending the Tribune varies from 5,000 to 6,000. I use 5,000 because that is what is cited by Allan, Galey, and Persinger because Persinger was one of the chief organizers of the Tribune.

27. Allan, Galey, and Persinger, "World Conference of International Women's Year," 40.

28. Cady, "Women's Year Conference in 3 Rings," p. 1.

29. From oral history interviews and written accounts, I have concluded that approximately 100–150 Chicanas from California attended the conference. Vásquez Robinson states that from 250 to 300 women, mostly Chicanas, attended the National Chicana Foundation meeting at the Tribune. An estimate of 100–150 from California would allow for an approximately equal representation from Texas.

30. Allan, Galey, and Persinger, "World Conference of International Women's Year," 40; Cady, "Women's Year Conference in 3 Rings"; Judy Klemesrud, "U.S. Group Assails Women's Parley: Feminists at Conference in Mexico Complain That It Ignores Real Issues," *New York Times*, June 22, 1975, p. 4.

31. "Calendar," *Xilonen* (Mexico City), June 20, 1975, pp. 7, 1. *Xilonen*, the name of the Tribune newspaper, was named after the Aztec maize goddess, also known as "the hairy one," because her hair resembled the fibers on unshucked corn. The Aztecs worshiped Xilonen to secure a good harvest. She was married to the Aztec god Tezcatlipoca, also known as "smoking mirror," god of night, north, and temptation.

32. "Calendar," *Xilonen*, June 24 and 26, 1975, p. 1. Two possible reasons for this shift in the conference structure are that it reflects the organization and agitation by members of the Tribune and that it reflects simple logistics. Not many organizations signed up for presentations before the conference but did so at the conference. These presentations then took place on the fourth day.

33. James Sterba, "Equal Rights Vital, U.N. Chief Asserts," *New York Times*, June 20, 1975, p. 1.

34. Cady, "Women's Year Conference in 3 Rings," p. 1.

35. Chicanas of La Raza Unida Party, "International Women's Year Conference: La Mujer Chicana," June 23, 1975, Año Internacional de la Mujer Mexicana Collection, Chicano Studies Research Center, UCLA.

36. Ignacio García, *Chicanismo: The Forging of a Militant Ethos among Mexican Americans* (Tucson: University of Arizona Press, 1998), 49. On the internal colonial model in Chicano/a history, see Mario Barrera, Carlos Muñoz, and Charles Ornelas, "The Barrio As Internal Colony," *Urban Affairs Annual Review* 6 (1972): 465–98; Tomás Almaguer, "Toward the Study of Chicano Colonialism," *Aztlán* 2 (Spring 1971): 7–20; Gilbert González and Raul Fernández, "Chicano History: Transcending Cultural Models," *Pacific Historical Review* 63 (November 1994): 469–97.

37. "Notes on People," *New York Times*, June 13, 1975, p. 1; Judy Klemesrud, "Americans Ease Stand at Women's Conference," *New York Times*, June 25, 1975, p. 1; Klemesrud, "International," 5.

38. Yolanda M. López, "A Chicana's Look at the International Women's Year Conference," *Chicano Federation Newsletter*, August 1975), p. 3, reprinted in Alma M. García, *Chicana Feminist Thought: The Basic Historical Writings* (New York: Routledge, 1997), 181–83.

39. Vásquez Robinson, "Are We Racist? Are We Sexist?" 2.

40. López, "A Chicana's Look "; Stanley Meisler, "Women's Parley Debate Pits Two U.S. Groups," *Los Angeles Times*, June 22, 1975, sec. I, p. 1.

41. "Therefore We Demand" [1975], Año Internacional de la Mujer Mexicana Collection, Chicano Studies Research Library, UCLA; Jane S. Jaquette, *What Do Women Want?* Womenfilming, 1975, videocassette.

42. Mujeres en Acción Solidaria, *ALERTA!* (Mexico City: June 26, 1975), pamphlet, Año Internacional de la Mujer Mexicana, Chicano Studies Research Library, UCLA. Full text in Spanish reads: "1.-El intercambio de experiencias y problemas que afectan a las mujeres en las diversas actividades en todo el mundo, profundizar en el análisis de la condición de la mujer y buscar la instrumentación adecuada para nuestra acción concreta y permanente. 2.-Apoyar la posición de los países que

dentro de la conferencia gubernamental relacionan la necesidad de los cambios estructurales a nivel interno e internacional para propiciar una efectiva transformación de la condicion de la mujer de todos los grupos sociales." English: "1. The exchange of experiences and problems that affect women in diverse activities all over the world, deepen the analysis of the woman's condition, and look for the adequate grouping of instruments for concrete and permanent action. 2. Support the position of countries in the governmental conference that espouse the need for structural changes on an internal and international level to propagate an effective transformation of the woman's condition in all social groups" (translation by author).

43. Judy Klemesrud, "U.S. Group Assails Women's Parley: Feminists at Conference in Mexico Complain That It Ignores Real Issues," *New York Times*, June 22, 1975, p. 4.

44. Cady, "Women's Year Conference in 3 Rings," 1.

45. Angela Gilliam, "Women's Equality and National Liberation," 217.

46. Vásquez Robinson, "Are We Racist? Are We Sexist?," 24. The meeting in question took place on Thursday, June 26, 1975, in Room 6 of the National Medical Center.

47. Paula Diehl and Guadalupe Saavedra, "Hispanas in the Year of the Woman," *Agenda* (Winter 1976): 18.

48. Ibid.

49. Betty Friedan, *Betty Friedan vs. the Third World* (cassette), BC2377, Pacifica Radio Archives, North Hollywood, Calif.

50. "Calendar," *Xilonen*, June 20, 23, 24, 25, and 26, 1975, p. 1. There were two general Tribune sessions per day, one at 10:00 A.M. and one at 1:00 P.M. from June 20 through June 27, 1975, as far as can be told from the calendar. Other topics addressed at the general sessions were building the human, agriculture and rural development; education; women and the environment; population and planned parenthood; women in public life; and peace and disarmament.

51. Corinne Sánchez, interview by author, April 4, 2002, San Fernando, Calif.

52. Herrera Rodríguez interview.

53. Quoted in Estelle B. Freedman, *No Turning Back*, 117. In *Let Me Speak* (New York: Monthly Review Press, 1978), Barrios de Chungara states that Betty Friedan accused her of being "manipulated by men" and of being too concerned with politics with her positions on development and poverty. See Angela Gilliam, "Women's Equality and National Liberation," 224.

54. López interview.

55. Anna Nieto Gómez, interview by author, June 1, 2002, Lakewood, California. I could find no corroborating evidence in newspaper accounts of the Tribune of this occurring, but I find it important to include this as evidence because it is not only the occurrence, but also the actual memory of it that is important. Other women who also attest to military presence at specific sessions at the Tribune are Lilia Aceves and Connie Pardo.

56. Nieto Gómez interview.

57. Sánchez interview.

58. Nieto Gómez interview.

59. Pardo interview.

60. *The Spirit of Houston: The First National Women's Conference: An Offi-*

cial Report to the President, the Congress, and the People of the United States (Washington, D.C.: National Commission on the Observance of International Women's Year, U.S. Government Printing Office, 1978), 114.

61. *Spirit of Houston,* 278.

62. Sandra Serrano Sewell, "President's Report," September 17, 1977, Comisión Femenil Mexicana Nacional Records, California Ethnic and Multicultural Archives, University of California, Santa Barbara, pp. 1–2.

63. *Spirit of Houston,* 298–99. The other Latina/Chicana organizations with official booths were the Chicana Caucus—National Women's Political Caucus, LULAC National Education Service Centers, Inc. (although this was not specifically woman-centered), and Puerto Rican Women, Cuban Women, Mexican Women.

64. Comisión Femenil Mexicana Nacional, *La Mujer: International Women's Year 1977,* brochure, Comisión Femenil Mexicana Nacional Records, California Ethnic and Multicultural Archives, University of California, Santa Barbara.

65. Comisión Femenil, "Report of the Conference," *La Mujer.*

66. Serrano Sewell interview.

67. Comisión Femenil, "Report of the Conference," *La Mujer.*

68. Marcie Miranda-Arrizon, "Building Herman(a)dad," (M.A. thesis, University of California, Santa Barbara, 1997), 73.

69. Serrano Sewell interview.

70. Ibid.

8. *The Star in My Compass: Claiming Intellectual Space in the American Landscape*[1]

The sixth-floor, walkup apartment in the South Bronx represented the center of my universe. On that warm, spring-like day the world was close to war, but this factor had a minimum effect on the sweetness of life at that very moment. Following the customary morning routine, a breakfast of buttered bread and warm milk laced with coffee, I sat beside my mother on the red, crushed velvet sofa set opposite tall twin windows that overlooked the neighboring tenement rooftops. The scarlet cushion fabric rubbed against the backs of my legs, making me itch and I gently shuffled my calves from side to side. "¿Qué dice, Mami? ¿Qué dice?" I repeated with four-year-old persistence. My mother glowed, pregnant with a new life, and fingered the newspaper draped across her lap. A slight hesitation, then concentrating on the page before her, she slowly related the comic strip antics of Archie and Veronica, and then Dagwood and Blondie. Gradually, index finger pointing the way, she reached my favorite—Little Lulu. She read in measured, heavily accented English, pronouncing each syllable as surely her third grade teacher in Mayagüez, Puerto Rico, had taught her to do.

If mother and I fully comprehended the funnies' alien words, harsh-sounding linguistic obstacles that conveyed a popular pastime in American culture, I cannot remember for sure. But what was clearly evident was that the cultural lessons I was determined to unlock in that foreign tongue held not an inkling of my own people's proud heritage. It would distance me for a long time from developing an appreciation for the connections between ancestral women on distant shores and those who, like me, would reach maturity in diaspora.

With time and a zealous Catholic school education, I became proficient in the English language. The written word flooded into my home via magazines, newspapers, and the treasured comic books my father salvaged while cleaning out the trains that came into Pennsylvania Station. Before my tenth birthday, small sister in tow, I would barge into the local public library hauling off every book within the limits of my restricted children's card. And while I reveled in this newly discovered world of words and wisdom, heroic adventures, time travel, distressed damsels, and foreign lands, not one book ever told me about me.

It was precisely because experiences like mine were common among the children of the pioneer migrant generation of Puerto Ricans who came to live in New York City during the twenties and thirties that heritage and education were of prime concern in pre–World War II communities. The cigar workers who were among the first Puerto Ricans to settle in the city at the turn of the century valued education highly. The tradition of *la lectura,* reading aloud to cigar workers in the tobacco factories of Puerto Rico and Cuba, found fertile ground in the fledgling New York *colonias.* Other examples of learning and instruction flourished in countless Puerto Rican and Hispanic associations that formed educational committees and study groups to provide intellectual sustenance and cultural continuity. Many prioritized the cultural welfare, including education, of continental communities in their by-laws. The *Liga Puertorriqueña e Hispana,* for example, lauded the founding of its educational center, a major objective in its 1926 Charter of Incorporation.[2] Organizational mission statements and programmatic plans stressed knowledge and celebration of one's language, history, and cultural heritage; many individuals carved out careers for themselves as community educators.

I would not know for decades that a woman named Pura Belpré was among the pioneers making an effort to educate young people in the early twenties.[3] The city's first Puerto Rican librarian, Belpré encouraged the New York Library system to collect books about Puerto Rican folktales and culture. An ardent storyteller and writer, Belpré wrote original stories, like the beloved *Pérez y Martina* about the elegant cockroach, Martina, who falls in love with Pérez, the shy mouse. Belpré translated treasured folktales, including the tales of the fabled trickster Juan Bobo, who always managed to get the best out of ridiculous situations.

Belpré taught classes at Union Settlement House to prepare student teachers, mostly Irish, Jewish, and Italian, to work with Spanish-speaking youngsters. She sponsored Hispanic cultural activities by organizing community and library programs, lectures, music recitals, and poetry readings. In her soft-spoken, ladylike way, she encouraged Spanish-speaking intellectuals, writers, and performers visiting the city to make guest appearances at the library. Public celebrations commemorated religious events such as Three Kings' Day, or historical fests like the Columbian discovery of Puerto Rico in 1493. These activities were intended to reinforce Hispanic culture and heritage and compensate for the invisibility of the subject in the public school curriculum. By the time I met Belpré at Brooklyn College in the late 1970s, she was a revered master teacher; a pioneering icon with an impressive record of achievement that helped advance the New York Puerto Rican community. When the diminutive, almost fragile, brown-skinned storyteller read *Pérez y Martina* aloud to a large audience of future bilingual teachers, she still commanded their attention as if they were children sitting on a library floor for story hour.

Except for my mother and large extended family, I did not have role models like Belpré. At the age of seven I was enrolled in the neighborhood parochial school, and my education under the custody of Dominican nuns took a different trajectory. Private schooling was made possible through my mother's sacrifices; her careful squirreling away of nickels and dimes made me feel guilty when I did not perform well. Beyond the protection of the home and familiar barrio streets, my initial encounters with ethnic diversity and multiculturalism happened in this school and opened new horizons. Before I realized it, I was "being raised" Irish Catholic!

One might ask how a light-skinned Puerto Rican girl, who could barely distinguish the *sh* in shore from the *ch* in chicken, got raised Irish Catholic. It happened almost automatically when you attended St. Anselm's Roman Catholic School in the South Bronx, at the dawning of the great population shifts from Puerto Rico to New York City. Unlike the parochial schools of today, St. Anselm's, or "St. Anne's Slums," as kids derisively called it, boasted a predominantly Irish American student population, a smaller concentration of Italian Americans, and an even less significant smattering of Puerto Ricans. Nurturing Irish antecedents and catering to a more established immigrant community, the school cultivated close ties to the old country and culture through its many activities. Among them, St. Patrick's Day was hailed with a flurry of arrangements every year that included two nights of musical entertainment, presented to captive audiences of parents, relatives, and friends. A tall, stern-faced music teacher, with a full head of graying ringlets that bounced in time to the music, instructed the children, regardless of race, gender, or ethnicity, in the intricacies of Irish reels and step dancing. Despite Miss O'Brien's valiant dedication, months of preparation often failed to clone miniature Ginger Rogerses and Fred Astairs, but the magnificent sight of high-kicking, step-dancing Irish girls in native attire was always worth the effort. In addition, the program included the crooning of traditional Irish songs until there was not a dry eye in the house—except perhaps for the Puerto Rican parents who came to savor the musical talents of their offspring but harbored little sentimentality over the Old Sod.[4]

In those days the nuns hovered over their charges like penguins protecting their young; indeed, these youngsters represented survival and continuity, for the children the nuns taught ensured cultural and spiritual bonds between Ireland and America for decades to come. Long before I knew anything about the political connections between Puerto Rico's colonial struggles and Ireland's—about women like Lola Rodríguez de Tió, Luisa Capetillo, and Lolita Lebrón; or about Don Pedro Albízu Campos and the Gaelic movement for liberation—I admired the tenacity of a people who so fiercely resisted acculturation. Engaged in the national business of Americanization, replete with civic duties, English-language dominance, democratic values, and worthy founding fathers, these teachers still *remembered* how to infuse pride in the "Old World" heritage. And so at some level I must have internalized the notion that you didn't have to give up one identity in order to assume another—that both strands could coexist without conflict. That understanding, however, would not manifest itself until I was much older.

Contradictions abounded for me and other Puerto Rican youngsters caught in an assimilationist one-way street. For the teachers and administrators, many of whom had not encountered a cohort of non-English-speaking youngsters in the classroom since the great immigrations of the early twentieth century, Puerto Rican children were virtually invisible; their rich multicultural and multiracial history, language, life-cycle commemorations, ritual kinships, and affirming institutions were inconsequential. Hundreds of Puerto Rican children became casualties of an Americanizing cultural onslaught that, coupled with intense wartime patriotism, absorbed them into a national ideal that promoted equality yet maintained a colonial stranglehold on Puerto Rico and sanctioned ethno-racial divisions on its own shores. Throughout those formative years I firmly embraced the American dream even as a nagging inner voice vacillated between my public and private beings, constantly questioning my own authenticity. I frequently snuck out for pizza, disparaging my mother's traditional foods; spoke English, consciously abandoning my Spanish foundations; and preferred American to Spanish movies, even though I worshipped Mexican film stars Jorge Negrete and María Félix. For most of my generation who experienced this painful dilemma, survival would rest on selective adaptation; the ability to pick and choose cultural elements from both cultures, blending "American" and Puerto Rican ways of being into something unique called U.S. Puerto Rican, *Boricua*, or *Nuyorican*. But it was, nevertheless, a rough job for a kid.

After the Great Migration of the 1950s and 1960s, diasporic communities proliferated, particularly in New York and the surrounding states, and began to forge links with the dominant American culture, but not without resistance and struggle. Their perseverance and mobilization brought about social changes that marked important contributions in several major arenas. Among these were Latin music and bilingual education. Puerto Ricans continued to care very much about education, and their involvement began to shift the paradigm of what and how students were taught in the public schools and later at the university level. The natural expansion of stateside barrios together with a highly visible increase in migration, a byproduct of the island's modernization and industrialization policies, meant sharp increases in the numbers of Spanish-speaking children enrolled in the public schools. Since 85 percent of the U.S. Puerto Rican community was concentrated in the city of New York, migrant and second-generation children would begin to overwhelm public instructional resources in urban areas that received large numbers of the group.

The first Puerto Rican teachers hired by the city to mediate between the public schools and the community became the precursors of bilingual education as it is practiced today. Their experiences provided models for bilingual professionals in New York City and for other Spanish-speaking communities in surrounding states. Mostly women, these young, enthusiastic educators connected the schools and the community by establishing rapport, cultivating reciprocity, and developing a bilingual communication network. They became cultural resources throughout the system, offering their expertise in sensitivity training and implementing programs that enhanced cultural awareness and self-respect. Activists in their professional organizations—the Society of Puerto Rican Auxiliary Teachers (SPRAT) the Puerto Rican Educators Association (PREA) and the Latino chapter of the United Federation of Teachers—these teachers created curricula, resource materials, and texts. Their mobilization provided the spaces in which the struggles for bilingual teacher accreditation were launched.

A little-known current in our history was the effort of the first bilingual professionals who simultaneously worked toward building informed communities. Among community parents, the teachers developed fervent and committed followers. The achievements of some of our best-known activists, like the organizer Evelina Antonetty, founder of the grass-roots organization United Bronx Parents, came from recruitment and experience.[5]

Among the first twenty teachers hired as substitute auxiliary teachers between 1949 and 1955, María E. Sánchez, a petite, dynamic redhead whom I would not meet until 1978, was typical of the women involved in this phase of community development.[6] Like others in her group, María was educated at the University of Puerto Rico. She moved to New York City shortly after her marriage and already had experience in classroom teaching. By 1958 she was appointed supervisor of District 14 in Brooklyn, charged with preparing other bilingual professionals for careers in city schools. She left the school system in 1972 because Brooklyn College recruited her to create a bilingual education program at the graduate and undergraduate levels. An astute pedagogue, well grounded in university politics, María became the second woman and third chairperson of the recently created Puerto Rican Studies Department, guiding it through a two-year battle that challenged administrative autocracy and solidified the rights of academic departments to select their own chairs. Among Professor Sánchez's colleagues, many bilingual educator-activists rose to prominence. Some directed bilingual programs, others became supervisors, and still others became principals in the public school system.

In spite of the dedication of a few Puerto Rican professionals, by the time I entered high school in the mid-fifties, stereotypical attitudes and distortions about Puerto Ricans had increased. Almost from the first discernable Puerto Rican presence in the United States, articles reeked with negative portrayals of our communities. The earliest scholarly account, Lawrence Chenault's *Puerto Rican Migrant* (1938), depicted Puerto Ricans as unambitious, unreliable, and pathologically sensitive individuals. Throughout the forties and fifties, the media referred to the group as the "Puerto Rican problem." *Daily Mirror* columnists Jack Lait and Lee Mortimer described them as "mostly crude farmers . . . (who) turn to guile and wile and the steel blade, the traditional weapon of the sugar cane cutter, mark of their blood and heritage."[7] The journalists opined: "They are . . . subject to congenital tropical disease, physically unfitted for the northern climate, unskilled, uneducated, non-English speaking and almost impossible to assimilate in an active city of stone and steel."[8] Another journalistic foray portrayed Puerto Ricans as catalysts in the loss of ground in educational standards: "because of the language problem, and when Puerto Rican children are in a majority on a street they can, like any such majority, make life almost unbearable for other children."[9]

Although pockets of responsible research (like C. Wright Mills's and collaborators' *Puerto Rican Journey* and *Up from Puerto Rico,* and the foundational work of Elena Padilla) began to appear in print in the fifties, negative and controversial writings titillated a reading public eager to believe the worst about the group.[10] For young Puerto Ricans grappling with identity and self-worth, one of the most damaging was Oscar Lewis's *La Vida.* I borrowed a copy from the library and felt its portrayal of Puerto Ricans, especially women, was insulting. Touted as an objective anthropological study, it overgeneralized both the island and diasporic realities from the experiences of one poor extended family engaged in prostitution as a way of life. Despite claims of impartial scholarship, Lewis studied a small sample and used a San Juan ghetto, the city's unofficial red-light district, as a representative site. While the work was generally well received at the time, one researcher later declared, "An account of a prostitute's family may produce a sensational best seller, but our studies of Puerto Ricans—employed, on relief, from the highland *jíbaro* background or from other strata—indicate it is not at all representative."[11]

Without doubt, such pervasive negativity affected the schooling of young Puerto Ricans. Overall, their invisibility in curricular content, methodology, texts, or materials frequently resulted in disaffected students. Pedagogical research asserted that teachers were indeed influenced by favorable and unfavorable stereotyping. When Puerto Rican students were perceived as culturally deprived nonachievers, teachers tended to have lower expectations. But when teachers were told that they were instructing high achievers, regardless of ethnicity, they expected and received more productivity from their students.[12]

Like the protagonist in Esmeralda Santiago's memoir, *Almost a Woman,* those of my generation who managed to attend and graduate from high school received a double message. You could succeed if you worked hard and earned a high school diploma, but not much was expected from you if you were Puerto Rican. Throughout the city, drop-out rates soared. Puerto Rican students were actively discouraged from entering academic programs, tracked instead into vocational or general courses of study that ultimately denied them access to higher education. Several of my cousins fell victims to prejudiced school counselors who justified tracking them into general diplomas on the perception that their families could not possibly afford the costs of a college or professional education.[13]

Women were also expected to follow traditional gender roles of marriage and motherhood, and schools offered few alternatives. They failed to provide leadership, role models, or incentives to do anything else. Absence from the curriculum, historical invisibility, negative stereotypes, and low teacher expectations meant that if I wanted to continue my education, to strive for that elusive American dream, I had to fight for it every step of the way. Although it was late in the semester of my senior year, I set out to explore my options. Seeking guidance about my academic future, perhaps even daring to articulate interest in college, I confronted the senior guidance counselors on the day before graduation from Bay Ridge High School. Preferring to comment on my "poor choice" of lipstick color, the counselors condescendingly informed me about the existence of a free city university system with a campus right there in the Borough of Brooklyn. If I could meet the standards, I might be admitted. Left to research college admissions on my own, I sought out the pertinent information, submitted an application, and was accepted at Brooklyn College, as a matriculated student at the start of the fall semester. At that time girls were required to have high school averages over ninety while boys could enter with GPAs in the high eighties. Lacking college role models in my family and facing low parental expectations for a college-educated daughter, I nonetheless became the first in the family to attend, and thus the trailblazer for my younger sister and brother. By the time I earned the baccalaureate degree, a mere 1 percent of the graduating classes of the entire CUNY system were Puerto Rican.

My first impression of Brooklyn College, nestled in what seemed to me a bucolic oasis that defied its urban location, was everything I could hope for. Granted, my frame of reference for institutions of higher learning was restricted to MGM movies like *Good News*, where June Allyson and Van Johnson did their famous "Varsity Drag," but I felt that I was on the brink of a wonderful adventure. Nonetheless, obstacles appeared at every turn. My bosses in the factory where I worked as a bookkeeper would have preferred that I dedicate all my time to their business, and "What are you going to college for? You'll only get married anyway" became a constant refrain. Few of my neighborhood friends were in school, so there was no one who could understand what I was doing. In time, I became socially and intellectually distant from family and friends as I struggled to open unknown paths for myself at Brooklyn.

If I could pinpoint the inception of any personal activist leanings, it would probably be during those college years. I soon discovered the hallowed halls were neither immune from the ethno-racial prejudice of the period nor eager to question social science dogma. In retrospect, I found it difficult to reconcile a nurturing home, the hub of an extended family, and community with social science rhetoric that frequently reinforced a notion of Puerto Rican downward mobility. The pervasive invisibility of anything Latino silently echoed its very absence throughout my education. I was drawn to piecing together evidence to counteract negative Puerto Rican images in the literature. Determined to make a difference in the lives of barrio students, the star in my personal compass pointed toward teaching as the viable medium for change. I believed that if I could give back to my community, influence just one student out of the many who would cross my path, I would be paying back not only for the omissions in knowledge, but also the opportunities given to me. Armed with the baccalaureate degree, I prepared to put my philosophy into practice. I taught high school English for four years, in working-class neighborhoods in New York, and later, Chicago, a feat my Uncle Fernando found most incongruous since I was teaching English to "Americans."

Two remarkable events occurred in 1971 that would further affect the implementation of my goals. The first involved my father, or "Popi," as he was known to his children and grandchildren. He came to live with us with plans to alternate domiciles between my family's in Long Island and my sister's in Boston. Living in households with school-age children and working husbands, Popi swiftly became the pivotal person in the running of each home. This extraordinary arrangement allowed me to enroll in graduate studies and my sister to go to law school. He was there when the children came home from school, kept food in the pantry, connected us to extended family, paid the newspaper boy, and fed the dogs. An adventurer who traveled the world over as a young merchant seaman, and a voracious reader throughout his entire life, my father became my touchstone particularly about Puerto Rican heritage and culture. Ironically, I had set out on a journey to find ancestral foremothers, but instead discovered a father—my resolute cheerleader and companion, but my toughest critic.

The second event in what would become a defining moment for me in my future intellectual work in ethnic studies began with a challenge. I sought admission to graduate studies in the History Department at the State University of New York at Stony Brook with a well-defined agenda in mind: to tell the story of the New York Puerto Rican community from my parents' pioneering generation to the present, to set straight the historical record, and to ensure that Puerto Ricans would forever find themselves in the national narrative. If Stony Brook could not help me achieve this goal, I would go somewhere else. The university accepted the challenge. And so began my intellectual journey into the study of Puerto Ricans, Latin Americans, and U.S. Latinos.

After the social reformations of the late sixties and early seventies, if Puerto Ricans appeared at all in college syllabi, it was usually in courses that perpetuated a deficit model in analyzing the group's thousands of adjustment "problems" in urban settings. The prevailing social science literature pictured a rural, alienated, dislocated community unable to cope with urban incertitude that was often marginal to the wider society. Moreover, Puerto Ricans appeared as victims or perpetrators of their deplorable situation, as isolated, ahistorical beings. The impact on nation building within the context of the colonial relationship between island and mainland was not mentioned, and burning issues of racialized groups in white America fell between the cracks. Especially lost was any understanding of Puerto Rican roots and their role in shaping the Americas.

The institutionalization of Puerto Rican studies on many campuses throughout the Northeast brought specific courses on island history to college curricula. They relied on importing academic talent from Puerto Rico to teach them but rarely included mention of the U.S. experience. With the exception of community studies courses, strongly focused on contemporary social issues, historical information was absent. Migration, a defining issue in U.S. Puerto Rican history, was treated as individually motivated. Analysis of migration endorsed a "push-pull" paradigm that ultimately argued for assimilation into mainstream culture in much the same way that prior immigrant groups had become hyphenated Americans.

The radical sociopolitical movements that helped establish the field also stimulated an ethnic and cultural revival motivating an increasing number of Puerto Ricans to write about themselves, validating their experiences through their own testimonies and biographies. Classics, such as Piri Thomas's *Down These Mean Streets*, Nicholasa Mohr's *Nilda*, and Edward Rivera's *Family Installments*, plumbed the individual search for identity and validation within the familial and broader community context. Considered another aspect of American immigrant literature, they soon gained legitimacy beyond ethnic studies. Similarly, the surge in popularity of social histories and gender and ethnic studies, coupled with English-language translations of critical island thinkers, articulated new ideas, important grounding for the study of U.S. Puerto Ricans. This creative output, and its social science research counterpart, brought fresh interpretations of U.S. diaspora communities and began to link the experiences of Puerto Ricans on both sides of the Caribbean. The literature affirmed self-determination, challenged absorption into mainstream society, defined new sources of knowledge (often within the experience itself), and defied conventional colonial ideologies. Novel theoretical frameworks and approaches laid the groundwork for alternative perspectives about migration and community. The historical documentation of continental communities became viable research material, and the resulting studies, many written by credentialed colleagues from both inside and outside the ethnic experience, significantly altered knowledge and learning about mainland Puerto Ricans in both island and U.S.-based scholarship. Such work shed light on U.S. Puerto Rican history and illuminated the multidimensional evolution of the interwar community in New York. The role of women in community building, issues of race and class, power relations, labor segmentation, organizations, and political structure became legitimate categories of analysis. As departments, programs, and research institutes fought for academic beachheads, practitioners of Puerto Rican studies charted their course and staked claims for future agendas.

My own work is historically situated within such trends. Although *From Colonia to Community* broke new ground in defining U.S. Puerto Rican communities, it complemented the collective building blocks of other scholars and archivists, all working toward one goal—the reconstruction and validation of community histories. The history of New York Puerto Ricans is cast in a revisionist mode that attempts to redefine the experience of the pre–World War II community viewed through the lens of those who lived it. Women are featured as key players in the saga and emerge as unsung heroes and internal leaders of a vibrant and dynamic episode in our past. Jesús Colón's essays, *The Way It Was and Other Writings,* documents activist, politically astute Puerto Ricans in barrios steeped in advancing the cause of the working classes and people of color in the struggle for equality. This volume is now included in the reading selections of advanced English placement examinations.[14]

But intellectual production presented merely one component of the revisionist enterprise. The establishment and maturation of departments and programs in often hostile institutional environs required enormous energy and political militancy, as did the institutionalization of the new knowledge at all educational levels. The concept of the scholar-activist was honed in these confrontations, and university academics emerged as battered veterans of turf wars. Scores of lecturers, instructors, and adjunct professors sacrificed opportunities to earn doctorates that would have ensured them of continued employment because of their involvement in the politics of ethnic studies. But the cost was often worth it, for, as we shall see, it helped establish interdisciplinary studies, departmental autonomy, and control over curriculum.

By the eighties I was an assistant professor at Brooklyn College in the Department of Puerto Rican Studies. With the unprecedented immigration and natural growth among Americans of Latin American and

Caribbean background, Latino studies could no longer be ignored. As activists cast from the cauldrons of the Chicano student movement, and its Puerto Rican counterparts, entered the ranks of university faculty, more attention focused on Latino history. From these developments, the U.S. Puerto Rican story emerged as a complicated one that incorporates the experiences of both conventional immigrants and of American people of color. It includes the dynamics of race and class and unfettered ties to the island nation. The second-largest among the U.S. Latino populations, Puerto Ricans have figured in the making of U.S. history since before the nineteenth century when the colony was still a major fortification in the defense of the Spanish New World Empire. The twentieth-century communities developed by U.S. Puerto Ricans bear witness to their place in American history, particularly from their direct participation in the nation's labor force and union movements, in creating community, in their commitment to bilingual and university education, and in politics. Efforts to close the gap between American constitutional guarantees and daily life in the barrios have led Puerto Ricans and other Latinos to struggle for justice, equality, and inclusion. Such historic endeavors have, in turn, strengthened American democratic principles.

The significance of Puerto Rican studies to the traditional social sciences and humanities cannot be denied, and its influence is clearly evident in American, Latin American and Caribbean, ethnic, Latino, and women's studies today. Philosophically, the underlying tenet in ethnic and women's studies is the union of learning, praxis, and community accountability. Academic departments and programs grew out of community with the understanding that institutional research would serve the needs of communities wherever they might be. Ethnic studies brought the Puerto Rican and wider Latino communities to the university and the university to the communities. In this way, Puerto Rican and Latino studies developed interdisciplinary expertise in the study of urban communities that today is being duplicated, or, some might say, co-opted, in other disciplines.

Migration, for example, is now a phenomenon understood within broad transnational structures; the concept of an integrated Puerto Rican community, island and mainland, has aided in shifting the paradigm from previous notions of immigrants permanently uprooting and transplanting. The notion that women have always worked is remarkably significant. Their contributions to the formal and informal economy, as salaried and unsalaried laborers, in and outside the home, have altered our concepts of the housewife in the traditional Puerto Rican family. The struggles for bilingual education, for example, spearheaded by Puerto Rican teachers in elementary education, have benefited countless numbers of new immigrants, not just Spanish-speaking children in the public schools of the northeastern United States. And more recently, the concept of cultural citizenship and a transnational Puerto Rican identity forms an important component in our understanding of the relationship between the island and continental communities. Described as a commuter nation, a people without borders, the experience is rooted in a nation with a shifting configuration of mainland settlements. As sociologist David Hernández points out, "One must begin to take the position that Puerto Rican identity is not a local or an insular matter but a transnational reality . . . that the perseverance of a dynamic Puerto Rican identity is in fact promoted by the continuous revitalization of ethnic symbols in which frequent back and forth movement to and from Puerto Rico plays a major role."[15]

My own work on U.S. Puerto Ricans was recognized by the New York State Department of Education, and in 1987 I was appointed to a five-year project to create an interdisciplinary curriculum on Latinos in the making of America. In 1989 I was called upon to advise the New York commissioner of education, Thomas Sobol, in his endeavors to infuse a multicultural focus into the state's social studies programs.[16] *The Curriculum of Inclusion*, an advisory report written by the Task Force on Minorities, chaired by Hazel Dukes, then president of the New York chapter of the National Association for the Advancement of Colored People, had created a furor both in the popular media and among university professionals. Torn apart by detractors for its "inflammatory" language about U.S. history and cherished American values, it gained notoriety throughout the nation.[17]

Caught in the middle of this conflict in New York State's own "culture wars," I found myself in the unenviable situation of evaluating *The Curriculum of Inclusion*, an advisory report written for Commissioner Sobol, the czar of the state's educational policies. Committed to offering as objective, honest, and informed an opinion as possible, I reread the report several times in a state of anxiety. I was not prepared for the large audience of state education personnel that greeted me the following morning. Members of the Task Force on Minorities, Commissioner Sobol, and three high-profile consultants—Asa Hilliard, known for the Portland African-American Baseline Essays; Diane Ravitch, adjunct professor at Columbia's Teacher's College; and psychologist Edmund Gordon of Yale University—were present. One by one, the other consultants presented their views on the report. The last to speak, I felt this was an opportunity I had prepared for all my life, a self-centered perspective that bolstered my ebbing confidence in the bold approach I wanted to propose. Convinced that the report had not gone far enough, I argued for the creation of a balanced curriculum created by a team of distinguished scholars that would include the experiences of all Americans, respect multiple perspectives, and embrace the vast body of knowledge on U.S. Latinos. To my relief and satisfaction the following year, Commissioner Sobol created a blue ribbon commission to review social studies as taught throughout the state and to develop a framework for curriculum development.

Almost from the start, the Social Studies Review and Curriculum Development Commission received negative media coverage. It was portrayed as Sobol's attempt to either ameliorate or to implement *Curriculum of Inclusion* ideology, but it actually was the commissioner's intention to distance himself from the stridency of the report, while acting on its critical insights, by bringing together "eminent scholars and educators[,] . . . distinguished scholars and teachers in relevant fields who represent a diversity of views and backgrounds" to review social studies in New York State.[18] I was one of twenty-four scholars and teachers selected from more than three hundred nominees. We were African Americans, Euro Americans, Latinos, Asian Americans, and Native Americans; university professors, teachers, and administrators; and public school and Ivy League representatives. Among the prominent scholars were sociologist Nathan Glazer, Harvard University; historian Arthur Schlesinger Jr., Graduate Center of the City University of New York; historian Kenneth Jackson, Columbia University; psychologist Edmund Gordon, Yale University; and political scientist Ali Mazrui, SUNY–Binghamton. To paraphrase the welcoming words of the commissioner, if we couldn't do it, no one could. He was referring to the intellectual and ethnically diverse makeup of the review committee charged with recommending what social studies should include and how the fields should be taught.

At stake was the definition of American society, and the political positions represented on the commission covered a wide spectrum of opposing ideas. The conservative tone set by Schlesinger posited "U.S. history as the making of a single nation with a common culture . . . primarily European—racially and culturally. . . . Despite problems, the West has been the major force for democracy." I more or less accepted the notion of a common culture, but from a different perspective. Can the representative culture be my own, I asked? In other words, where did Latino and other people of color fit in? We questioned whether indeed Americans shared a common culture, or rather common understandings and beliefs. Mazrui concluded by calling into question "two sociological myths" of "shared ancestry and collective purpose. If we are going to en-

gage in ancestor worship (for example, the Founding Fathers) . . . we need
to be more inclusive of our ancestors. Second, we need wider participation to justify the claim to collective purpose." From that point forward
I knew the dialogue would be thoughtful, that we would learn from one
another, be willing to compromise, and strive for consensus by working
through our differences. For many of us who had devoted our lives to
promoting concepts of American diversity and multiple perspectives, this
was indeed an opportunity to make a difference. As Catherine Cornbleth,
professor in the School of Education at the University of Buffalo, wrote,
"subsequent meetings of the Review Committee can be characterized as
a roller coaster in slow motion—with highs and lows, twists and turns,
but moving slowly and occasionally doubling back on itself."[19]

Nine months later, before a standing-room-only crowd of journalists,
educators, state personnel, and the New York State Board of Regents,
Dr. Sobol presented our report, *One Nation, Many Peoples: A Declaration of Cultural Interdependence.* In my mind, the opening salvo in the
document's preamble said it all. "The United States is a microcosm of
humanity today. No other country in the world is peopled by a greater
variety of races, nationalities, and ethnic groups. But although the United
States has been a great asylum for diverse peoples, it has not always been
a great refuge for diverse cultures."[20] The document affirmed multiculturalism and multiple perspectives, acknowledged racism, and recognized
the continuing struggle to close the gap between democratic ideals and
practices.

But Sobol's ideals, and those of most of the members of the commission, were once again crushed by an intense negative reaction by
the media that unleashed another battle in the ongoing national culture
wars. *One Nation, Many Peoples,* thought too radical by the media, was
basically repackaged in subsequent recommendations. Approved by a 12
to 3 vote, it nonetheless became New York State education policy. In a
statement written by Cornbleth, Susan Sagor, and myself, we supported
both the process and the report. "Given the diverse backgrounds of the
committee members, the consensus that was reached represents well
the strengths inherent in diversity and the unity which can emerge."[21]

After the report's release, my husband and I spent a leisurely weekend
visiting small towns and villages in upstate New York. Everywhere we
went, local papers printed slanted accounts of the report and its genesis.
Nevertheless, I could not have been prouder of the experience and our
accomplishments. I felt what my inner voice confirmed, that we had
won the day for the "good guys."

I began my journey in a period of irrelevancy for Puerto Ricans in the United States, most evident in the popular media and educational curricula. A personal, intellectual undertaking of discovery, I arrived at the present heightened awareness of self and community. The subject itself has become a legitimate field of study. My journey crossed intellectual borders, scaled barriers, and took scores of unusual twists and turns, but it ultimately converged with the collective actions of those who, like me, sought to advance educational horizons for future generations of Puerto Ricans and other Latinos. My generation also represented that transitional group that bridged feminist ideology with traditional concepts of womanhood. Many of my counterparts, usually light-skinned and unaccented-English-speaking, opted for total assimilation into mainstream America. But many others did not. Like me, they stayed the course, or returned, committed to ensuring a place in the dialogue so that their personal experiences translated into scholar activism—the political tool to forge a people's legacy.

Afterthoughts

The rain finally came to an end. I wiped the round, white table on the deck, fully intending to use the remaining daylight hours of what was rapidly becoming a glorious fall afternoon to work on the presentation. This was my favorite place to work. The parklike backyard provided privacy, a solitude not totally removed from the outside world. Children's voices could be heard comfortingly at play out in the front court, reminding me of other days when my own daughters' playful squeals were what I listened for. A bee circled my chair, and for a brief moment I wondered whether it was an ancestral spirit come back to prod new insights I might have forgotten. What else needed to be told? So much had happened, and yet the struggles continued. How could you tell the personal stories of so many men and women—our fathers, sisters, friends, and foremothers—so that they could never be erased from memory? What did their joys, struggles, decency, and courage have to do with the big story? How could we interlace intergenerational connections and make them meaningful, so that our young people could drink in their nourishment? In the final analysis, isn't the big story made up of the personal accounts of each and every one of us? I shivered, aware of the lengthening shadows and coolness in the air. Gathering my papers, I rose from the table and went indoors.

Notes

1. Portions of this paper have been presented at the Encuentro Feminista, Interamerican University, San Germán, Puerto Rico, April 1998; and at the CARNAL symposium, Université de Provence, September 1997. The paper also draws upon Virginia Sánchez Korrol, *Teaching U.S. Puerto Rican History*, AHA Series on Diversity (Washington, D.C.: American Historical Association, 1999).

2. Virginia Sánchez Korrol, *From Colonia to Community: The History of Puerto Ricans in New York City*, 2d ed. (Berkeley: University of California Press, 1994), 154.

3. Lisa Sánchez González, "Pura Belpré: The Children's Ambassador," in *Latina Legacies: Identity, Biography and Community*, edited by Vicki L. Ruiz and Virginia Sánchez Korrol (New York: Oxford University Press, 2005).

4. A great deal of this information was inspired by my sister, Aura Sánchez Garfunkel, who first wrote about our being raised Irish Catholic in the Streetfeet Women, *Laughing in the Kitchen* (Boston: Talking Stone Press, 1998).

5. Antonetty's career as a radical organizer is legendary. The library and archives of the Center for Puerto Rican Studies at Hunter College, City University of New York, is named after her.

6. María was chairperson of the Puerto Rican Studies Department at Brooklyn College for fifteen years and was responsible for laying the academic foundations. See Virginia Sánchez Korrol, "María E. Sánchez," in *Latinas in the United States: A Historical Encyclopedia*, edited by Vicki L. Ruiz and Virginia Sánchez Korrol (Bloomington: Indiana University Press, 2006).

7. Gerald Meyer, "Marcantonio and el Barrio," in *Centro Bulletin* (New York: Centro de Estudios Puertorriqueños, Hunter College, CUNY, 1992), 76–77.

8. Ibid.

9. Christopher Rand, *The Puerto Ricans* (New York: Oxford University Press, 1958), 5. The bias of mass media encouraged internal divisions among Puerto Ricans, turning some established migrants against recent arrivals.

10. Joseph P. Fitzpatrick, *Puerto Rican Americans: The Meaning of Migration to the Mainland* (Englewood Cliffs, N.J.: Prentice-Hall, 1971); C. Wright Mills et al., *The Puerto Rican Journey* (New York: Harper & Row, 1950); Elena Padilla, *Up from Puerto Rico* (New York: Columbia University Press, 1958); and Oscar Lewis, *La Vida* (New York: Random House, 1965).

11. Clara E. Rodríguez, "Puerto Ricans in Historical and Social Science Research, Working Paper #57" (New York: Russell Sage Foundation, 1994).

12. Sonia Nieto writes extensively on this topic. See "Puerto Rican Students in U.S. Schools: A Troubled Past and Search for a Hopeful Future," in *Handbook of Research on Multicultural Education*, 2d ed., ed. James A. Banks and Cherry A. McGee (San Francisco: Jossey-Bass, 2004), 515–41.

13. When my Harvard-educated sister—a lawyer and former Peace Corps director on Palau and elsewhere in Micronesia—was in junior high school, she was counseled against taking the entrance test for the High School of Science in spite of her high GPA. The rationale was that she shouldn't put herself through that ordeal; she was a girl and could attend the local district high school. My younger brother's chronic cutting of classes was supported by his high school science teacher who ran the lab. My brother spent most of his class time helping, or

hanging out, in the lab—because, after all, he was not expected to go to college. Years later I met this teacher, who was stunned to find out that Ramon was *my* brother and apologized for not being tougher on him.

14. Sánchez Korrol, *From Colonia to Community.* Jesús Colón and Edna Acosta-Belén, eds., *The Way It Was and Other Writings* (Houston, Tex.: Arte Público Press, 1993). I refer to two publications only, but the work of Puerto Rican and Latino scholars is as much in the public arena as it is in the intellectual. Maintaining viable departments of Puerto Rican and Latino studies requires exceptional expertise in the politics of academe.

15. David Hernández, "Puerto Rican Geographic Mobility: The Making of a De-territorialized Nationality," *Latino Review of Books* 2, no. 3 (1996–1997): 5.

16. Spearheaded by the New York State Department of Education the Ibero-American Heritage Curriculum Project, *Latinos in the Making of the United States of America, Yesterday, Today, and Tomorrow* was an international, inter-disciplinary project to integrate the study of Ibero-American heritage and culture into classroom instructional programs. It targeted the Columbus Quincentenary for its unveiling. Its membership came from six countries, including Puerto Rico, Spain, and Portugal, and educators from Arizona, California, Florida, New Jersey, New Mexico, and Texas. I was on the international advisory panel.

17. *The Curriculum of Inclusion* was a report, not a curriculum. The "inflammatory language," for example, included the following statement: "African-Americans, Asian-Americans, Puerto Rican/Latinos, and Native-Americans have all been victims of a cultural oppression and stereotyping that has characterized institutions—including the educational institutions—of the United States and the European-American world for centuries." See Catherine Cornbleth, *The Great Speckled Bird: Multicultural Politics and Education Policymaking* (New York: St. Martin's Press, 1995), 96.

18. "Board of Education Selects Committee to Oversee Project for Understanding Diversity," New York State Education Press release, July 27, 1990.

19. Cornbleth, 105.

20. New York State Social Studies Review and Development Committee, *One Nation, Many Peoples: A Declaration of Cultural Interdependence,* June 1991, p. xi.

21. *New York Times,* June 21, 1991. In her book, Cornbleth states that 322 pages of newspaper clippings collected in five booklets testify to the intensity of the debate.

CONTRIBUTORS

GABRIELA F. ARREDONDO is associate professor in Latin American and Latina/o studies at the University of California, Santa Cruz. She is the coeditor of *Chicana Feminisms: Disruption in Dialogues* (2003) and the author of *Mexican Chicago: Race, Identity, and Nation, 1919–1939* (2006).

JOHN R. CHÁVEZ is professor of history at Southern Methodist University. He is the author of *The Lost Land: The Chicano Image of the Southwest* (1984) and *Eastside Landmark: A History the East Los Angeles Community Union* (1998). He and Neil Foley coauthor *Teaching Mexican American History* (2002).

MARISELA R. CHÁVEZ is assistant professor of Chicano/Latino studies at California State University, Dominguez Hills. She wrote "'We Lived and Breathed and Worked the Movement': The Contradictions and Rewards of Chicana/Mexicana Activism in El Centro de Acción Social Autónomo (CASA), Los Angeles, 1975–1978," in *Las Obreras: Chicana Politics of Work and Family* (2000).

YOLANDA CHÁVEZ LEYVA is associate professor of history at the University of Texas, El Paso. She is completing a scholarly monograph on children's immigration experiences in El Paso at the beginning of the twentieth century. She has also a book of poetry entitled *A Tejana in Tenochtitlan.*

MARÍA E. MONTOYA is associate professor of history and American culture at New York University. The author of numerous articles, she wrote *Translating Property: The Maxwell Land Grant and the Conflict over Land in the American West* (2002).

LYDIA R. OTERO is assistant professor in the Mexican American Studies and Research Center at the University of Arizona. Her research concentrates on the histories of diverse ethnic groups in the Southwest, with an emphasis on Chicanas/os, gender and racial formations, border, urban, cultural and social history. Her chapter, "Refusing to be Undocumented: Mexican Americans in Tucson during the Depression Years," is in *Visions in the Dust: Arizona through New Deal Photography* (2005).

VICKI L. RUIZ is professor of history and Chicano/Latino studies at the University of California, Irvine. She is the author of *Cannery Women, Cannery Lives* (1987) and *From Out of the Shadows: Mexican Women in Twentieth Century America* (1998). She is the coeditor of *Unequal Sisters* (with Ellen DuBois) and *American Dreaming, Global Realities* (with Donna R. Gabaccia). With Virginia Sánchez Korrol, she coedited *Latina Legacies: Identity, Biography, and Community* (2005) and *Latinas in the United States: A Historical Encyclopedia* (2006).

ELIZABETH SALAS is associate professor in American ethnic studies at the University of Washington. She wrote *Soldaderas in the Mexican Military: Myth and History* (1990) and has published articles on New Mexico Hispana and Washington State Chicana politicians.

VIRGINIA SÁNCHEZ KORROL is professor emerita in the Department of Puerto Rican and Latino Studies at Brooklyn College, CUNY. She is the author of *From Colonia to Community: The History of Puerto Ricans in New York* (1983; 2d ed., 1994) and the coauthor (with Marysa Navarro) of *Women in Latin America and the Caribbean* (1999). She and Vicki L. Ruiz coedited *Latina Legacies: Identity, Biography, and Community* (2005) and *Latinas in the United States: A Historical Encyclopedia* (2006).

CARMEN TERESA WHALEN is associate professor of history at Williams College. A labor historian, she is the author of *From Puerto Rico to Philadelphia: Puerto Rican Workers and Postwar Economies* (2001) and coeditor of *The Puerto Rican Diaspora: Historical Perspectives* (2005).

INDEX

Esparza, Paul, 113
Espiritu, Yen Le, 4
Esquibel Tywoniak, Frances, 154
ethnicity: diversity of, among Chicago immigrants, 95; diversity of, among coal miners, 14, 18–20, 24–26, 29, 29–30, 38–39; divisions over, among coal miners, 38; elements in cohesiveness of, 46–47; and feminism, 185. *See also* race; *specific ethnic and racial groups*

factory workers, 83, 106, 107, 109, 123, 203. *See also* garment industry
Falikman, Moe, 137
family. *See* nuclear family
Family Installments (Rivera), 205
farmworkers: exclusion of, from child labor laws, 83, 88, 160; gender differences in work of, 86, 158, 162; housing for migrant, 156, 157, 164, 165; industrialization of, 19, 98, 154; Latina politicians on issues of, 164–66; Latinas' background as, 6, 13, 154–69; Latinas' work in, 104, 155–56, 161; Latinos' work in, 76–77, 154–57, 161; in Puerto Rico, 123; and voting, 163–65; working conditions for, 161, 164, 165
fathers. *See* generations; men
Felipa's (shop), 165
Félix, María, 200
feminists, 6, 171–90, 211
fences (in coal camps), 24, 25, 32, 33–35
Fergusson (major), 47
Fernández Bautista, Esperanza, 154–55
Fernández Ramírez, Fausto, 155
Figueroa, José, 130
First World women, 174–75, 179. *See also* United States
"floating borderlands," 152
Flores, Agapita, 112
Flores, Lauro, 168n2
Flores, Rosie, 124–25
Flores, Rubén, 112
Flores, Ruth, 112

Flores-Ortiz, Yvette, 114n7
foliage (in coal camps), 31, 32, 33, 34, 35, 35, 36. *See also* vegetable gardens
Ford, Henry, 18
Ford Foundation, 178
Fortieth Street (New York City), 126
Ft. Lewis (Washington), 156
Frederick (Colorado), 32
Freedom Socialist Party, 162
Frémont, John C., 57
Fremont House (Tucson, Arizona). *See* Sosa-Carrillo-Fremont House
Fresno (California), 170
Friedan, Betty, 183, 184, 187
From Colonia to Community (Sánchez Korrol), 206
From Puerto Rico to Philadelphia (Whalen), 3
Fuentes, Leticia Jacobs, 55

Gadsden Purchase, 47, 63
Gamboa, Erasmo, 153, 168n1
García, Bernice, 160
García, Dolores G. Viuda de, 80
García, Esperanza, 155–56
garment industry, 100, 121–47; assembly (section) work in, 134–35; making of whole garment in, 124, 135; segmentation of, 125–26, 142
gender: discrimination on basis of, 162, 173, 180, 182, 183, 185–86, 188, 203; dual wage system associated with, 90n23, 97–98, 110, 157, 162; and education, 85–86, 88, 203; as factor in migration, 1–2, 71–73, 79–80, 97–107; and family relations, 162; and farmworkers' work, 86, 158, 162; as issue in Chicano organizations, 162, 171, 179; role reversals in, as political gambit, 164. *See also* Latinas; Latinos; men; women
generations: as factor in Latina migration, 1, 5–6; mixing of, in coal mines, 29–30; support between, for advancement, 156–59, 196–98, 204; tensions between, over *mujeridad*, 95, 107, 112–13. *See also* children

Gilliam, Angela, 183
Glassberg, David, 47
Glazer, Nathan, 209
globalization, 2, 5, 7, 122, 141–43
gold rushes, 153, 155
Goldstein, Marcus S., 73
Gomez, Manuel A., 130
González, Gilbert, 2
Good News (film), 203
Gordon, Edmund, 208, 209
grassroots activism (defined), 52. *See also* activism
Great Depression: and Colorado coal miners, 13–14; Latinas' occupations during, 102, 105
Greek immigrants, 19, 29
Greyhound Bus Station (Tucson, Arizona), 54
Grijalva, Raúl, 68n69
Guadalajara (Mexico), 99, 100
Guanajuato (Mexico), 77, 95
Guayama (Puerto Rico), 122
Guerrero (Mexico), 101
Guerrero, Eva, 105
Guerrero, Frank, 105
Gulf Oil Corporation, 178
Gutiérrez, Dora, 99
Gutiérrez, Janie, 159
Gutiérrez, Margarita, 99
Gutiérrez, Xavier, 99

Haas, Dorothy, 53
Haida people, 152
Half-Moon Chinese Food (Tucson, Arizona), 51
Hall of All Nations (Chicago), 112
Hardin (Montana), 165
Harlem (New York City): garment industry in, 126, 127, 131, 140
Harris, Rosalind, 178
Hart, Elva Treviño, 154
Hayden, Dolores, 46, 57
head taxes, 79
Herberg, Will, 129
Hernández, Celia, 101–3, 102
Hernández, David, 208
Herrera, Juan Felipe, 168n2
Hezeta, Bruno de, 152

Hidalgo (Texas), 100
"hidden transcripts," 55
Las Hijas de Cuauhtémoc, 173
Hill, Herbert, 141
Hilliard, Asa, 208
Hinojosa Chinas, Julia, 75
Hispanas: as a term, 3. *See also* Latinas
Hispanic: as a term, 151–52, 160, 164, 167. *See also* Latinas/os
historic preservation: of Latino communities, xi, 5, 44–68
Historic Zone Ordinance (Tucson, Arizona), 60
homemaking (unpaid work), 207; as a gendered occupation, 85–87, 155, 159; by Latinas in company towns, ix, 4, 5, 13–43; and *mujeridad*, 158; not recognized as work, 84, 86. *See also* child care; cooks; domestics; laundry; vegetable gardens
honor (of family), 112
housing: in boxcars, 77, 103–4, 108, 155; in company towns, ix, 4, 5, 13–43, 33–36; discrimination in, 131, 133, 142; for migrant farmworkers, 156, 157, 164, 165; tents as, 14–15, 37, 156, 157. *See also* homemaking; rent control; segregation
Houston (Texas): Chicana conference in, 171–72; National Women's Conference in, 174, 188–90
la huelga: as a term, 173
Huerta, Dolores, 170
Hughes, Anastasia Santa Cruz, 48
Hungarian immigrants, 124
Hutar, Patricia, 181
Hymer, Evangeline, 85

Idaho, 154
identity (Latina): as bordered, 5–6; as complicated by being identified as American, 6, 7, 172, 173, 179–83, 186–87, 190; as gendered and ethnoracial, 4, 7; and memory, 4, 5, 7, 57; region's importance in, 1–5, 47, 61–62, 172–73, 208. *See also* masculinity

Mexico: attempts to preserve history of, in Tucson, 44–68; and Bracero Program, 154–55; Carmen de Blasco on, 93; Chicanas' experiences in, x, xi, 6, 7, 170–95; Chicanos' embrace of culture of, 173; coal miners from, 1, 5, 13–43; migrants from, in Washington State, 151, 153, 154, 166, 167; military repression in, 186–87; nostalgia for, 176; 1910 revolution in, 75–78, 81, 82, 106; troops from, in Arizona, 47; and U.S. imperialism, 2, 8n5; Washington State's distance from, 156; and women's rights, 93–94, 98, 101, 186–87. *See also* Latinas/os; Mexicans; migration; *specific places in*

Mexico City (Mexico), xi, 6, 7, 71, 101, 170–95

Meyer Street (Tucson, Arizona), 50, 51

Michigan, 95. *See also* Detroit (Michigan)

Michoacán (Mexico), 95

Migrant Education Program (Washington), 167

migration of Latinas (diaspora): airborne, 122; and Americanization, 8n2; by children, xi, 5–7, 71–92, 155; class as factor in, 1, 72, 73, 80–81, 207; gender as factor in, 1–2, 71–73, 79–80, 97–107; generation as factor in, 1, 5–6; male emphasis in scholarship on, 72, 96, 103, 107, 113–14; motivations for, xi, 1, 2, 80, 81, 123; of Puerto Ricans to the U.S., 122–27, 197, 200, 204, 205; region as factor in, 1–4, 7; and transnationalism, 207–8; wage work as factor in, 1, 6, 76–77, 95, 123; to Washington State, 154, 155–56. *See also* transnationalism

milliners, 109

Mills, C. Wright, 202

miners' clubs, 16, 20–21, 24, 28

mines: Latinos' work in, 76, 77; as men's space, 19–20, 23, 24, 27, 29–30. *See also* coal miners

Minority Women's Plank (National

Women's Conference, 1977), 189, 190

Missouri, 105

modernization (mass culture): as influence on women's behavior, 95, 97, 107, 112, 113; in Puerto Rico, 200. *See also* industrialization

Mohr, Nicholasa, 205

Monserrat, Joseph, 132

Montaño, Ann, 56

Monterrey (Mexico), 78

Montes, Clotilde, 109

Montoya, María E., xi, 3, 5, 13–43

Mora, Pat, 3–4

morality (for women), 72, 73, 88, 94–95, 102–3. *See also* prostitution

Morenci (Arizona), 105

Moreno, Dorinda, 176

Morgan, Harry, 78

Mormon battalion, 59

Mortimer, Lee, 201

mothers. *See* children; generations; marriage; women

Mount Vernon Ladies' Association, 46

El Movimiento Estudiantil Chicano de Aztlán (MEChA), 162, 167

La Mujer: International Women's Year 1977 (brochure), 188–89

mujeres decentes, 95. *See also* morality (for women)

mujeridad concept, 93–120

Muños, Carmen, 91n38

Muñoz, Guadalupe, 80

Muñoz, Manuel, 91n38

Musquiz, Bertha ("Rosita"), 102

My History, Not Yours (Padilla), 7

NAACP, 141, 208

Naco (Arizona), 84

Narváez, Alex, 167

National Association for the Advancement of Colored People (NAACP), 141, 208

National Association of Cuban Women, 189

National Chicana Coalition (IWY Tribune), 183

paternalism: in company towns, 16, 18, 19, 23, 39; in ILGWU, 139–40, 142

Peck, Gunther, 42n7

Peña, Ada, 183–84

Pennsylvania: garment industry in, 123, 126, 127, 133, 135, 140

Perera, Ana María, 189

Pérez, Concepción (Caroline), 100–101

Pérez, Emma, 4

Pérez, Juan, 152

Pérez y Martina (Belpré), 197, 198

Persinger, Mildred, 178

Peru, 54, 152–53

pesticides, 161, 164, 165

petitions (against urban renewal), 56, 59

Philadelphia (Pennsylvania), 123

Pinkerton Agents, 14

pioneers: Mexican, in Washington State, 151, 153, 154, 166, 167

Piscitello, Joseph, 127

place. *See* region; *specific places*

"Plan for the Preservation, Restoration and Uses of the Plaza de la Mesilla Area, within the Pueblo Center Redevelopment Area," 56–57

playgrounds, 74

plazas, 5, 32, 44–68. *See also* property ownership: communal

Poder Femenino, 177

political activism: among Latinas, 6, 44–68, 158–68, 170–95

prayer committees, 54

La Prensa (Spanish-language newspaper), 130

Prentice, Margarita López, 163–64, 166

Prentice, William C., 164

Presidential Advisory Commission on International Women's Year, 181

pressers (in garment industry), 125, 126

Primero (Colorado), 13–14, 20–43, 21, 24–28, 25, 26, 33–35

property ownership: communal, 32, 45, 46–47; private, 22, 32, 35

prostitution, 72, 73, 88, 111, 202

Protestantism, 21, 38, 54

Pueblo (Colorado), 19

Pueblo Center Redevelopment Project (Tucson), 45, 47, 54, 56

Puerto Rican Educators Association (PREA), 200

Puerto Rican Journey (Mills), 202

Puerto Rican Migrant (Chenault), 201

Puerto Rican Studies, 201, 205–8, 211

Puerto Rico: commonwealth status of, 2; cultural pride in, 197–99, 204–8; female senators from, 189; impact of U.S. imperialism on, 2, 8n5, 199, 205; industrialization in, 123, 200; memories of, 4; migrants from, x, xi, 6, 121–47, 196–213; reading in, 197; stereotypes about people from, 142, 201–2, 204–5; union visits to, 130, 131–32; U.S. garment industry in, 123, 124, 141. *See also* Boricuas; Latinas; migration

Puertorriqueño/a: as a term, 2. *See also* Latinas

Quincy (Washington), 162–63

Quincy City Council (Washington), 163

Quintanilla, Abraham, 156

Quintanilla, Selena, 156

Quintero, Michaela, 84

Quintero, Mr., 110

race: children as crossing boundaries of, 73, 79, 80; in company coal towns, 19, 20, 24–26, 29–30, 35; in garment industry, 128–29, 140; as IWY issue, 178, 182–85; Tucson boosters' use of, 50; as U.S. issue, 199, 205, 207, 210. *See also* Anglos; discrimination; ethnicity; mestizaje; segregation; *specific races*

Radical Women (Freedom Socialist Party), 162

railroads: boxcar housing for employees of, 77, 103–4, 108, 155; as bringing Anglos to Tucson, 47; as

Steinem, Gloria, 184
Stone, Frank R., 73
Stone Avenue (Tucson, Arizona), 49
strikes: children's support for mothers', 162; by coal miners, 14–16, 20, 38–41; by dressmakers, 121–22, 133–41; women's support for husbands', 38–40, 40, 128. *See also huelga*
suit industry, 125
Sunnyside (Washington), 161

table metaphor (for corporate union), 17–18
Tacoma (Washington), 155
Tapia, Davíd, 99
Task Force on Minorities (New York State), 208
Taylor, Paul S., 77, 108
teachers: in coal camps, 30–31, *31, 33, 37*; Irish, 198–99; Puerto Rican, 204–13. *See also* education; schools
El Teatro Campesino, 170
Tejano/a: as a term, 3. *See also* Latinas
tents, 14–15, 37, 156, *157*
Tepic (Mexico), 80
Texas: agriculture in, 77, 156; Chicana activists from, 177; on child labor, 82–83; Latina migrants in, 95, 97, 100, 103, 105, 155–57, 162–63. *See also specific places in Texas*
Texas Rangers, 155
Texas Raza Unida Party, 180
Third World, 172–75, 179, 181, 183, 186–87, 191n5. *See also specific Third World countries*
Thirty-fifth Street (New York City), 124, 126, 127
Thomas, Piri, 205
Tijuana (Mexico), 170
timber industry, 19
Tinsman, Heidi, 7
"To Live in the Margins" (Sánchez), 4
Toppenish (Washington), 156–57, 163, 165
Torin (Mexico), 106
Torres, Alva Bustamante, 5, 44–46, 51–62, *63*

Torres, Arthur, 51
Torres, Luisa, 163
town halls, 21
Translating Property (Montoya), 3
translational (defined), 8n2
translocal (defined), 9n11
transnationalism: within the Americas, 7, 167, 205–8; Chicanas' attempts to establish, with Mexican women, 171–76; defined, 9n11; family networks as example of, 81–82, 84, 97; and globalization, 2, 5. *See also* migration
Tratado de la Mesilla, 47, 63
Treaty of Guadalupe Hidalgo, 8n5
Tribune (Mexico City), 170–74, 177–88
Trinidad (Colorado), 13, 19
Trinidad Pickwire, 16
Tucson (Arizona): contested images of the West in, 44–68; early population of, 49; Latinas' attempts to preserve the Mexican history in, xi, 5, 44–68; Spanish presidio in, 44, 47, 65n17
Tucson Advertising Club, 61
Tucsonans: as a term, 63n1
Tucson Community Center, 45
tucsonenses, 44–63; as a term, 63n1
Tucson Heritage Foundation, 67n57
Tucson Historic Committee, 59, 61
Tucson Mountain Men, 59
Tucson-Pima Historical Commission, 60
Tyler, Gus, 131

Udall, Morris, 57
UFW. *See* United Farm Workers Union
U & I Sugar Cane Company, 154
UMW. *See* United Mine Workers
undergarment manufacture, 125
Union Settlement House, 197–98
United Bronx Parents, 201
United Charities (Chicago), 104
United Farm Workers Union (UFW), 162, 170, 173
United Federation of Teachers, 200

The University of Illinois Press
is a founding member of the
Association of American University Presses.

Composed in 9.5/12.5 Trump Mediaeval
by Jim Proefrock
at the University of Illinois Press
Manufactured by Sheridan Books, Inc.

University of Illinois Press
1325 South Oak Street   Champaign, IL 61820-6903
www.press.uillinois.edu